I0046136

NEW DIRECTIONS IN ASIA-PACIFIC ECONOMIC INTEGRATION

China National Committee for Pacific Economic Cooperation (CNCPEC)

The China National Committee for Pacific Economic Cooperation is a national organization established in 1986 in accordance with the PECC Charter, which comprises tripartite representatives from government, business and industry, academic and other intellectual circles, all participating in their private capacities. The objective of the National Committee is to seek and promote economic cooperation and prosperity within the Pacific region. The CNCPEC secretariat is located in Beijing at the China Institute for International Studies.

United States Asia Pacific Council (USAPC)

A network of private American citizens, the United States Asia Pacific Council promotes the constructive engagement of the United States with the Asia-Pacific region. An East-West Center-sponsored and administered program, established with the encouragement of the Department of State, the Council provides the framework for US engagement in the Pacific Economic Cooperation Council.

East-West Center

The East-West Center promotes better relations and understanding among the people and nations of the United States, Asia, and the Pacific through cooperative study, research, and dialogue. Established by the US Congress in 1960, the Center serves as a resource for information and analysis on critical issues of common concern, bringing people together to exchange views, build expertise, and develop policy options. The Center has research, residential, and conference facilities in Honolulu, and a Washington, DC, office that focuses on preparing the United States for an era of growing Asia Pacific prominence.

New Directions in Asia-Pacific Economic Integration

Ambassador Tang Guoqiang
Peter A. Petri
EDITORS

China National Committee for Pacific Economic Cooperation
(CNCPEC)
United States Asia Pacific Council (USAPC)

EAST-WEST CENTER
COLLABORATION · EXPERTISE · LEADERSHIP

Copyright © 2014 by the East-West Center

New Directions in Asia-Pacific Economic Integration
Ambassador Tang Guoqiang and Peter A. Petri, editors

ISBN 978-0-86638-250-2 (print) and 978-0-86638-251-9 (electronic)

The views expressed in this volume are those of the authors and not necessarily those of the sponsors or the publisher.

Free electronic files of the volume are available on the East-West Center website.
EastWestCenter.org/Publications

Publications Office
East-West Center
1601 East-West Road
Honolulu, Hawai'i 96848-1601
Tel: 808.944.7145

EWCBooks@EastWestCenter.org

Find the East-West Center website at EastWestCenter.org

Contents

Introduction / 1
*Ambassador Tang Guoqiang, Chair, China National Committee
for Pacific Economic Cooperation*

THE TRANS-PACIFIC PARTNERSHIP NEGOTIATION

1　The Trans-Pacific Partnership: Looking Ahead to Next Steps / 9
Deborah Kay Elms, Director, Asian Trade Centre in Singapore

2　Japan's Approach to the TPP / 23
*Masahiro Kawai, Project Professor, Graduate School
of Public Policy, University of Tokyo*

3　Canada and the TPP: Short-Term Tactics and
Long-Term Strategy / 44
*Hugh Stephens, Vice Chair, Canadian National Committee
on Pacific Economic Cooperation*

4　Chile and the TPP: Waiting for Outcomes / 54
Rodrigo Contreras, Chile's former lead TPP negotiator

5　How Far Away Is China from the TPP? / 66
*Zhang Jianping, Director, Institute for International Economic
Research at the National Development and Reform Commission*

6 The TPP, China, and FTAAP: The Case for Convergence / 78
Peter A. Petri, Professor of International Finance,
Brandeis International Business School
Michael G. Plummer, Eni Professor of International
Economics, The Johns Hopkins University, SAIS
Fan Zhai, Managing Director and Head of the Asset Allocation and
Strategic Research Department, China Investment Corporation

THE REGIONAL COMPREHENSIVE ECONOMIC
PARTNERSHIP NEGOTIATION

7 The Regional Comprehensive Economic Partnership:
An Initial Assessment / 93
Ganeshan Wignaraja, Director of Research,
Asian Development Bank Institute

8 East Asian Multi-Track Regional Partnership / 106
Djisman Simandjuntak, Senior Economist and
Chairman of the Board of Directors, Center for Strategic
and International Studies Foundation

9 A Stages Approach to Regional Economic Integration
in Asia Pacific: The RCEP, TPP, and FTAAP / 119
Shujiro Urata, Professor of International Economics,
Waseda University

10 The RCEP: A Chinese Perspective / 131
Quan Yi, Editor-in-Chief, Asia-Pacific Economic Review

11 South Korea's Recent FTA Policy: A Personal Viewpoint / 138
Inkyo Cheong, Professor of Economics, Inha University

12 Australia's Free Trade Agreements with Japan
and South Korea: Lessons for the Future / 150
Christopher Findlay, Executive Dean of the Faculty
of the Professions, University of Adelaide

13 APEC in 2014: Meeting New Challenges / 163
Zhang Yunling, Director of International Studies,
Chinese Academy of Social Sciences

14 US Economic Strategy in the Asia-Pacific Region:
Promoting Growth, Rules, and Presence / 169
Matthew P. Goodman, William E. Simon Chair in Political
Economy, Center for Strategic and International Studies

15 Where to with Cooperation Across Asia and the
Pacific Now? / 180
Peter Drysdale, Emeritus Professor of Economics,
The Australian National University

16 Placing Increased Priority on Services in APEC / 193
Sherry Stephenson, Senior Fellow, International Centre
for Trade and Sustainable Development

17 Connecting APEC Economies Through Infrastructure,
Governance, and Social Inclusion / 208
Tan Khee Giap, Co-Director, Asia Competitiveness Institute, Lee
Kuan Yew School of Public Policy, National University of Singapore
Yap Xin Yi, Research Assistant, Asia Competitiveness Institute, Lee
Kuan Yew School of Public Policy, National University of Singapore

18 APEC's Role in Promoting Asia-Pacific Regional
Economic Integration / 224
Liu Chenyang, Director and Professor of APEC
Study Center of China, Nankai University

TOWARD CONVERGING FRAMEWORKS

19 The TPP and RCEP: Prospects for Convergence / 235
Robert Scollay, Director, New Zealand APEC Study Centre

20 Asia-Pacific Economic Integration: Projecting the
Path Forward / 246
*Jeffrey J. Schott, Senior Fellow, Peterson Institute
for International Economics*

21 Regional Economic Integration Strategy of South Korea / 254
*Sangkyom Kim, Senior Research Fellow (on leave),
Korea Institute for International Economic Policy*

22 How to Push the WTO Doha Round in the Current
RTA Talks? / 267
*Winichai Chaemchaeng, Director of the International Institute
for Asia-Pacific Studies, Bangkok University*

23 The Asia-Pacific Cooperation Agenda: Moving from
Regional Cooperation Toward Global Leadership / 279
Charles E. Morrison, President, East-West Center

Contributors / 287

Acronyms

ACI	Asia Competitiveness Institute
ADB	Asian Development Bank
AEC	ASEAN Economic Community
AIIB	Asian Infrastructure Investment Bank
APEC	Asia-Pacific Economic Cooperation
ASEAN	Association of Southeast Asian Nations
BIT	bilateral investment treaty
BOT	build-operate-transfer agreement
CEPEA	Comprehensive Economic Partnership in East Asia
CETA	Canada-EU Trade Agreement
CGE	computable general equilibrium
CJK FTA	China-Japan-Korea FTA
CMIM	Chiang Mai Initiative Multilateralization
CSIS	Center for Strategic and International Studies
DSM	dispute settlement mechanism
EA	East Asia
EAFTA	East Asia Free Trade Area
EAS	East Asia Summit
EFTA	European Free Trade Association
EG list	APEC List of Environmental Goods
EPA	economic partnership agreement
EU	European Union
FDI	foreign direct investment
FTA	free trade agreement
FTA	free trade area
FTAAP	Free Trade Area of the Asia-Pacific

GATS	General Agreement on Trade in Services
GATT	General Agreement on Tariffs and Trade
GCC	Gulf Cooperation Council
GDP	gross domestic product
G-20	Group of Twenty Finance Ministers and Central Bank Governors
GVC	global value chain
IP	intellectual property
IPR	intellectual property rights
ISDS	investor-state dispute settlement
ITA	Information Technology Agreement
KORUS FTA	Korea-US FTA
LDEs	least-developed or less-developed economies
MAFF	Ministry of Agriculture, Forestry, and Fishery
MDB	multilateral development bank
MERCOSUR	South American Common Market
METI	Ministry of Economy, Trade, and Industry
MFN	most-favored nation
MNC	multinational corporation
MTS	multilateral trading system
NAFTA	North American Free Trade Agreement
NAMA	nonagricultural market access
NGO	nongovernmental organization
OECD	Organisation for Economic Co-operation and Development
PECC	Pacific Economic Cooperation Council
P4	Pacific 4 (Chile, Brunei, New Zealand, and Singapore)
R&D	research and development
RCEP	Regional Comprehensive Economic Partnership
REI	regional economic integration
ROO	rules of origin
RTA	regional trade agreement
S&D	special and differential treatment
S&T	science and technology
SME	small- and medium-sized enterprises

SOE	state-owned enterprise
SPS	sanitary and phytosanitary measures
TBT	technical barriers to trade
TPA	trade promotion authority
TPP	Trans-Pacific Partnership
TRQ	tariff rate quota
TRIPS	Agreement on Trade-Related Aspects of Intellectual Property Rights
TTIP	Transatlantic Trade and Investment Partnership
UNESCO	United Nations Educational, Scientific, and Cultural Organization
USTR	Office of the US Trade Representative
WTO	World Trade Organization

Introduction

Ambassador Tang Guoqiang, Chair,
China National Committee for Pacific Economic Cooperation

The year 2014 marks the twenty-fifth anniversary of the first APEC Ministerial Meeting and the twentieth anniversary of APEC's Bogor Goals. It's time to shape the future by building on past achievements. If we look at the past 25 years of economic cooperation and integration in the Asia-Pacific region, I think it can be roughly divided into three stages.

The first stage started in 1989, when the Asia-Pacific Economic Cooperation (APEC) Ministerial Meeting was held in Canberra, Australia, marking the official inception of Asia-Pacific regional economic cooperation and integration. The climax of this period was the announcement of the Bogor Goals by APEC leaders, who were committed to realizing trade and investment liberalization by 2010 in the industrialized economies and by 2020 in the developing economies. However, the East Asia financial crisis of 1997 and the failure of the Early Voluntary Sectoral Liberalization program cast a pessimistic outlook for economic integration and cooperation in the Asia-Pacific region.

The second period started in 1997 and lasted until the global economic crisis in 2008. During this period, economies in East Asia—especially Northeast Asia—initiated a new wave of regionalism, with ASEAN as the driver. The United States under the George W. Bush administration explicitly practiced the strategy of competitive liberalization. Some economies in the region, such as South Korea, Singapore, and Chile, successfully engaged the big economies in various bilateral free trade agreements (FTAs). Still, some smaller economies formed groups, such as the Trans-Pacific Strategic Economic Partnership (P4). Both China and Japan proposed future directions for East Asia regionalism, with one preferring the East Asia Free Trade Area, while the other favored the Comprehensive Economic Partnership of East Asia.

The third stage features mega-regional trade agreements (RTAs). When the US government announced that it would join the Trans-Pacific Partnership (TPP), first by the Bush administration in 2008 and then by the Obama administration in 2009, the third stage of regional economic cooperation and integration was ushered in. East Asia came up with a new design named the Regional Comprehensive Economic Partnership (RCEP), with ASEAN playing a central role. At the same time, the Latin American members of the Pacific region started the Pacific Alliance, another mega-RTA with great prospects. Paradoxically, these mega-RTAs reflect the need for deeper regional economic integration on the one hand, while creating a situation of fragmentation on the other. Twenty-five years ago, when APEC was just founded, there were only three cooperation forums and three free trade agreements in the Asia-Pacific region. Now there are 25 cooperation mechanisms and 56 FTAs.

In retrospect, Asia-Pacific regional economic cooperation and integration has grown much deeper since the 1980s, when the Pacific Economic Cooperation Council (PECC) was promoting the effort as a tripartite, nongovernmental regional organization. Although APEC has encountered challenges, it has developed a strong economic growth strategy, enabling the Asia-Pacific region to act as an engine for the global economy and giving it a more prominent position in the global economic landscape. APEC has worked to bring about the big changes of economic transformation and reform. It has pursued important visions, with the Bogor Goals at the heart. APEC was the first to set out the ambitious goal of a Free Trade Area of the Asia-Pacific (FTAAP), thus greatly boosting trade and investment liberalization and facilitation in the Asia-Pacific region and advancing regional integration. It has pooled the efforts of both developed and developing members to advance economic and technical cooperation, enhancing trade and development capabilities of its members. It has always stayed the course in its pursuit of regional economic cooperation and integration.

However, if regional economic cooperation is to go further, it is imperative that APEC champion regional economic institution building;

promote sound interactions between competitive mechanisms in an open, inclusive, cooperative, win-win, transparent, and flexible manner; and prove its credibility with the Bogor Goals and a meaningful post–Bogor Goal agenda.

It is high time for APEC to become an incubator of big ideas and work out a meaningful and credible roadmap toward the realization of an FTAAP. In the past eight years, the APEC-branded FTAAP has developed into a far-reaching vision and worthy objective. Numerous studies have also shown that an FTAAP will bring about maximum economic welfare to the Asia-Pacific region.

In practical terms, there is a sound basis for cooperation among APEC members on creating an FTAAP. First, both developed and developing economies in the region are committed to economic restructuring and reform. Second, APEC has made well-known progress in macroeconomic policy coordination, trade and investment liberalization and facilitation, connectivity, and ecotechnology, as well as functional cooperation. Third, the bilateral and regional free trade arrangements have established new areas, new standards, and new methods, which can serve as very good inputs in the design of long-term goals. Finally, the TPP, the RCEP, and other regional free trade agreements can be useful references for a new regional arrangement.

Therefore, actions should be taken to substantiate the FTAAP idea. People cannot wait for another eight years of merely talking about the concept. On the basis of consensus, an FTAAP roadmap should be created, defining its objectives and principles, and a draft 10- to 15-year timetable designed for achieving an FTAAP. In the roadmap, we also need to identify a series of actions that can be taken, each based on stocktaking. To make the roadmap credible and meaningful, a few deliverables, such as a feasibility study, should be launched in 2014 and implemented consecutively by the hosts of subsequent APEC meetings.

APEC should also play a constructive role to improve the smooth interaction between the TPP and the RCEP. Given the overlapping memberships, the TPP and the RCEP are actually complementary arrangements. They both have the same ultimate objective of economic integration at a higher level and with a greater scope. They may not completely converge, but they may well coexist to satisfy the varying needs of the economies.

There are also areas shared by the two, and in these areas, attempts should be made to harmonize the rules.

In this connection, it may be possible to create and launch an FTA information exchange mechanism to facilitate communication and interaction among the TPP, the RCEP, and other free trade arrangements—to learn from, promote, converge with, and complement each other.

Whatever way forward, one thing is essential. That is the intellectual input needed for making well-informed policy decisions. The Pacific Economic Cooperation Council (PECC) and its 26 members and associate members have been committed to this practice over the years. Last year, following PECC's renewed commitment to the vision of an open and integrated region at the general meeting in Vancouver, a bilateral meeting between the China National Committee for Pacific Economic Cooperation (CNCPEC) and the United States National Committee for Pacific Economic Cooperation took place. In the meeting, Dr. Charles Morrison endorsed my proposal that PECC-member committees take the initiative to reenergize the intellectual contribution process. We agreed to do something together to promote regional economic cooperation in ways that align with the PECC tradition. In July 2013, Professor Peter Petri sent me a joint action plan for the year 2014, when China plays host to the APEC meetings. One of the suggestions was a joint publication on regional economic integration.

The success of the international symposium New Development and Future Direction of Asia-Pacific Regional Economic Integration, which was hosted by my committee in Beijing on November 14–15, 2013, reinforced our idea to do so. Then, the APEC 2014 Symposium, which was hosted again by my committee back-to-back with the APEC Informal Senior Officials Meeting, gathered many important views about the future of APEC. Armed with new insights, we were determined to continue with our plan of publishing a book of essays, with Peter and me as coeditors. The East-West Center, headed by Dr. Charles Morrison, generously financed the publication of the present book.

The contributors were all participants of the above-mentioned two symposiums. It was not only challenging to secure them for the events, but also extremely challenging to get them to carve out time in their busy schedules to develop these articles, which are based on their presentations.

Yet each of them did. Peter and I would like to extend our sincere thanks for the invaluable contributions made by the many participants. By the way, it should be acknowledged that the views of the contributors are their own. They do not represent the views of the CNCPEC, the United States Asia Pacific Council (USAPC), the East-West Center, or the PECC.

Last but not least, I would like to give thanks to the people on both sides who worked hard on various aspects of this book, especially Peter. Besides his personal participation in our academic activities, his great efforts in planning, efficient coordination, and careful review of the drafts have made the present book a reality.

Beijing, June 2014

The
Trans-Pacific
Partnership
Negotiation

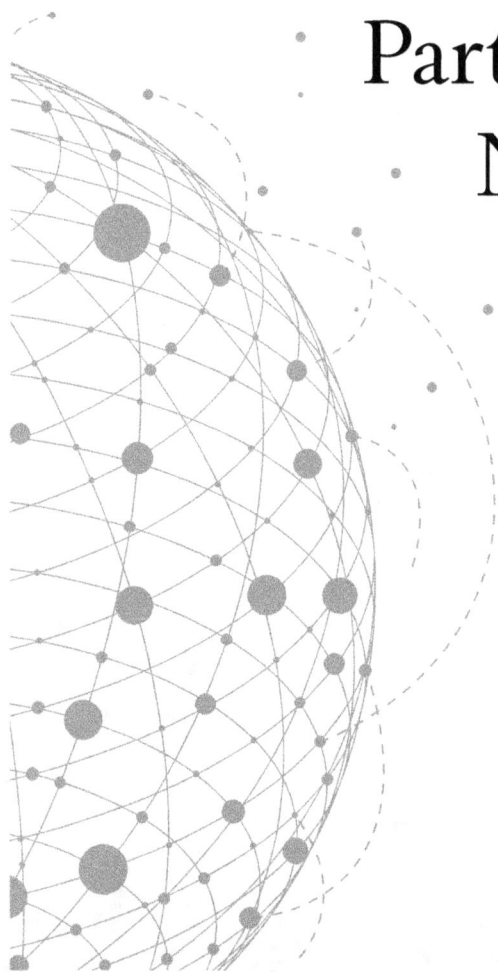

1

The Trans-Pacific Partnership

Looking Ahead to Next Steps

Deborah Kay Elms, Director, Asian Trade Centre in Singapore

THE UNFINISHED BUSINESS IN THE END GAME

After more than four years of negotiations, officials have been scrambling to conclude the Trans-Pacific Partnership (TPP) among the current 12 participating members: Australia, Brunei, Canada, Chile, Japan, Malaysia, Mexico, New Zealand, Peru, Singapore, the United States, and Vietnam. After dozens of rounds of very complex bargaining across an expanding set of members, negotiators are down to the final political decisions on how deep, wide, and ambitious the TPP agreement will ultimately become.

Most of the final sticking points could have been (and were) predicted at the outset of the negotiations. Rather than rehash specific problem areas, such as sugar, dairy, rice, intellectual property rights, or the environmental chapter (Elms 2013a, Schott et al. 2013), the focus here is on some of the broader issues that remain in the negotiations.[1] This chapter discusses the context of the negotiations, the concept of a "living agreement," and the importance of creating a TPP Secretariat, and it engages in a discussion of future admission procedures for new members.[2]

These broader issues are likely to be critical to the future success of the TPP. Many of these ideas were discussed at length at the very outset of negotiations, starting in March 2010 in Melbourne. However, once officials began getting serious about the technical issues, most of the deeper concerns fell by the wayside. As officials limp toward the finish line, the urgency in finding creative solutions to these far-reaching aspects of the agreement has only increased.

THE CLUSTER APPROACH

One of the biggest challenges in getting the TPP to reach the highest aspirational goals of the "twenty-first century, high quality" agreement set forth from the beginning has been prodding trade officials to think as broadly as possible about the implications of their actions. Since the TPP-12 has been so active in negotiating free trade agreements (FTAs) in the past, many of the officials involved view the TPP as just another trade agreement, albeit one that is bigger and harder to negotiate than many of the others.

In the initial round of negotiations in Melbourne, officials wanted to think creatively. Rather than split themselves into traditional "chapters" for discussions (goods, services, investment, intellectual property, etc.), they tried dividing themselves into clusters. These clusters were supposed to consider overarching themes that ran across multiple issue areas and that might better conform to the "real world" of business than past FTA practices. However, the cluster idea quickly broke down once the discussions started moved into substantive areas. Officials reached for the familiar settings of traditional chapters, and the whole "cluster" approach was rapidly abandoned.

The only exception was the "horizontal" chapter, where nearly everything new and innovative about the TPP was tossed. This included ideas such as fostering small- and medium-sized enterprises, encouraging supply chains, bringing about regulatory coherence, and all things related to development and cooperation.

A moment's reflection, however, will suggest that this approach was also going to be problematic. Placing all these diverse issue areas into one basket left a handful of officials grappling with a wide range of topics and concerns. To compound the difficulties, these were all issues that had never before been addressed in a trade agreement—mostly because they were extremely tough to tackle. Now they were all bundled together and handed to one team.[3] It is therefore not particularly surprising that the results from the horizontal chapter will be deeply disappointing to many.

The efforts to assist small- and medium-sized enterprises quickly devolved into a website.[4] Much of the "meat" of the supply chain/business connectivity issues got pulled out and placed elsewhere in the agreement. This is fine, except that many in the supply chain industry, particularly those in logistics, have argued for years that the primary problem for supply chain operators is precisely that their issues fall in between ministries and, therefore, are never appropriately managed by anyone. The TPP was supposed to represent a rare opportunity to pull together a host of issues into one place and keep governments focused on this critical web of interlocking elements for business in the twenty-first century. By pulling these items out of their own special "chapter" and placing them back into various substantive chapters, such as goods or services, some of the synergies that were supposed to be unlocked by bundling them together will have been lost.

The regulatory coherence agenda may be the most disappointing of all. Whenever officials in the TPP have been asked about the twenty-first century components of the agreement, they cite regulatory coherence. The idea was that all the economies would try to harmonize standards in food, agriculture, and other areas if such a thing were possible. If not, they would at least try to accept as small a set as possible of compatible, multiple standards. As an example, if Economy A permitted a certain type of food safety inspection for apples, Economy B would be willing to accept this certification, even if their own apple inspection might be different. They would not be forced to harmonize standards to the same degree (which was seen as *too* ambitious), but they would go beyond what is typically found in an FTA—especially one with multiple parties.

The November 12, 2011, the Trans-Pacific Partnership Leaders' Statement highlighted regulatory coherence in particular, noting that members pledged to "work to improve regulatory practices, eliminate unnecessary barriers, reduce regional divergence in standards, promote transparency, conduct our regulatory processes in a more trade-facilitative manner, eliminate redundancies in testing and certification, and promote cooperation on specific regulatory issues."

Such high ambition proved problematic to implement. It was especially difficult to get regulators from different ministries and agencies to cooperate with trade officials in the TPP around a broad agenda of increasing market access for members. In the end, the TPP chapter on regulatory coherence will be about the institutional framework for coherence. It will contain information on inquiry points and procedures for obtaining information and promoting transparency. It will not really discuss standards at all. Some of this material got put into the specific chapters on sanitary and phytosanitary standards (SPS) or technical barriers to trade (TBT). But in general, it proved too difficult to get regulators to cooperate in the TPP.[5] The final result will be much less ambitious and twenty-first century than the early rhetoric would have suggested.

A LIVING AGREEMENT

All is not yet lost. One of the best ideas of the TPP from the beginning was to create the TPP as a "living agreement." The idea gained momentum after officials observed problems in the World Trade Organization's (WTO) Information Technology Agreement (ITA), which was being renegotiated at the same time that the TPP was getting underway. In the ITA, the electronics sector was liberalized and unleashed tremendous growth, especially in Asia. However, officials soon came to recognize that it had a serious flaw—given the method of negotiations (a positive list), technology was only liberalized if it was included on the list (c.f., Beltz 1997, Lee-Makiyama 2011, Lin 2011). This meant that as new technology was developed, it was not automatically included for market opening. Over time, and in a rapidly evolving industry, the ITA became less and less relevant as fewer and fewer traded products were covered. Record players might be eligible, but not smart phones, for example. Getting economies to sit down and reopen negotiations also proved extremely difficult and tedious.

It is true that FTAs usually have a clause for regular reviews. However, in practice, such reviews are frequently not held or are largely superficial. Even when economies take the review process seriously, the revisions undertaken generally consist of changes to the legal language of the document to bring sections into conformity with one another, or to try to bring different FTA provisions into compliance with one another. But periodic reviews have not, so far, been used for major renegotiations of an FTA.

Officials are not oblivious to these problems in other agreements. There are generally two different approaches taken to avoid creating obsolete commitments in "modern" FTAs. First, officials try to negotiate on the basis of a "negative" list. This approach means that new sectors are automatically opened for partner preferences, unless members specifically meet and declare reservations to opening the sector. The TPP uses a negative list for both services and investment, partly as a mechanism for remaining relevant in the future without the need for complex revisions to the agreement. It ensures that new industries and sectors are automatically opened for investment or foreign competition.

Second, most next-generation FTAs have complex committee structures built into their agreements from the beginning. The parties may agree to create a general trade committee that meets every year or every two years. This is supplemented with specific committees on goods, services, investment, government procurement, and so forth. These subcommittees or working groups are also scheduled to meet regularly—often every two years.

However, while these committees have made arrangements to meet, the actual practice of holding consistent, productive meetings has yet to be seen. In many of the latest generation of FTAs, it is frankly too soon to tell how well these committee structures will work because many have only just been completed and no reviews have been held. If there is an obvious flaw in the agreement, the committees will allow the parties to correct the problem. But modifications or improvements to the agreement to make it work better overall are less likely to happen. In most cases, committee meetings will probably be short affairs attended by junior staff.

Recall the promiscuity of many TPP members, as they signed multiple FTA agreements. Chile has agreements with 60 economies. By the time it joined the TPP, Mexico had 12 FTAs linking 44 economies. By 2013, Singapore had 20 agreements, with another 5 under negotiation. Many of these deals come with complex committee structures for management. In most of the TPP economies, some portion of their trade ministry officials could spend their whole careers just preparing for one FTA committee review after another.

Because of this, TPP officials suggested a slightly different approach early on in the talks. This FTA would become a "living agreement." This meant that it would not just be opened for annual reviews. Instead, it would be up for regular and ongoing discussions and revisions going forward. In this way, the TPP would never be out of date.

From an institutional perspective, a benefit of a living agreement is that TPP member economies would dedicate specific individuals to oversee and monitor their TPP commitments. The TPP would not just be examined in the every-two-years committee period.

A living agreement could, for example, take the rather limited framework for regulatory coherence in the original TPP document and, over time, turn it into something much more substantial.[6] Regulators from across the TPP economies could engage in ongoing meetings and become accustomed to coordinating their regulations with one another before proceeding with changes that might impact the membership. New elements like sub-federal–level entities or states could be added to the government procurement commitments relatively easily under a living agreement provision. Reservations in specific service sectors or subsectors could be removed over time without requiring a wholesale renegotiation of the agreement.

The idea of the living agreement was discussed at length early on in the TPP negotiations. It was then largely dropped from conversations for most of the next three years while officials moved on to more substantive conversations about specific chapters. At the time of the endgame negotiations in 2014, it is not clear whether the idea will survive at all, or whether it will simply be a puffed up or enhanced version of the regular FTA review mechanisms.

A TPP SECRETARIAT

If it is to survive and be meaningful, a living agreement cannot be managed without a robust secretariat dedicated to supervising the TPP agreement. The intention of the TPP is to continue to expand in the future—at least in terms of membership. If the living agreement idea gains traction, the issue areas and coverage of the agreement will also increase over time.

Even if it does not expand any further, the TPP includes nearly 30 chapters and 12 member economies. Many of the rules go well beyond anything promised in the WTO or other FTAs. Commitments will be phased in over the implementation period(s), with different start dates likely for many members. This will add to the complexity of administering the agreement.

The TPP will require a dedicated staff to monitor implementation and reach out to the business community in each of the member economies. Otherwise, the provisions negotiated at great cost and difficulty through so many years are likely to be underutilized.

For example, many of the commitments in the agreement go well beyond obligations made in the WTO. This will make it impossible to use WTO dispute settlement for many issues in the TPP. Like most FTAs, the TPP has its own dispute settlement mechanism (DSM). However, unlike most FTAs, the TPP DSM has been designed to be actively used. Managing dispute cases will require an institutional structure. If the DSM picks up momentum over time, the case load could increase. It might even be possible to imagine a scenario under which the TPP develops a standing dispute system (more similar to the WTO).

Even leaving dispute settlement aside, such a complicated agreement cannot be managed by trade officials in the Asia desk, as in many other bilateral FTAs. Existing regional FTAs do not extend nearly as far, nor do they include such deep, behind-the-border commitments. The fact that these FTAs have worked without a secretariat is not a convincing argument for managing the TPP in the future. As it stands, many TPP officials have already complained about the difficulties of coordination in the negotiation stage.

Some have suggested that the APEC Secretariat could be used as the TPP Secretariat. After all, the TPP is officially one of the four possible pathways to the Free Trade Area of the Asia-Pacific (FTAAP) for APEC.[7] So far, all TPP members are also APEC members. The accession clause for the TPP privileges APEC members as well.[8] Leaving aside the issue of whether or not the TPP might eventually become the FTAAP, let us focus instead on whether or not the APEC Secretariat could do double-duty as the TPP Secretariat as well.

There are at least three reasons why using APEC is problematic. First, APEC's own statement of purpose is to "serve as an incubator of ideas." This function would be lost if the secretariat were to become somehow divided between staff responsible for monitoring the TPP, and staff incubating ideas in a nonbinding manner. APEC already has a very complex organizational structure of its own, and an extremely small secretariat staff to manage hundreds of meetings and thousands of participants in a rotating set of locations.

Second, not all of the APEC members are also members of the TPP. It is highly likely that the non-TPP members of APEC would find the suggestion to convert APEC into the TPP Secretariat quite objectionable. Even if only a portion of the APEC Secretariat was kept busy with TPP tasks, it would run the risk of diluting the non-TPP portion of the agenda.

Third, two of the possible pathways to the FTAAP are currently in play—the TPP and the Regional Comprehensive Economic Partnership (RCEP). The RCEP involves 16 parties in Asia, and may also need a secretariat at some point in the future, depending on if this agreement also progresses to become a kind of deep integration effort similar to the TPP. But this would mean that the APEC Secretariat would effectively be split into three different elements—a nonbinding ideas hub in APEC, the deeply ambitious TPP, and the (slightly?) less ambitious RCEP.

It is possible to argue that, in the long run, these functions might merge again in the FTAAP. In the meantime, the costs involved in setting up the institutional structure of a TPP Secretariat could be significant. However, even if the TPP eventually evolves into the FTAAP, such an outcome is likely to be well over a decade (and more likely two decades) away. In the interim period, businesses could substantially benefit from a strong institutional structure to effectively implement the complicated TPP agreement.

In short, using the APEC Secretariat as the TPP Secretariat is a poor idea. The two ought to coordinate, but they must remain separate to provide the best service to both institutions. The TPP needs its own dedicated secretariat to manage this complex, binding agreement.

ACCESSION OF NEW TPP MEMBERS

In addition to the institutional issues around a secretariat, another broader, long-term issue that must be sorted out prior to closure of the TPP agreement is the procedures for accession of new members. Under the current "rules," new members have been admitted after first applying to the current members. Each prospective member must then engage in a series of bilateral meetings to discuss possible irritants in the relationship that may prove problematic for the group as a whole. These issues may require resolution or progress toward resolution prior to entry to avoid having them interfere negatively on negotiations with others. Finally, the whole TPP membership has to collectively approve the new member for admission. New members must then wait for final domestic procedures to be completed before they are allowed to see the negotiating texts and formally sit down with other members at the table.[9]

A further informal provision introduced when Canada and Mexico joined in late 2012 prevented new members from "reopening" any closed chapters or provisions that had already been agreed upon by the existing members. Outstanding issues (those remaining in square brackets, which is how negotiators signal disagreements over specific points in a text) could be discussed and new issues tabled, but anything resolved could not be taken up again.

Taken as a package, these accession procedures suggest that, going forward, the next tranche of TPP members will have no room for negotiating on the TPP rules. New members will engage in bargaining over their own market access commitments in goods, services, investment, government procurement, and so forth, but they will have no input into the rest of the document.

From the perspective of those who have just spent more than four years negotiating over every comma, clause, and paragraph in the existing agreement, such provisions make a great deal of sense. They do not see any need for new members to be able to reopen any portion of the document that was finally nailed down. After all, many probably feel that the agreement was open to new members (particularly from APEC economies) at any point starting in 2008. If any new economy had wanted to enter at the negotiating stage, they could simply have put their hand up, gotten in, and negotiated for whatever priorities they might have wanted.

However, a lack of flexibility collides with one important political reality. The TPP would be substantially strengthened if China—currently with world's second-largest economy—enters. After all, one of the most important factors driving this mega-regional is the opportunity to knit together global value chains in a seamless trade agreement that contains not just tariff reductions but also substantial behind-the-border provisions. Since many of the presumptive second tranche of members, such as China, South Korea, Hong Kong, and Chinese Taipei, are deeply enmeshed in value chains across the Asia-Pacific region, getting them into the TPP would provide significant economic benefits (Wignaraja 2013; Baldwin and Kawai 2013; Petri, Plummer, and Zhai 2012).

For China, in particular, joining the existing TPP with no opportunity at all for discussing any of the existing provisions may present political difficulties at the domestic level. This suggests that current TPP members would be wise to think carefully about a mechanism that would apply specifically to the first batch of new entrants in the next tranche of negotiations. To write into the agreement that accession terms are to be negotiated later with each new entrant will be unacceptable to many. Some sort of clarity, therefore, is needed on what sort of accession provisions will be required of new aspirants.

One suggestion is that officials think creatively now about a clause that gives certain measures of flexibility to the first set of members entering the TPP. Such a clause will not allow a wholesale rewriting of the agreement, but might allow for some modest changes, or perhaps participation in writing new rules or new chapters. Done carefully, it would satisfy the demands for new members to put their collective stamp on the agreement, while not prolonging new negotiations.

Such a mechanism would also encourage any economy considering membership to declare its interest. This would have the added benefit of getting all potential new members into the deal at the same time. The alternative could be to add new members on an ongoing and regular basis, which would be deeply problematic.

Some sort of clause in the agreement that privileges entrants in the first wave of new applicants could be extremely helpful in pushing TPP expansion in the near term. The clause does not need to allow wholesale changes to the existing text, but some ability to show flexibility may be necessary to encourage new entrants. Otherwise, entry becomes a "take it or leave it" proposition and increases the risk that prospective members may opt to "leave it."

CIRCLING BACK TO THE LIVING AGREEMENT

Managing revisions is tricky, of course. It also comes with one final caveat for officials. Although there are some strong incentives to create a living agreement overall that allows for general flexibility and improvements to the document going forward, there is at least one challenge to be addressed. For economies that require a ratification procedure for approval of the TPP, there is, presumably, some threshold level of change than cannot be exceeded in the document before it triggers a new ratification process. In other words, it remains to be worked out how much change can take place within the TPP in terms of revisions to the text, rules, schedules, commitments, new members, and so forth without going back to member-state domestic procedures for ratification. These conditions should be specified as clearly as possible in advance of closing the agreement so that members know what to expect from one another in the future.

CONCLUSIONS

Pressure has been building for closure of the TPP. Getting the deal done is important. The economic benefits from this 12-party agreement are likely to be substantial. But the TPP is not just another FTA. It represents the chance to set a trade agenda for the future across a wide range of topics for economies throughout the Asia-Pacific region. This means that the agreement should not be settled in haste. More importantly, it also means that key decisions need to be reached about broader issues related to the institutional structure of the TPP. These decisions must be made now, before the deal is closed, on issues such as creating the TPP as a living agreement, setting up a TPP Secretariat, and clarifying entry conditions for future members. These choices must be made deliberately and carefully, even while officials are struggling to get closure on the most highly sensitive issues remaining in settling the agreement. It will not be easy, but wise decisions are necessary now to ensure the long-term success of the TPP.

NOTES

1. To show how deep and enduring the sticking points have been in these talks, the book by Lim, Elms, and Low (2012) is likely to have highlighted nearly every problem area still contested in October 2013, although the book was completed by the team of authors very early in 2012.

2. See also a longer version in "The Trans-Pacific Partnership Agreement: Looking Ahead to the Next Steps," Asian Development Bank Institute Working Paper Series, No. 443, December 2013.

3. Of course, officials will quickly argue that they had other individuals they could engage as resources whenever and wherever needed. But I believe that history will show that most of the teams on the horizontal chapter managed the bulk of the details on their own.

4. And, I would argue, this is even worse than it sounds—unless the TPP creates a meaningful secretariat, such a website will rapidly collapse since no one will be responsible for maintaining it.

5. If the living agreement idea takes off, this may not be a fatal blow, as regulators would meet regularly to discuss changes and, perhaps, move toward harmonization.

6. Other than the European Union, perhaps the closest trade agreement to a "living" agreement idea is the Australia–New Zealand Closer Economic Relations (Leslie and Elijah 2012). Another potential model might be APEC itself, where commitments made by member states evolve over time. The difference, of course, with APEC is that APEC is not binding.

7. The others are what is now called the Regional Comprehensive Economic Partnership (RCEP) or ASEAN-Plus-Six, consisting of the 10 members of ASEAN plus China, Japan, South Korea, India, Australia, and New Zealand; ASEAN-Plus-Three; and "other."

8. The relevant clause is drawn from the original P4 agreement and reads, "The Agreement is open to any APEC economy or any other State (Article 20.6), subject to terms to be agreed among the Parties."

9. In practice, this basically means that if a new member did not have clearance from the US Congress in the form of existing coverage under trade promotion authority (TPA), the new member had to wait for the Office of the US Trade Representative (USTR) to inform Congress of the intention to begin negotiations. New members then wait 90 days for comments inside the United States before US domestic procedures were considered concluded. For the existing members, Malaysia already "had" approval under a stalled bilateral negotiation and could join the talks almost immediately, but Japan, Mexico, and Canada did not and had to wait 90 days before entry. This was true even though TPA technically was expired, since the USTR was acting "as if" TPA rules were in place for TPP negotiations. For details on what is now called TPA, see Destler 2005, Fergusson et. al., 2013.

SOURCES

Baldwin, Richard E. and Masahiro Kawai. 2013. *Multilateralizing Asian Regionalism*. ADBI Working Paper No. 431.

Beltz, Cynthia. 1997. "Global Telecommunications Rules: The Race With Technology." *Issues With Science and Technology* 13 (3): 63–70.

Destler, I.M. 2005. *American Trade Politics*, 4th Edition. Washington, DC: International Institute for Economics.

Elms, Deborah. 2013a. "The Trans-Pacific Partnership Negotiations: Some Outstanding Issues for the Final Stretch." *Asian Journal of WTO and International Health Law and Policy* (AJWH) 8 (371).

———. 2013b. "The Trans-Pacific Partnership Agreement: Looking Ahead to the Next Steps." Asian Development Bank Institute Working Paper Series, No. 443, December.

Fergusson, Ian, William H. Cooper, Remy Jurenas, and Brock R. Williams. 2013. *The Trans-Pacific Partnership Negotiations and Issues for Congress.* CRS Report No. 7-5700. Washington, DC: Congressional Research Service.

Kawai, Masahiro, and Ganeshan Wignaraja. 2011. *Asia's Free Trade Agreements: How Is Business Responding?* Northhampton, MA: Edward Elgar.

Lee-Makiyama, Hosuk. 2011. "Future-proofing World Trade in Technology: Turning the WTO IT Agreement (ITA) into the International Digital Economy Agreement (IDEA)." *Aussenwirtshaft* 66 (3): 279–322.

Leslie, John, and Annmarie Elijah. 2012. "Does N=2? Trans-Tasman Economic Integration as a Comparator for the Single European Market." *Journal of Common Market Studies* 50 (6): 975–993.

Lim, C.L., Deborah Elms, and Patrick Low, eds. 2012. *Trans-Pacific Partnership: A Quest for a 21ˢᵗ Century Trade Agreement.* Cambridge, UK: Cambridge University Press.

Lin, Tsai-Yu. 2011. "Systemic Reflection on the EC-IT Product Case: Establishing an 'Understanding' on Maintaining the Product Coverage of the Current Information Technology Agreement in the Face of Technological Change." *Journal of World Trade* 45 (2): 401–430.

Petri, Peter, Michael Plummer, and Fan Zhai. 2012. *The Trans-Pacific Partnership and Asia-Pacific Integration: A Quantitative Assessment.* Washington, DC: Peterson Institute for International Economics.

Schott, Jeffrey, Barbara Kotschwar, and Julia Muir. 2013. *Understanding the Trans-Pacific Partnership.* Washington, DC: Peterson Institute for International Economics.

Wignaraja, Ganeshan. 2013. "Regional Trade Agreements and Enterprises in Southeast Asia." Asian Development Bank Institute Working Paper Series, No. 442.

2

Japan's Approach to the TPP

Masahiro Kawai, Project Professor, Graduate School
of Public Policy, University of Tokyo

INTRODUCTION

Japan joined the Trans-Pacific Partnership (TPP) negotiations in July 2013 despite strong opposition from the domestic agricultural lobbies. Since then, it has been negotiating on trade and investment rules with other member economies multilaterally, and on trade liberalization measures with other members, particularly the United States, bilaterally. The TPP is expected to be a comprehensive, high-quality, twenty-first century free trade agreement (FTA), which covers 21 areas—market access, rules of origin, services, investment, intellectual property rights, competition policy, government procurement, the environment, labor, and other areas. These are truly twenty-first century issues needed to support supply chains developed in the Asia-Pacific region.

The TPP is important for Japan, and will help to achieve economic recovery after two decades of stagnation and to restore sustained growth. It is part of the "Abenomics" growth strategy. In addition, pursuing the TPP is consistent with Japan's economic partnership agreement (EPA) policies toward East Asia through the Regional Comprehensive Economic Partnership (RCEP), and toward the EU through the Japan-EU EPA. The TPP and the economic partnership agreements attempt to further connect Japan with the major centers of the world economy and, thus, to generate significant economic benefits for Japan.

This paper attempts to answer several key questions: What is the progress so far from the Japanese perspective? What are important challenges for Japan to successfully complete a TPP agreement? What is next after the TPP?

JAPAN'S ECONOMIC CHALLENGES AND TRADE POLICY STRATEGY

The Japanese government considers it vital for the economy to recover from two decades of economic stagnation. Without growth, Japan cannot solve various important problems, such as securing and expanding employment, maintaining a reliable social security system in an aging society, and reducing public debt to a sustainable level.

From international comparative perspectives, the Japanese economy has been relatively closed in terms of trade and foreign direct investment (FDI). Figure 1 demonstrates that Japan's trade (both exports and imports) and FDI stock (both outward and inward), measured as a ratio of GDP, are low. This suggests that Japan can further open its economy and integrate itself with the global market and to enhance its growth potential.

Traditionally, Japan has been trading with and investing in the United States and Europe. But in recent years, its trade and FDI relations with emerging economies in Asia have deepened. Japanese multinational corporations (MNCs) were the first that developed extensive production networks and supply chains throughout emerging Asia, helping to create "factory Asia" through advanced technological capabilities. Figure 2 shows that Japan's trade dependence on China has been rising rapidly, as have fears of overdependence on China and the perceived "China risk."

As a result of heavy investment in Asia's emerging economies, Japanese firms have accumulated sizable FDI stocks in emerging Asia, which have exceeded those in the United States and Europe (see Figure 3A). Figure 3B demonstrates that the computed rate of return on FDI is higher in emerging Asia—with the exception of those years immediately following the Asian financial crisis—than in the rest of the world.

Trade/GDP (%)

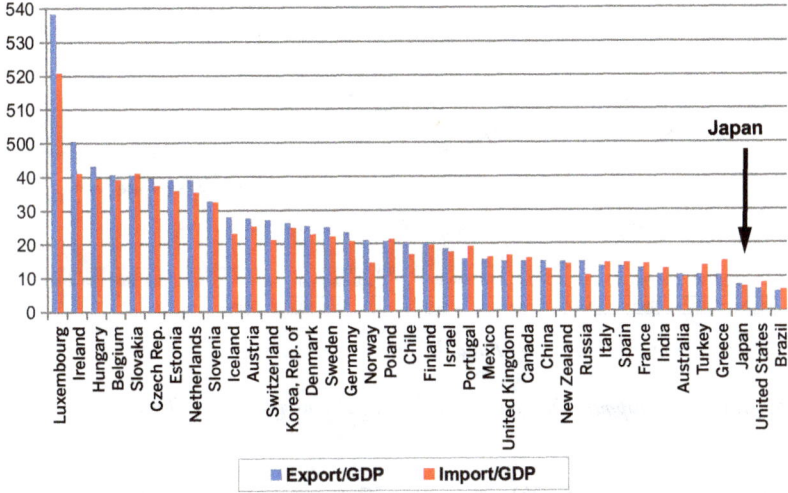

FDI (stock)/GDP (%)

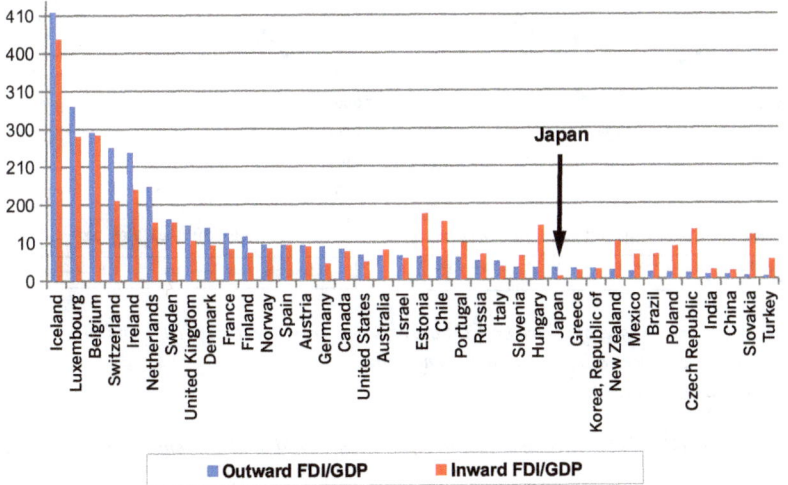

Source: International Monetary Fund, International Financial Statistics; United Nations Conference on Trade and Development.

FIGURE 1 *Japan's Trade/GDP and FDI (Stock)/GDP Compared Globally*

Exports

Imports

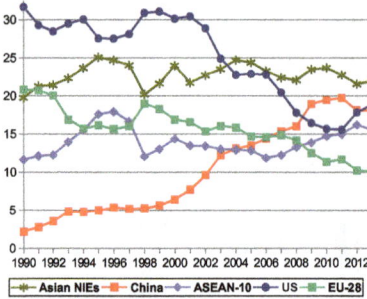 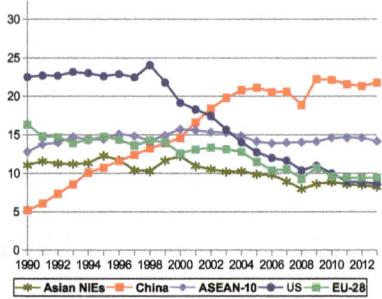

Source: International Monetary Fund, Direction of Trade Statistics.

FIGURE 2   *Geographical Distribution of Trading Partners for Japan's Trade (%)*

3A. FDI (stock)/GDP (%)

3B. Computed rates of return (%)

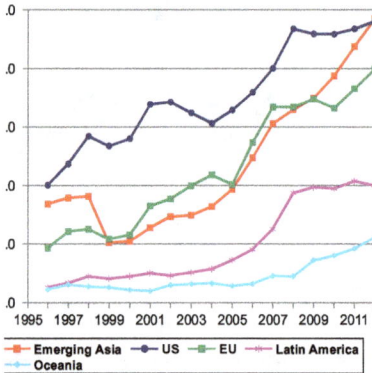 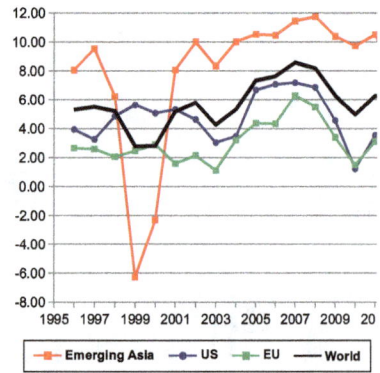

Note: Computed rates of return on FDI are obtained from the stock of FDI and investment income flows reported in the balance of payments.
Source: Bank of Japan.

FIGURE 3   *Global Comparison of Japan's FDI (Stock)/GDP and Computed Rate of Return*

This suggests the continued importance of emerging Asia for Japanese businesses.

Given that mature markets in the United States and the EU remain important for Japanese MNCs, and that emerging Asia has been growing rapidly, it is natural for Japan to focus its trade and FDI policies on strengthening economic ties with the United States, the EU, and emerging Asia.

Japan's Trade Strategy

Japan had long taken a policy of liberalizing trade through the GATT/WTO. In about 2000, however, Japan shifted from a WTO-only approach to a multi-track approach that uses both the WTO process and economic partnership agreement (EPA) policies.

So far, Japan has implemented 13 EPAs with 1 region (ASEAN) and 12 economies (7 ASEAN economies, Mexico, Chile, Switzerland, India, and Peru). Japan has just concluded an EPA with Australia and is now under official negotiations with Canada, Colombia, the EU, the GCC, and Mongolia, as well as with other ASEAN-Plus-Six economies (for a RCEP), China and South Korea (for a trilateral EPA), and 11 Asia-Pacific economies (for the TPP).

Until recently, several problems have stymied Japan's EPA approach. One problem has been the low trade coverage of its EPA partners, which at only 19 percent is lower than other developed economies (see Figure 4A). This reflected the fact that Japan had never forged EPAs with its major trade and FDI partners—the United States, the EU, and China. Recent efforts to start negotiations on the TPP, the Japan-EU EPA, the China-Japan-Korea FTA (CJK FTA), and the Regional Comprehensive Economic Partnership (RCEP) are potential solutions for addressing this problem. Indeed, these EPAs provide excellent opportunities for Japan to further connect with the United States and the Pacific side of Latin America, the EU, and China. They will also help Japan in achieving greater openness in its economy and greater diversification of its trade and FDI relationships.

Another problem has been that Japan's FTA/EPA liberalization ratio has been low, in the range of 84 percent to 88 percent (see Figure 4B). This is in sharp contrast with the liberalization ratios of most of its trading partners. For example, the United States, the EU, South Korea, Malaysia, and a few others have consistently achieved liberalization ratios of more than 95 percent. The low liberalization ratio in Japan is a result of protecting too many products, mainly in the agricultural sector.

4A. FTA/EPA trade coverage ratio (%)

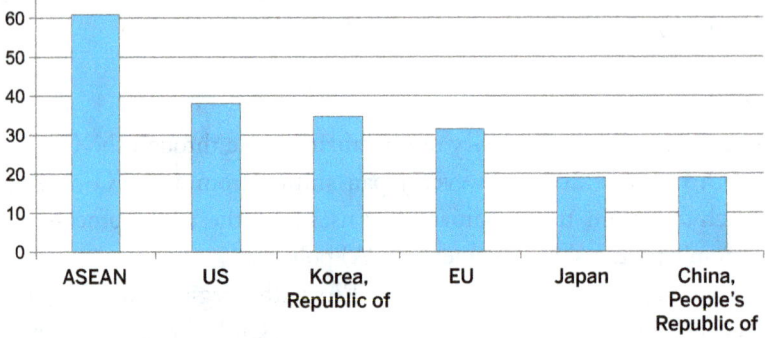

4B. FTA/EPA liberalization ratio (%)

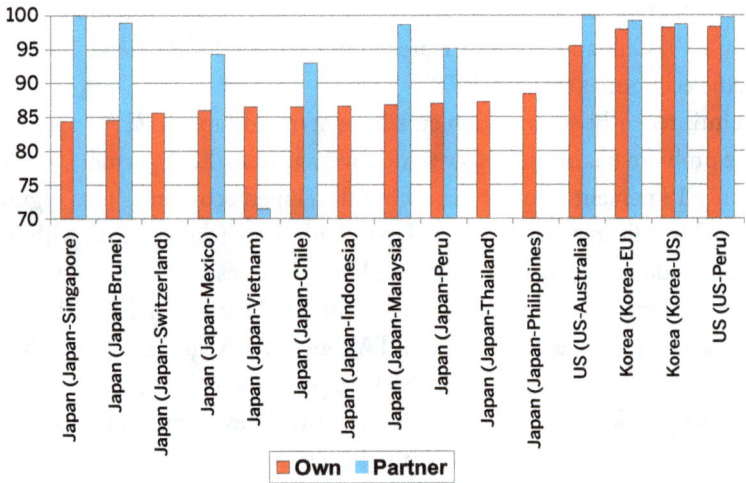

Note: The FTA/EPA trade coverage ratio is trade with FTA/EPA partners as a ratio of total trade. ASEAN data include intra-ASEAN trade, while EU data exclude intra-EU trade (if intra-EU trade was included, the ratio would be 76%). The FTA/EPA liberalization ratio is the number of tariff lines to become zero in ten years as the ratio of total number of tariff lines. Source: Calculated from International Monetary Fund, Direction of Trade Statistics; Cabinet Office, Government of Japan.

FIGURE 4   *Characteristics of Japan's EPAs: International Comparisons*

The elimination of tariffs has been hampered by policy considerations toward the agricultural sector, which has been regarded as internationally noncompetitive and in need of tariff protection. An important challenge for Japan is how to strengthen productivity and competitiveness of its agricultural sector so that it could withstand pressures from greater market opening and see eventual elimination of tariffs.

HIGHLIGHTS OF THE TPP

The TPP is often characterized as a comprehensive, high-quality, twenty-first century free trade agreement (FTA). This means that it aims to eliminate all tariffs in principle, and includes trade and investment rules that strongly support international supply chains. Twelve APEC economies are currently negotiating on the TPP, and South Korea, the Philippines, and Thailand may join in the near future. The negotiations cover 21 areas (with 29 chapters), including market access to goods (tariff elimination), rules of origin, services, investment, and so forth.[1]

One of the distinct features of the TPP is the diversity of its negotiating members, which include developed and developing economies, as well as agricultural exporting and importing economies.[2] Reaching a meaningful, high-quality agreement among them has been a difficult task, though some progress has been made. The most contentious issues have been market access, intellectual property rights (IPR), competition policy (particularly state-owned enterprise [SOE] reform), government procurement, investment (particularly the investor-state dispute settlement [ISDS] system), the environment, and labor. Table 1 provides a summary of the issues and different views among the negotiating members.

Market access issues are negotiated bilaterally between a pair of economies under the TPP framework.[3] The most serious bilateral negotiations have been taking place between the United States and Japan. Japan has been aggressive about opening US markets for manufactured products, particularly automobiles and home electric appliances, while it is defensive about protecting its own agricultural product markets. As another example, Vietnam has been aggressive about opening US markets for textiles, while the United States has been defensive.

TABLE I   *Contentious Issues in TPP Negotiations as of June 2014*

Areas	Economies most involved	Issues
Market access	US vs. JPN	The US claims that Japan's tariffs on agricultural products should be substantially reduced. Japan claims that auto tariffs in the US should be eliminated.
Intellectual property rights	US (JPN) vs. MAS & VIE	The US claims that data for pharmaceutical products and copyrights (for novels, movies, music, etc.) should be protected for a long period, while Malaysia and others claim that such protection should be for a short period.
Competition policy	US (AUS, JPN) vs. MAS, VIE, BRU	The US claims that policies that favor SOEs (such as subsidies) should be abolished to establish a level playing field against private firms, while Malaysia and others argue against such a claim.
Government procurement	SIN (US, JPN) vs. MAS, VIE, BRU	Singapore and others argue that government procurement should be opened to foreign firms, while Malaysia and others are reluctant.
Investment	US (JPN) vs. AUS (NZL, MAS)	The US and others argue that an investor-state dispute settlement (ISDS) system should be introduced, while Australia and others are against it.
Environment	US (CAN, JPN) vs. VIE, MAS	The US and others argue that environmental standards for firm activity should be improved, while Vietnam and others are reluctant.

Note: *AUS=Australia, BRU=Brunei, JPN=Japan, MAS=Malaysia, NZL=New Zealand, SIN=Singapore, US=United States, VIE=Vietnam.*
Source: *Compiled by the author from various sources.*

Trade and investment rules are negotiated multilaterally among all economies. On IPR issues, the United States currently protects data for new pharmaceutical products for five years (as do Malaysia, Vietnam, Australia, and New Zealand) in principle, but insists that the protection period should be lengthened to 10 years. On copyright protection for novels, movies, and entertainment products, the United States argues for the protection period to last for 70 years (as done in the US, Singapore, Australia, Chile, and Peru), while Mexico protects for 100 years and other economies (Japan, Malaysia, Vietnam, New Zealand, Brunei, and Canada) offer 50 years of protection.

Ensuring a level playing field in markets where state-owned enterprises (SOEs) have significant presence is also a contentious issue. Malaysia and Vietnam are vehemently resisting US demands that SOEs should stop receiving favorable treatment from the government. The Malaysian government claims that such reforms would force it to reconsider its long-standing policy of promoting indigenous Malays and, thus, could change the foundation of the society.

Government procurement is another sensitive area. Economies that have opened procurement processes in their central governments and, at least partially, in their local governments include Japan, the United States, Australia, Canada, and Peru. Economies that have opened their central government procurement to foreign firms are Mexico, Chile, New Zealand, Singapore, and Brunei.[4] For those economies that have not opened any procurement—namely, Malaysia and Vietnam—the challenges are significant.

Developing-economy members may need somewhat different treatments in most of these areas. For example, the protection period for data of some pharmaceutical products (to combat contagious diseases, for example) may have to be shorter in developing economies than in developed ones, as the former need low-cost generics. A sufficiently long period should be allowed for SOE reforms in developing economies. It is noted that Malaysia and Vietnam represent the interests of many developing and emerging economies, a role that China would play if it were a negotiating member of the TPP.

Income Gains under Alternative TPP Scenarios

A study by Petri, Plummer, and Zhai (2012) has examined the impact of the TPP and other scenarios on incomes of TPP member economies, as well as others. Figure 5A demonstrates that the TPP has a positive impact on world income, measured by the percentage change in 2025 from baseline scenarios, but that this impact is less than that of the RCEP and much less than that of a Free Trade Area of the Asia-Pacific (FTA-AP). Thus, the study suggests that once the TPP has been agreed upon, APEC members should combine the TPP with the RCEP to forge an

5A. TPP, RCEP, and FTAAP (US$ Bill)   **5B. Alternative TPP scenarios (% GDP)**

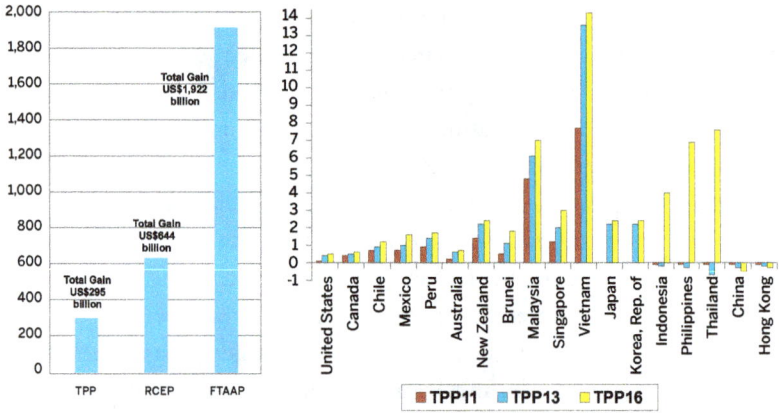

Note: *Effects of various FTA scenarios (TPP, RCEP, and FTAAP in Figure 5A; TPP-11, TPP-13, and TPP-16 in Figure 5B) on world income (5A) and on individual economies (5B) in 2025 in terms of percentage changes from baseline scenarios. TPP-11 excludes Japan, TPP-13 includes South Korea, and TPP-16 further includes Indonesia, the Philippines, and Thailand.*
Source: *Petri, Plummer, and Zhai (2012).*

FIGURE 5   *Income Gains under Alternative Scenarios*

FTAAP, as this would generate higher income from a world perspective. Figure 5B shows that Malaysia and Vietnam, which are engaged in many contentious negotiations with the developed economies, will actually be big winners as a result of the TPP. They are advised to conclude the TPP by pursuing domestic reforms, which would lead to agreement on contentious trade and investment rules. In addition, the study shows that as membership grows, income gains for each member will also rise.

OPPORTUNITIES AND RISKS OF TPP FOR JAPAN

Japan decided to join TPP negotiations in July 2013 in the midst of extensive domestic debate. The business sector strongly supported participation in TPP negotiations, while the agricultural lobbies were strongly opposed to such a move. A central feature of Prime Minister Shinzo Abe's growth strategy, announced in June 2013, included economic partnerships such as the TPP.

Opportunities for Japan

As a key pillar of the growth strategy, the TPP can (1) stimulate foreign firms' investment in Japan; (2) increase Japanese producers' access to goods and services markets in member economies with whom Japan has not had EPAs, particularly the United States; and (3) provide more confidence for Japanese multinational corporations investing in member economies through more equal treatment of foreign investment and IPR protection in host countries. It also provides opportunities for Japanese small- and medium-sized enterprises to conduct business through simpler trade procedures and movements of business people.

But the largest intangible benefit for Japan would be that it could participate in designing trade and investment rules for the twenty-first century Asia-Pacific region. As the TPP is potentially a step toward an FTAAP, the rules under the TPP will likely form the basis for future common rules in the Asia-Pacific region.

The TPP can have other benefits as well. It can strengthen Japan-US political relationships and allow diversification of Japan's trade, given the fear of overdependence on China and the perceived China risk. It also rectifies Japanese firms' disadvantageous positions in the US markets relative to South Korean firms, which enjoy preferential tariffs. The TPP negotiations can induce China to be more firmly committed to RCEP negotiations, as well as push the EU to accelerate official negotiations on a Japan-EU economic partnership agreement. Finally, the TPP provides an opportunity to reform and strengthen Japan's agricultural sector in a fundamental way.

The advantageous position given to South Korean firms is worthy of further explanation. With the implementation of the South Korea-US (KORUS) FTA in January 2012, Japanese firms have become less competitive in the US market relative to South Korean manufacturers. South Korean firms now enjoy preferential tariffs in the United States (and in the EU with the implementation of the South Korea–EU FTA in July

2011), while Japanese firms do not. For example, Japanese car producers face a 2.5 percent tariff on automobiles and a 25 percent tariff on trucks, while South Korean producers face zero tariffs. Tariffs are levied on Japanese producers of bearings (9 percent), polyethylene and polyester (6.5 percent), and color televisions (5 percent), while their South Korean counterparts can export tariff-free. The TPP can correct this imbalance.

Initial Concerns about the TPP

While Japan's government decided to join TPP negotiations, various concerns were expressed by the public about possible negative consequences of the TPP.

First, the TPP would require the immediate tariff elimination on all products, thereby exposing domestic noncompetitive sectors—such as the agricultural sector—to fierce competition from abroad and resulting in the collapse of these sectors. If the agricultural sector is severely affected, food self-sufficiency would also be further reduced and food security threatened.

Second, the TPP would weaken the Japanese social security system, particularly its universal health and medical insurance system, because it would allow private firms to enter the medical industry (such as hospital management). In addition, higher protections of pharmaceutical IPR would lead to higher costs of medical drugs (such as generics). Critics argued that a private sector–driven health and medical system could create a huge divide between the haves and the have-nots, and reduce the quality of services to low-income people. According to them, this would not be consistent with the idea of a universal healthcare system. Compounding the problem, less-qualified medical professionals might immigrate from abroad, reducing the overall quality of medical services in Japan.

Third, insurance services provided by Japan Post Insurance (JPI) and cooperative credit institutions would be prohibited from receiving favorable treatment from the government, and would be required to behave as if they were private entities. The reason is that JPI, as a government-owned insurance provider, enjoys a number of statutory, regulatory, and other governmental privileges. Cooperatives offering insurance also enjoy business, tax, and regulatory advantages over foreign insurance providers, which would distort market competition with the private sector.[5]

The fear is that once these insurance providers stop receiving favorable treatments, people in local or remote areas might lose access to such services as a result of their transformation into private-like entities.

Fourth, the TPP would open local government procurement to foreign firms, shifting business opportunities away from domestic firms. It would allow foreign investors' legal disputes against the state to expand and might undermine national sovereignty. In addition, the TPP might also allow more imports of unsafe food because of relaxed food safety standards.

Most of these initial concerns were based on misinformation and/or misunderstanding of the TPP. As information on the bilateral negotiations between the United States and Japan has been revealed, most of these concerns have dissipated. However, concerns over the negative impact of the TPP on agriculture have persisted, and they deserve further attention.

Economic Impacts of the TPP on Japan

Government reports about the impact of the TPP on agriculture have been contradictory. The Ministry of Agriculture, Forestry, and Fishery (MAFF) emphasized serious negative impacts, while the Cabinet Office and the Ministry of Economy, Trade, and Industry (METI) reported positive impacts.

MAFF estimated that the TPP would cause significant damage to both Japan's agriculture and the overall economy. Under the assumption that all tariffs on agricultural imports were eliminated, the report found that agricultural production would decline by 4.1 trillion yen, the value of multifunctional agriculture would drop by 3.7 trillion yen, employment opportunities would be lost in the amount of 3.4 million jobs, and GDP would decline by 7.9 trillion yen. The food self-sufficiency rate would decline substantially, from 40 percent to 14 percent.

A Cabinet Office report (2010 supported by Kawasaki 2011) concluded that Japan's participation in the TPP, and its elimination of tariffs, would raise real GDP by 0.48 percent to 0.65 percent (see Figure 6).[6] It also found that Japan's nonparticipation in the TPP (while South Korea implemented FTAs with the United States, the EU, and China) would cause a decline of Japan's real GDP by 0.13 percent. The reason for this

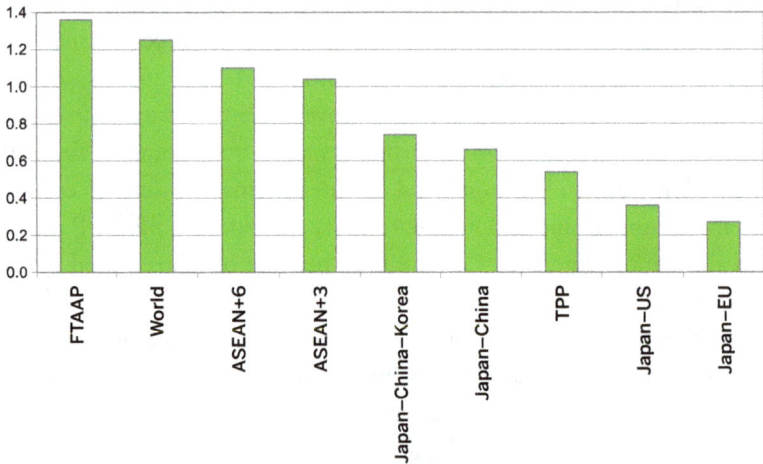

Source: Kawasaki (2011).

FIGURE 6 *Benefits of Various FTA Scenarios for Japan (% of GDP)*

is that Japan's exports and production of automobiles, electric and elec-tronic products, machinery, and other manufacturing goods will decline, as firms in these sectors lose market shares in the United States, the EU, and China due to competition from South Korean firms. These negative impacts on the manufacturing sector would be large if Japan did not participate in the TPP.

An analysis conducted by METI showed that Japan's failure to par-ticipate in the TPP and conclude EPAs with the EU and China (while South Korea implemented FTAs with China in addition to the United States and the EU) would reduce Japan's real GDP by 1.53 percent in 2020, relative to the benchmark case. There would be a loss of 812,000 jobs. Japan's exports, production, and GDP would all decline.

An additional finding was that Japan's participation in the TPP would make a notable difference to some Asian members, particularly Vietnam and Malaysia. The reason for this is that the economic size of Japan is large enough to create additional benefits to smaller developing econo-mies. Thus, Japan's participation in the TPP benefits not only Japan, but also developing member economies in Asia.

PROGRESS ON THE TPP NEGOTIATIONS

The most difficult issue for Japan in its bilateral negotiations with the United States has been the tariff reduction of agricultural products, particularly pork and beef. The second difficult issue is the auto market in both Japan and the United States. The results of bilateral negotiations between the United States and Japan are important for the TPP negotiations as a whole, given that the combined GDP of the two economies accounts for more than 80 percent of the total GDP of all negotiating members.

Tariff Reductions on Agricultural Products

The Japanese government identified five critical product categories to be protected from tariff elimination. These were rice, wheat, beef and pork, dairy products, and sugar. The five categories include 586 tariff line products. Table 2 shows that there are altogether 9,018 tariff line products in Japan. Of these, 8,089 tariff line products have been subject to tariff elimination (with the maximum potential liberalization rate of 89.7 percent) and the remaining 929 tariff line products—including the five critical product categories (586 tariff line products) and other sensitive products (343 tariff line products)—have never been subject to tariff elimination.

The bilateral negotiations have revealed that the United States is not particularly interested in opening the Japanese rice market. Rather, it is interested in opening the pork and beef markets and, to a lesser extent, the dairy product market. The United States is the largest producer of beef in the world, and the second-largest producer of pork (following China). It exports about US$7 billion worth of beef and US$6 billion worth of pork. Japan is the largest importer of US pork. Figure 7 shows that in the Japanese beef market, Japanese producers are the largest supplier (accounting for 42 percent), followed by Australian (36 percent) and US (15 percent) producers. In the Japanese pork market, Japanese producers account for 55 percent of total supply, and the United States is the largest foreign supplier of pork, accounting for 18 percent of the market. For US producers of pork and beef, Japan is indeed one of the most attractive markets in the world.

TABLE 2 *Classification of Japan's Import Products*

Products that have never been subject to tariff elimination (929 tariff lines, 10.3%)	Five critical product categories (586 tariff lines, 6.5%)	Rice (58) Wheat (109) Beef (51) and pork (49) Dairy products (188) Sugar (131)	
	Other sensitive product categories (343 tariff lines, 3.8%)	Agricultural, forestry, and fishery products (248)	Fishery (91) Beans (16) Konjak (3) Prepared food (30) Plywood (34)
		Manufactured products (95)	
Products that have been subject to tariff elimination (8,089 tariff lines, 89.7%)			
Total number of Japanese imports (9,018 tariff lines)			

Source: Compiled by the author from various sources.

Market for beef (thousand tons)   Market for pork (thousand tons)

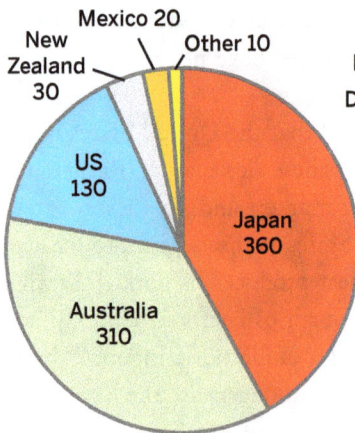

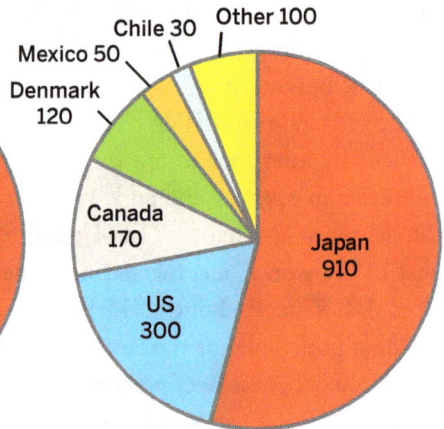

Source: Ministry of Agriculture, Forestry, and Fishery.

FIGURE 7 *Japanese Markets for Beef and Pork: Major Supplier Countries, 2012*

The United States and Japan have been negotiating intensively on the extent of tariff reductions, the time frame for tariff reductions, conditions for triggering safeguard measures, and use of low- or zero-tariff import quotas. Japan would like to protect their beef and pork producers by maintaining high tariffs, pursuing gradual reductions over long time periods (more than 10 years), and adopting easily usable safeguard measures.[7] In contrast, the United States would like to open the Japanese beef and pork markets by reducing tariffs as deeply and quickly as possible, and by constraining implementation of safeguard measures. It appears that it would not insist that tariffs be completely eliminated on the five critical agricultural categories, as long as US producers can meaningfully increase exports of their products.

In the case of rice and wheat, it is likely that the current high tariffs will remain, while Japan will introduce special tariff-free import quotas for US rice and wheat under private trading. For dairy products, Japan is considering setting up low- or zero-tariff import quotas on cheese. Sugar has not been discussed.

Thus, tariff reductions are expected for beef and pork, but tariff elimination is unlikely to occur. This poses a problem with regard to the liberalization ratio for Japan. To achieve a high liberalization rate, such as 95 percent or higher, tariffs need to be eliminated among the five critical product categories and other sensitive categories that have never been subject to tariff elimination. It turns out that of the five critical product categories (586 tariff line products), 181 tariff line products have not been imported over the 2008–2012 period, and can potentially be subject to tariff elimination. If the Japanese government can further identify 269 tariff line products for tariff elimination from these critical and sensitive categories, the liberalization ratio could reach 95 percent.

Japanese and US Automobile Market Issues

The United States has been insisting that the Japanese automobile market is closed. Figure 8 shows that Japanese automobiles account for 95.5 percent of the Japanese market, and foreign automobiles account for only 4.5 percent. In contrast, US automobiles account for 47 percent of the US market and Japanese automobiles account for 35 percent of the US market. The United States interprets these figures as an indication that Japan's automobile market is closed, while the US market is open. As Japan's tariff on auto imports is zero, the United States argues that nontariff barriers to trade are responsible. That is, Japan's automotive regulations—such as safety standards—make it hard for US autos to be imported. They argue that auto sector rules and regulations in Japan are often developed in a nontransparent manner without consultation with foreign producers. In addition, Japan provides preferential treatment to a specific car segment, the tiny kei (light) car, which is manufactured only in Japan. Japanese automakers, on the other hand, believe that the Japanese market is fully open, and wonder what the United States really wants. Although it seems to want Japanese safety standards to be relaxed and the preferential treatment of light cars to be dismantled, it is not clear whether US auto sales in Japan would expand even with these changes.

Japanese automakers would like to see auto tariffs in the United States (2.5 percent for automobiles and 25 percent for trucks) eliminated. The United States seems to be agreeable, but tariff elimination could take place over the longest possible time frame allowed under the TPP, such as 20 years. This is not an acceptable proposition for Japan.

CONCLUSIONS

Japan needs to further open its economy and integrate with the global economy, particularly the United States, the EU, and emerging Asia. The TPP, now led by the United States, aims to achieve high levels of openness among like-minded economies and is a key step toward an FTAAP, together with a RCEP. Japan can benefit from joining the TPP because it affords greater market access, protection of its investment abroad, enforcement of IPR rules, and attraction of foreign investment.

The bilateral negotiations between the United States and Japan have revealed that the TPP would not require immediate elimination of tariffs on all products, but that many exceptions could be allowed. Japan's rice tariffs will most likely remain untouched. The US auto market will likely achieve zero tariffs on Japanese autos, but over a long time period. These developments run counter to initial expectations of the TPP. Nonetheless, the progress that has been made should be valued highly.

Japanese auto markets (2010) US auto markets (2010)

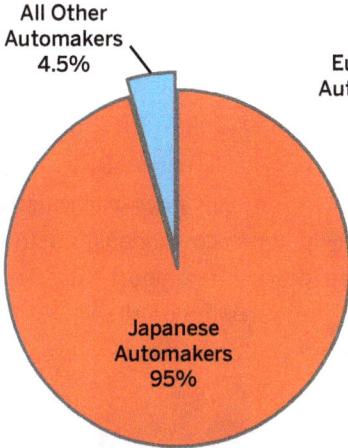

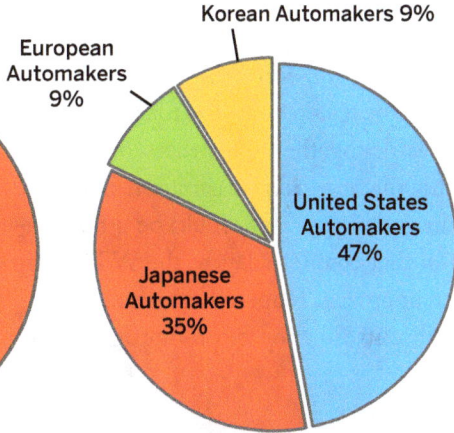

Source: Japan Automobile Manufacturers Association for Japan's data; Automotive News Database 2010 sales for US data.

FIGURE 8 *Auto Markets in Japan and the US*

A major challenge for Japan to successfully complete the TPP is to improve the productivity and competitiveness of the agricultural sector, particularly beef and pork producers, through comprehensive reforms. Japanese authorities may consider changing the mode of protection away from border measures (such as tariffs and quotas) to domestic measures (such as income transfers) if agricultural protection is to continue long term. It is important for Japan to open the beef and pork markets to the maximum extent for the benefit of domestic consumers, and to see tariff elimination on autos in the United States within the shortest possible time frame. Another challenge is to remove or reduce behind-the-border regulations, which would also be required for a Japan-EU EPA.

The US negotiators must obtain trade promotion authority (TPA) to make sure that the TPP will be ratified without major problems and delays. Otherwise, other negotiating members might not be able to make maximum possible concessions as the US Congress could force renegotiation without the TPA.

Once the TPP is implemented, the Asia-Pacific economies need to connect the TPP with the RCEP to forge a greater FTAAP. This is likely to take the form of an increasing number of RCEP members joining the TPP. In this sense, the TPP has the role of setting a benchmark that other developing and emerging economies, such as China, India, and Indonesia, will eventually accept.

The next step would be for member economies of the TPP and TTIP to work together to further connect the two mega-regionals, starting with the adoption of common trade and investment rules, particularly rules of origin. This would be a bottom-up approach to global integration that counterbalances the WTO's top-down, often poorly functioning approach. Hopefully, this process will put pressure on the WTO to restore its function of promoting global integration without discrimination.

NOTES

1. There is a discussion in the US as to whether the TPP should include a currency manipulation clause. Currency manipulation is said to be present when foreign exchange market intervention prevents currency appreciation in the presence of a large current account surplus.

2. In the case of the US-EU FTA, called the Transatlantic Trade and Investment Partnership (TTIP), negotiating members are all developed economies and relatively homogeneous. In this sense, given the diversity of WTO members, the TPP could be a model for future multilateral trade and investment liberalization. This model might be pursued by a future WTO, if the organization could be significantly reactivated and remodeled.

3. This means that any one country's agreed on tariff tables will not be common vis-à-vis TPP partner members. The US, Canada, and Mexico have taken the approach that each economy's tariff tables can be different depending on bilateral partners, which was essentially the approach adopted by NAFTA. Australia, New Zealand, and Singapore, on the other hand, take the view that each economy should establish common tariff tables vis-à-vis all TPP bilateral partners. The former approach can easily accommodate exceptional treatments vis-à-vis particular partners, while the latter approach tends to limit such treatments. Japan appears to prefer the former approach for agricultural products, and the latter for manufactured products.

4. Japan, the United States, Canada, and Singapore are signatories of the WTO Agreement on Government Procurement (GPA) of April 1994 (signed by 15 parties, including Hong Kong, South Korea, and Chinese Taipei in Asia).

5. As a result, the United States wants JPI not to provide new or modified products, such as cancer insurance, until level playing fields have been established between JPI and US insurance suppliers (like Aflac). JPI seems ready not to introduce new insurance products.

6. The Cabinet Office report also estimated the benefit of forming an ASEAN-Plus-Three FTA to be 1.04% of real GDP, the benefit of ASEAN-Plus-Six FTA to be 1.10% of real GDP, and the benefit of forming an FTAPP to be 1.36% of GDP. These are typically smaller than the Petri-Plummer-Zhai estimates.

7. When imports of a certain product surge in value within a short period of time, the importing country's government can invoke safeguard measures by applying high tariffs on the product.

SOURCES

Cabinet Office, Government of Japan. 2010. "EPA ni kansuru kakshu no shisan (Various Simulations on EPAs)." October 27.

Kawasaki, Kenichi. 2011. "Determining Priority among EPAs: Which trading partner has the greatest economic impact?" RIETI Column 318, May 31.

Petri, Peter A., Michael G. Plummer, and Fan Zhai. 2012. *The Trans-Pacific Partnership and Asia-Pacific Integration: A Quantitative Assessment*. Policy Analysis in International Economics No. 98. Washington, DC: Peterson Institute for International Economics and East-West Center.

3

Canada and the TPP

Short-Term Tactics and Long-Term Strategy

*Hugh Stephens, Vice Chair, Canadian National Committee
on Pacific Economic Cooperation*

There are valid questions about whether it will be possible to bring
the Trans-Pacific Partnership (TPP) to a successful conclusion within
a reasonable time frame, but Canada is firmly committed to—and
needs—a successful outcome, despite its early ambivalence toward
the agreement. There are still a number of difficult issues to be dealt
with in the negotiations, made more complex by the addition of new
participants such as Japan and the narrow room for maneuver of US
negotiators, given the administration's lack of trade promotion authority
(TPA) from Congress, and considerable congressional opposition to
granting such authority. Given all these concerns, one might well ask:
why was Canada so keen to join the TPP, and why is it so committed
to the TPP now?

THE STAKES FOR CANADA

For Canada, the TPP is both an end in itself (that is, a vehicle for
trade liberalization and job growth), and a means to an end, which is
to reestablish Canada's economic credentials in the Asia-Pacific region

generally. The TPP is rightly seen as one of the vehicles that could become the foundation for a Free Trade Area of the Asia-Pacific (FTAAP). The other, at the moment, is the Regional Comprehensive Economic Partnership (RCEP) process, an ASEAN-centered plurilateral negotiation that includes all 10 ASEAN states, plus China, South Korea, Japan, India, Australia, and New Zealand. Canada and the United States are excluded. The Pacific Economic Cooperation Council (PECC) has estimated—based on economic modeling work done by Peter Petri and Michael Plummer—that a 12-economy TPP (including Japan) will lead to economic gains of US$295 billion by 2025. The RCEP will lead to gains of almost double that amount, totaling US$500 billion, owing in part to higher existing barriers in the RCEP economies that will be removed. The real payoff, however, comes with a combined TPP and RCEP in the form of the FTAAP, which will bring gains of US$1.9 trillion in 2025.

In addition to being a potential pathway to the holy grail of the FTA-AP, the TPP has a very real significance for Canada beyond protecting its access to the US market. A key player for Canada is Japan. Japan's (and potentially South Korea's) entry into the TPP was a significant factor in Canada's decision to seek participation. Japan is Canada's fourth-largest export market, but much of Canada's exports to Japan compete directly with the United States. While Canada and Japan have launched bilateral negotiations, there is no guarantee that this process will be successful. It is important, therefore, for Canada to be at the TPP table with Japan, along with the United States, engaged in a process where the removal of trade barriers to the Japanese market is being discussed.

With a population of only 35 million, Canada learned a bitter lesson from its experience with South Korea, which lost interest in concluding a deal with Canada once the South Korea–US and South Korea–EU deals were completed. Canada, as a smaller economy, does not have the same negotiating leverage as the United States, yet obtaining access to the South Korean market for those Canadian products, such as pork and beef, that compete directly with similar or identical US products was an essential negotiating objective for Canadian officials. Canada's unwillingness to settle for second-best, combined with South Korea's lack of interest and opposition from some auto manufacturers based in Canada, led to the current impasse. (Since the original date of writing, Canada and South Korea have successfully concluded their bilateral FTA, with agreement reached on March 11, 2014). Canada needs to avoid a similar outcome in its negotiations with Japan, where the attraction of the US market for Japan may trump interest in doing a bilateral deal with Canada. Recent indications of South Korea's willingness to join the TPP provided an added lever that Canada apparently used as a way to break the South Korea–Canada logjam.

CANADA'S DELAYED PARTICIPATION

When Canada was officially invited to join the negotiations in Los Cabos, Mexico, in June 2012, it marked (for Canada) an important milestone on what had become a long and tortuous road to participation. Canada's invitation came a day after the invitation was extended to Mexico, and the hitch in what was supposed to have been a simultaneous invitation demonstrated the difficulty that Canada faced in convincing the US administration—and some other TPP economies—that its presence would be a positive element toward a successful outcome. At the same time, it seemed to reflect the reality of Canadian ambivalence toward the TPP process.

The fact that Canada was not openly welcomed is somewhat surprising given its economic heft (by most counts, it is the world's tenth- or eleventh-largest economy) and its massive trading relationship with the United States. In fact, in his letter to Congress seeking approval for the administration's invitation to Canada to join the TPP negotiations, then US Trade Representative Ron Kirk noted that US exports to Canada totaled US\$337 billion in 2011, the largest export market for US goods. He went on to say, "We have conducted in-depth discussions with Canada about the standards and objectives that the TPP countries are seeking, particularly in those areas where the standards and objectives are higher than those that exist in the North American Free Trade Agreement (NAFTA). Canada has assured us of its willingness to negotiate on these issues and its preparedness to achieve these high standards together with other TPP countries."[1]

But Canada was a latecomer, and had to work overtime to push its way into the negotiations. Its Asia credentials had lapsed. Although Canada has had a long history of engagement with Asia—going back to the days of the Colombo Plan in the 1950s, becoming an ASEAN dialogue partner in 1977, being a founding member of the Pacific Economic Cooperation Council (PECC) in 1980, and being a founding member of APEC in 1989—in recent years, it has neglected to maintain its previous level of engagement with Asia. Part of the reason can be blamed on a series of minority governments from 2004 through 2011, which resulted in a degree of political uncertainty and relative lack of interest in foreign policy and trade issues on the part of Canadian political leaders—other than in the war in Afghanistan, which became a significant political liability as Canadian casualties mounted. Even though Canada launched FTA negotiations with Singapore in 2001 and with South Korea in 2004, these negotiations did not make progress. When Canada was offered a chance in 2005 to join the then Pacific 4 (P4), the precursor to the TPP, it wasn't interested. Even after the United States breathed new life into what became the TPP, Canada's attention was elsewhere.

ROLE OF THE UNITED STATES

For Canada, the overriding policy issue has always been access to the US market. This was the driving motivation for the Canada-US FTA in 1989 that developed into NAFTA. Instead of focusing on the TPP negotiations, it was all too easy for Canadians to focus on the huge US market just next door. In addition, there were concerns in Canada that "sensitive" issues, such as supply management in dairy, would have to be addressed if it entered into talks with economies like Australia and New Zealand. Moreover, the United States had—and still has—ongoing concerns in Canada regarding a number of trade issues, such as its cultural exception, and Canada was concerned that these might be reopened. As a result, during the early phases of the TPP, Canada showed no interest. The 2008 global financial crisis changed Canadian attitudes, as it changed much else.

The slowdown in the US economy in the wake of the financial crisis, combined with the growing economic clout of Asia, became a wake-up call impossible to ignore. The business community was calling for bold moves to get Canada back in the game in Asia. The Conservative government of Stephen Harper had positioned itself as the party of economic growth and jobs, and—after a series of minority governments—it finally won a majority in 2011. Part of Prime Minister Harper's economic platform was to push for trade liberalization across the board. In May 2009, negotiations were launched with the EU on a Canada-EU Trade Agreement (CETA). Other initiatives followed: a bilateral framework was established with the United States to discuss border issues that impeded trade, and a full-court press was mounted to get Canada into the TPP. But despite Canada dropping broad hints that it would be open to an invitation to join the talks, the welcome mat was not rolled out. Apart from New Zealand's well-known antipathy to Canada's supply-managed dairy policies, the US response was guarded—and distinctly cool.

Several reasons have been advanced for the lack of enthusiasm on the part of the United States for Canadian participation. Despite their NAFTA partnership and the fact that the vast majority of Canada-US trade crosses the border without problems, there have been a number of bilateral disagreements. The United States may have felt that these issues would not be helpful additions to the TPP negotiating agenda. In the eyes of some in Washington, DC, Canada would be more of a hindrance than a help. One of the principal areas of concern was intellectual property (IP) rights protection, where US copyright industries were unhappy with Canada's weak copyright regime, as well as issues regarding the length of protection for pharmaceutical patents. There was no doubt concern that Canadian insistence on protecting its "cultural industries" could potentially contaminate negotiations with some of the other TPP economies in ways that would not be helpful to the United States. Finally, adding a new and potentially "difficult" partner part way through the negotiations would do nothing to speed up what was already becoming a protracted process. Canada was reluctant to openly profess interest lest it be publicly rebuffed. Finally, at the Honolulu APEC Summit in November 2011, Prime Minister Harper took the plunge (presumably after getting the signal that the United States would not oppose Canada's and

Mexico's TPP applications)[2] and declared the TPP to be a process "that Canada was interested in moving forward on." Canada's International Trade Minister Ed Fast was dispatched on a trans-Pacific odyssey of epic proportions, visiting all TPP capitals in the space of a few months. In each, he secured either supportive or benign statements regarding Canadian participation. This admirable demonstration of determination did not go unnoticed, and the effort to "surround" the United States by getting other partners on board was partially responsible—along with heavy Canadian lobbying of both government and business groups in Washington, DC—for securing the full support of the Obama administration and in successfully navigating the congressional approval process. Many US businesses with operations in Canada (and Mexico) were becoming concerned that the exclusion of their Canadian operations from TPP preferences could complicate supply chains. There was additionally the opportunity to update and complete some of the unfinished business of NAFTA. Canada could even be helpful in some areas, such as the controversial investor-state provision, given its experience with such a regime in NAFTA.

OPPOSITION IN CANADA

After the announcement that Canada would be joining the negotiations (once the necessary consultation with Congress had been completed), a vocal and active anti-TPP chorus emerged in Canada. This was fueled largely by those with a mistrust of trade liberalization generally (such as anti-WTO groups), but also because of the terms on which Canada was admitted—the so-called "take it or leave it" provisions. The "anti-just-about-everything" nature of the opposition was perhaps best summed up by a quote from the advocacy group the Council of Canadians. The TPP, said the group, "could lead to the dismantling of Canada's important supply management regimes for dairy, poultry, and egg production; the race-to-the-bottom potential in a proposed regulatory harmonization chapter; extreme intellectual property protections for big drug companies that would limit access to life-saving medicines; investor-state provisions that would allow companies to sue governments over rules to protect the environment; government procurement restrictions, and copyright rules that undermine Internet freedom."[3] These same voices are now busy denouncing the Canada-EU Trade Agreement (CETA), on which agreement in principle was announced on October 18, 2013. That agreement maintained Canada's supply management system, but allowed for a doubling of European quotas for cheese; opened subnational government procurement to European companies; and extended the patent protection period for pharmaceutical drugs to partially cover the lengthy patent approval process.[4] The offset, of course, is improved market access for 35 million Canadians to a market of 500 million, including better access in the areas of automotive products, beef and pork, and financial services. The outcome of CETA offers some indications of where Canada may be prepared to make concessions in the TPP negotiating process, but these will necessarily be part of larger trade-offs.

TPP OUTCOMES

It seems clear that despite the high-blown rhetoric about TPP negotiating partners having to put everything "on the table," and talk of a "gold standard, twenty-first century" agreement, the reality will be somewhat different. Everything may in theory be on the table, but some things will fall off as part of the negotiating process. Don't expect US sugar quotas to go away, or Canada's supply management system to be dismantled, or Australia to sign on to investor-state provisions, or Vietnam to put its state-owned enterprises (SOEs) under full market discipline. Don't expect all the TPP economies to meet the sort of IP standards the United States would like, or US trade remedy laws to be made subordinate to a TPP dispute settlement mechanism. There is now talk in the US Congress of a "currency manipulation" provision being added to the agreement, a move that would surely be a deal breaker given the vagueness of definitions in this area, and the potential for misuse of such a clause.[5] On the other hand, if the TPP can achieve progress in a substantial number of areas by rationalizing the conflicting rules of origin that exist across the region and simplifying supply chains, strengthening investor protection generally and improving respect for intellectual property laws, addressing e-commerce issues and opening services markets, it will have made a significant contribution to trade liberalization in the region.

The biggest gains will come from dismantling the import barriers that exist in the Japanese market. Their removal will benefit Japan significantly,[6] and will also bring important benefits to Japan's trading partners. Given the nature of the TPP negotiations, the bilateral US-Japan talks within the TPP framework will be critical to achieving the fullest possible economic gains for all members. Despite Japan's predictable reluctance to make any significant movement on key agricultural commodities, and ongoing US concerns over the balance in auto trade with Japan (concerns that are linked to the so-called "currency manipulation" clause favored by many members of Congress), the importance of achieving even a partial breakthrough in the US-Japan bilateral talks is critical if the US administration is to win trade promotion authority from Congress, and both the Obama and Abe administrations are acutely aware of this. The rest of the TPP partners are watching and waiting to see how and when the United States and Japan can resolve their differences, so that their own negotiations with Japan can be finalized. At that point, there is a reasonable prospect that the agreement will be able to proceed to its final phase.

The gains that Canada can expect to achieve from the agreement are dependent in large part on successfully opening the Japanese market, as well as the productivity gains that will accrue from opening its own market. Indeed, the Canadian Council of Chief Executives has published a study arguing the benefits of "unilateral disarmament" (i.e., unilateral removal of tariffs) for Canada, which it claims could generate CA\$20 billion in economic gains, approximately five times the value of the CA\$4 billion a year that Canada currently collects in customs revenues.[7] These gains would more than double the estimated gains to Canada from the TPP, using Petri and Plummer's calculations. Realistically, neither Canada nor any other TPP partner is going to unilaterally open its market, so gains will have to be based on the mutual concessions achieved within the TPP. The TPP started with a high level of ambition with regard to tariff removal, and the gains to be achieved will be significant as long as economies follow through on commitments to comprehensive coverage. Additionally, Petri and Plummer have pointed out that as much as 20

percent of additional gains will be brought about by investment liberalization through the increase of foreign direct investment (FDI) flows.
Individual investment liberalization agreements, such as the one Canada
has reached (but not implemented) with China,[8] have the potential to
bring about positive investment results. However, as the Canada-China
bilateral has shown, such bilateral agreements can fall hostage to other
unrelated issues, and are not a substitute for a regional investment liberalization regime. To achieve the benefits that will come with a successful
TPP, and potentially an FTAAP in the future, Canada recognizes that it
needs to be part of the process, and the TPP at the moment is the only
negotiating forum where it has a seat at the table.

CONCLUSIONS

The success of the TPP is still an open question. The TPP may not be
concluded, and if it is, the results may be less than originally hoped for.
Ratification will be politically difficult, not only for the United States,
but also for some of the other TPP partners. There will be vocal opposition on the part of a number of special interest groups. Despite these
challenges, for Canada—not part of the RCEP or any ASEAN-Plus
agreement, and not part of the East Asia Summit—the TPP is the best
available forum on offer. It cannot afford to squander this opportunity.
Now that it has proven the skeptics wrong and found enough common
ground with the EU to initial an agreement, Canada will be pushing
hard to conclude the TPP as early as possible. Through its EU agreement, Canada has already signaled where it may have some negotiating
flexibility, and Canadian trade negotiators will work hard to ensure that
Canada stays in the game and comes home with positive gains that it can
sell to the provinces and business community, particularly with reference
to Japan. Beyond any specific improvements in market access to TPP
economies, Canada will use its reasserted Asia-Pacific presence through
the TPP to push for a broader role generally and to reach beyond the
TPP to China, South Korea, Indonesia, India, and others. That is the
ultimate end game for Canada, and it is why the TPP has strategic significance well beyond its immediate economic impact.

NOTES

1. Ambassador Ron Kirk to Speaker John Boehner and Senator Daniel Inouye, July 10, 2012.

2. "The United States welcomes the interest of Canada and Mexico, our neighbors and largest export markets, in seeking to join the Trans-Pacific Partnership talks," said Ambassador Kirk. "We look forward to initiating consultations with them, and with Congress and our domestic stakeholders, and to discussing the TPP's high standards for liberalizing trade and specific issues of concern to the United States. These will include stronger protection of intellectual property rights, additional specific opportunities for US goods, services, and investment, and the elimination of various nontariff barriers." From the website of the Office of the US Trade Representative, "Statement by US Trade Representative Ron Kirk on Announcements from Mexico and Canada Regarding the Trans-Pacific Partnership," November 13, 2011.

3. The Council of Canadians website, www.canadians.org, accessed November 25, 2012.

4. See http://www.theglobeandmail.com/news/politics/eu-harper/article 14924915/.

5. See http://www.theglobeandmail.com/report-on-business/economy /leave-currency-manipulation-out-of-trade-talks-ed-fast-urges /article14563787/.

6. Peter A. Petri and Michael G. Plummer, "The Trans-Pacific Partnership and Asia-Pacific Integration: Policy Implications," Policy Brief No. PB 12–16, Peterson Institute for International Economics, June 2012, Table 1.

7. See http://www.theglobeandmail.com/report-on-business/economy /study-recommends-canada-remove-all-trade-tariffs/article18598773/; http://www.ceocouncil.ca/wp-content/uploads/2014/05/Should-Canada-unilaterally-adopt-free-trade-Ciuriak-and-Xiao-May-20141.pdf.

8. See http://www.international.gc.ca/trade-agreements-accords-commerciaux /agr-acc/fipa-apie/index.aspx?lang=eng.

4

Chile and the TPP

Waiting for Outcomes

Rodrigo Contreras, Chile's former lead TPP negotiator

The project of establishing a free trade zone around the Asia-Pacific region is an ambitious and important undertaking. Indeed, in 2004, the president of Chile proposed the idea of making a large FTA within the framework of APEC. Chile then initiated negotiations with the P4 economies (Chile, Brunei, New Zealand, and Singapore), developing a very comfortable agreement for all participants. A distinctive characteristic of these agreements was the potential for growth in the future.

SIGNIFICANCE OF THE TPP

In terms of its macroeconomic dimensions, the TPP is a very attractive area. It produces 38 percent of total worldwide GDP, and about 73 percent of Asia-Pacific GDP, and it has a population of 800 million people. For Chile, the TPP represents around 40 percent of total exports, while TPP economies account for 33 percent of investments into Chile and 16 percent of Chilean investments abroad.

After the stagnation of negotiations under the World Trade Organization (WTO), plus the lack of binding commitments in the APEC framework and the poor trading policies of the United States, the TPP initiative appears very promising. It would be an ambitious alternative to the WTO and move the US agenda forward, and it could serve as the seed for a future FTA among the APEC economies. Expectations, then, are very high.

In one scenario of success, the TPP could link the interests of South Korea, Chinese Taipei, and at least three more ASEAN economies, as well as several Latin America economies, starting with Colombia. The goal is to reach 19 economies of the Asia-Pacific region, which will create a very prominent future for this project.

OBJECTIVES AND CONTENTS OF THE TPP

When the negotiations began, the participating economies of the TPP did not yet have enough clarity about the contents of the future agreement. All the participants recognized where they wanted to go, but they didn't know how to best craft the contents to get to that point.

The distinctive characteristic of these negotiations was to create a next-generation agreement. Although at the beginning no one could explain what this affirmation implied, now that details of the contents are being hammered out, the agreement provides concrete direction.

The main guideline of the TPP is to alleviate trade problems, which all concern the inconveniences or barriers that affect trade, investment, and services flows among the economies. In relation to this, it is important to consider that most trade problems evolve over time. If past barriers were mainly related to tariffs, today's problems will be related to quotas, import licenses, distribution channels, and behind-the-border barriers, among others. Each economy's problems and solutions depend on its degree of openness and development, which vary widely.

There are very open and nonaligned countries, such as Chile, Singapore, New Zealand, or Peru; large, liberal economies with strong internal policies, such as Mexico, the United States, Japan, or Australia; and, finally, highly planned and directed economies, such as Vietnam, Malaysia, or Brunei.

In formulating the benchmarks, it should be taken into account that each economy will weigh numerous possibilities to address their objectives. While objectives in negotiations can be legitimate, if the costs for the other parties are too high, it doesn't make sense to push so hard.

OBJECTIVES AND BALANCE OF POWER OF EACH ECONOMY IN THE NEGOTIATIONS

In the real world, even having apparently common objectives is not enough to reach agreement. Differences in power among negotiators can change the way those objectives are actually addressed. In terms of how power in the room is balanced and how consensus is reached, plurilateral negotiations can resemble bilateral negotiations more than multilateral negotiations. This failure in the system harms small countries far more than powerful countries.

The lack of natural consensus in plurilateral discussions can also damage the multilateral system. Plurilateral negotiations can promote specific disciplines to global agreements, despite the fact that these provisions would fail to achieve consensus in multilateral discussions, and do not even represent consensus in a small group.

In any group of economies there are subgroups with particular objectives and interests in negotiations. In the TPP, we can define three groups of economies: one is seeking market access, another has systemic interests, and a third group wants to develop new trade rules.

In the group of economies seeking to gain market access through negotiations, we could put New Zealand, Vietnam, Malaysia, Japan, Mexico, Canada, and Australia. The first four do not have free trade agreements with the United States, which is a significant objective for them, and the rest are looking to improve access for their products through new or existing agreements.

In the second group of economies, we can put Chile, Brunei, Peru, and Singapore. All of them have traditionally or recently opted for openness, several have trade agreements with their main trade partners, and all consider this agreement to be a good way to improve their individual agreements, as well as to reduce the impact of the "spaghetti bowl" and contribute to a better multilateral system.

The third group is integrated primarily by the United States, and even if they are seeking market access for their products in Asia (as are all the rest), they are mainly looking to develop new rules that will address the trade problems they are facing and improve their competitiveness.

Directly related with the expectations of reaching each of these objectives is the disposition of the participants to compromise in order to achieve a successful agreement.

We must keep in mind the difference in power of each participant, in part based on the different backgrounds they bring to trade agreements, but mainly based on the size of each economy. We can't dismiss the fact that the United States is three times larger than the second-largest economy in the group, Japan. In theory, all economies in the negotiations have the same weight, but at the end of the day, that is not the reality.

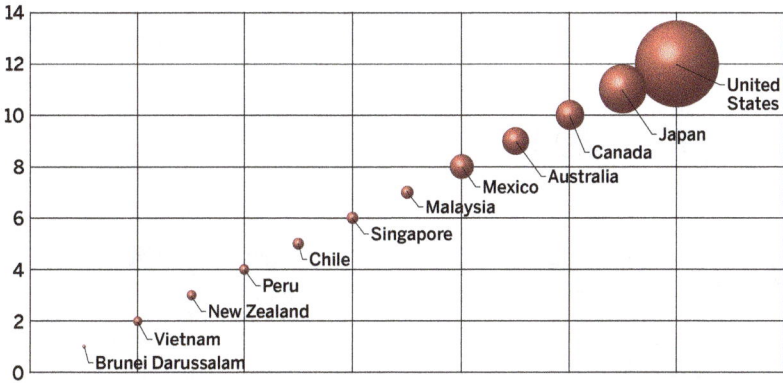

FIGURE 1 *Relative Dimension Based on the GDP*

When groups of economies with different objectives/interests are crossed with power players in the negotiation process, certain results are likely to occur. The most powerful economies, as well as the more determined, will impose the agenda and the terms of the final negotiations.

THE TPP'S MAIN CONTENTS AND POSSIBLE OUTCOMES

A free trade agreement represents a huge assemblage of chapters on a multitude of different matters relating to the trade in goods, the trade in services, investment, intellectual property, labor, the environment, and legal issues, among others. Thus, it is very difficult to make a detailed analysis in a few words, especially considering that there is no public

Systemic Approach
Chile
Canada
Brunei
Peru
Singapore
Percentage of TPP GDP 3%

Market Access
New Zealand
Vietnam
Malaysia
Japan
Mexico
Australia
Percentage of TPP GDP 38%

+

Create new rules for trade
United States
Percentage of TPP GDP 59%

=

Percentage of TPP GDP 97%

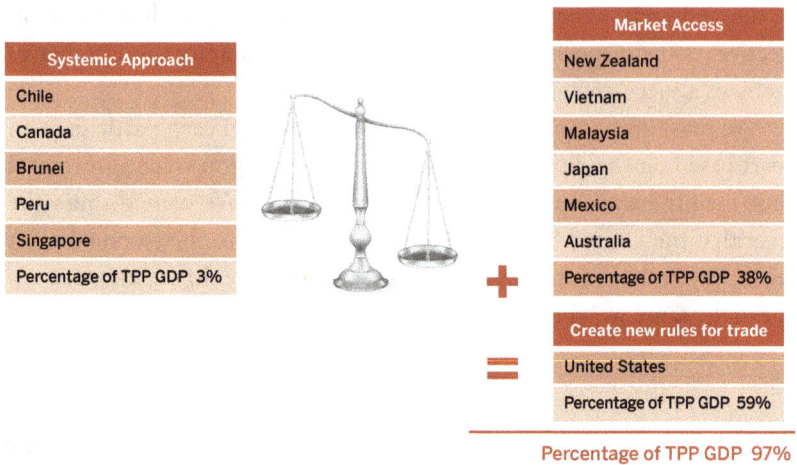

FIGURE 2 *Percentage of TPP GDP*

information released about the agreement's contents. For that reason, the following comments are based on the available information.

Trade in Goods

Trade in goods is an issue that has at least two main areas. The first is related to the disciplines for trade, mainly nontariff barriers to trade, such as export subsidies, distribution channels, or any export or import restriction. The second big area is related to the reduction of tariffs between economies. Even if, in principle, all the economies have a common objective, the sensitive sectors (products) of each can create bottlenecks in the negotiations.

In terms of disciplines, progress is being made in the first important area, which is related to restrictions and discriminatory treatments to imports inside each economy.

In respect to distribution channels and government presence in trade areas, discussions veer toward eliminating any interference in order to avoid discrimination of private imports once the product has been introduced in each economy. If this goal is reached, it would be a step forward in trade liberalization.

The requirements for licensing are usually used as a trade policy measure and as a way to control trade flows. Under the TPP, as with the WTO, it is very important to use licensing, and especially to add components of transparency for its use. Without transparency, any tariff concessions could be lost by export prohibitions.

Export subsidies are, in general, terms that are considered negative for trade agreements, and we could expect a compromise concerning the nonapplication of subsidies in the free trade area. Certainly one of the most powerful agreements that could be reached would be the control of internal supports, but acceptance seems to be very difficult to achieve in all the TPP economies.

Tariff elimination is a primary interest of all the participants; represents a clear concession that is reflected in reductions of trade barriers, which bring immediate gains; and has a positive impact on the competitiveness of the economies. While tariff elimination is the most visible result in any trade agreement, and would be good news for most of the economies involved, that would not be the case for Chile, which has FTAs with all the participants.

A basic requirement to be part of the TPP was to be committed to liberalizing the tariffs for all products. But we have heard repeatedly about the difficulty some economies have to committing to full liberalization, including the economies of Japan, the United States, Canada, Vietnam, and others. As a result, we can expect that exceptions in tariff liberalization will become a reality.

Rules of Origin

Rules of origin are very technical issues, and constitute one of the key chapters of this agreement. Considering that the main objective is to bring order to the "spaghetti bowl" of FTAs, to help construct global chains of production in the region, and to create a free trade zone, the rules of origin must operate in an open way in order to ensure the flexibility required today. To think that they have to be applied with the restricted vision developed 20 years ago is a big mistake that would severely and permanently damage this agreement.

The section of the chapter that relates to the framework for the application of rules by product seems to be nearing an end. But the section related to specific rules by products, and the way they are materializing and accumulating, seems to be reaching a breaking point. Controversial sectors such as automotive and textile products are seen from both a defensive point of view, in the case of the Americas, and from an offensive point of view in the case of Asia.

Sanitary and Phytosanitary Issues and Barriers to Trade

Expectations in these two areas were very high, but the application of norms as a trade policy instrument is, unfortunately, rarely used. Advancements in transparency and the development of common criteria for decisions would be satisfactory results from the negotiations, but those seem unlikely to happen because of a lack of consensus among the participating economies.

In the case of sanitary and phytosanitary measures (SPS), gains could be made by improving transparency concerning the procedures, and by including a dispute settlement mechanism for solving plurilateral problems inside the group.

The case of trade barriers, on the other hand, is a little different because of expectations to include particular agreements about good practices for certain industries, which could impact SPS.

Investment

In terms of investment clauses, they should follow the same direction as the North American Free Trade Agreement–Plus (NAFTA-Plus) design.

While there is a general concern, mainly from the Asian economies, about assuring a wide framework of protection for foreign investors, it is helpful to realize that investment and services disciplines are uncommon in Asian trade agreements. Additionally, there appear in the public discussion at least two areas of concern: the free flow of capitals and, a big concern for Australia, clauses about investor-state dispute settlements.

Trade Facilitation

Every economy shares the objective of trade facilitation, which is why it appears on WTO, APEC, and, of course, the TPP forums. There are practical problems that affect exports and imports in their day-to-day movements. The difficulty this issue poses is clarifying the scope and extent of commitments, which is not clear even under the WTO's technical barriers to trade. It is difficult to evaluate the possible results of other negotiations because previous standards have been very low.

Intellectual Property

The intellectual property chapter covers copyrights, patents, trademarks, geographical indications, and mechanisms for implementation, including Internet environments.

The background in all these matters is the desire to create protections for creators, and to improve compliance by users, especially in Internet environments. This chapter models itself on World Property Intellectual Organization–Plus (WIPO-Plus) agreements, and aims to not only comply with multilateral compromises, but also to improve upon them.

The big question is whether there is a consensus about the level of desired protection. A legitimate question to ask is whether the economies understood what improvement would actually look like, and if they were interested in making the same advancements. As an example, there seems to be asymmetrical interests in favor of patents and copyrights in relation to geographical indications.

A horizontal area is intellectual property applied to Internet environments. The Internet Age has been as transformative as the Industrial Revolution. It has changed communications (from expensive and limited to free and integrated), compressed financial transactions (from weeks to fragments of seconds), increased trade of products by previously unimaginable magnitudes (the world's products, culture, and knowledge at your fingertips). The latter, in fact, may be the most powerful and democratic consequence of the Internet. For small- and medium-sized enterprises and entrepreneurs, it serves as an inexhaustible information resource and a way to provide services to nearly everyone, in any place on the planet.

The effort to rule this media becomes an enormous and onerous challenge, one that Chile did not anticipate when negotiations began. Past experiences have been disastrous, with the Anti-Counterfeiting Trade

Agreement (ACTA) being a prime example. To try to interfere in the creation, education, and trade patterns generated by the Internet is a daunting challenge and heavy responsibility.

An argument to increase protection is that it would increase innovation. But it is impossible to raise the level of innovation in the developing economies without appropriate policies and incentives. Moreover, extending the rights of creators without providing previous incentives would block any possibility to develop knowledge.

New Matters
The main characteristic of the TPP agreement is that it would address matters of actual trade, such us trade facilitation, small- and medium-sized enterprises, regulatory coherence, and more. While this objective is very positive, the final evaluation would depend on the degree of commitments achieved on each chapter.

Other Issues
Some other issues have also been mentioned, such as the possibility of having disciplines to rule the participation of state-owned enterprises on the market, systems of reimbursement of medicines, or supervision of the currency exchange systems. All of these matters, again, are positive objectives, but it is difficult to advance any because participants' interests are, in some cases, contradictory.

CHILE IN THE TPP

Chile is a small country that made the decision to have a free market economy more than 30 years ago. While this decision created initial difficulties for some production sectors, many industries—including the fruit, wine, and salmon industries—launched into a process of evolving competitiveness.

Chile is not a big player in the international economy, with just 0.36 percent[1] of global GDP, a population of 0.25 percent of world inhabitants, and exports of 0.38 percent in relation to population. To synthesize these figures, Chile is only the thirty-sixth economy in the world. As a small economy in the international context, Chile is unable to impose rules on all of the other economies.

Consistent with being a liberal economy, Chile fosters the external sector and promotes exports (68 percent openness today[2]), with a high composition of raw materials and semi-elaborated products, and around 53 percent of exports composed of copper and related minerals. It is a country that does not impose barriers to imports, and rarely uses trade defense tools.

With a small geographical area and a very exposed economy, Chile needs trade rules that assure a minimum of governance and stability to its model. That is the reason that Chile plays an active role in the WTO and maintains a consistent unilateral policy with very low, even nonexistent, trade barriers. The main component of its trade policy has been the negotiation of bilateral trade agreements.

In bilateral trade policy, Chile has an outstanding record. It has 23 trade agreements in force with 60 countries, having started in the early 1990s with a set of agreements within the region, and continuing to negotiate agreements with economies throughout North America, Europe, and Asia. Today, Chile has access to 62 percent of the global population, representing 86 percent[3] of world GDP. This opens up the possibility of sending 93 percent of Chilean exports under preferential agreements. Based on those figures, we can infer that Chile has established a successful process.

In terms of public policy, it is very difficult for a developing economy to consider the perspective of one that has reached state-of-the-art levels in trade. The main problem is that bilateral options have been maintained for so long, it has created great disparity in the contents between agreements. Even focusing on the same matters illuminates differences among the agreements, and generates what is often known as the "spaghetti bowl." But what is worse, this phenomenon of market segmentation occurs as a consequence of the application of restrictive bilateral rules of origin.

The above-mentioned issues suggest that there are many things to improve in terms of trade policy. The actual system, even if it has driven good results in increasing trade flows, is far from what economic theory indicates should be achieved, or what a multilateral system should strive to be.

The way to level the field in terms of coverage among Chile's free trade agreements—and transition from the restrictive characteristics of the bilateral agreements to the optimum characteristics of the multilateral system—is to take the plurilateral path. That is why Chile and other economies that have exhausted their bilateral policies are working on projects such as the Pacific Alliance and the Trans-Pacific Partnership (TPP) agreement.

The P4 agreement, along with the APEC experience, represents a solid rock to build an ambitious initiative like the TPP. But it is important to keep in mind that in the real world, many good ideas are dismissed because of practical problems. There are basically two threats that are generating instability in the TPP process: the first is the assumption that everyone has agreed upon the initial contents, and the second is the assumption that all the economies possess the same negotiating power in a plurilateral system. Given that neither assumption is true, the attractive TPP project faces difficult moments and searching questions.

The most important gains for Chile are not in the tariff-elimination process, as it has agreements with all the economies involved. The gains, rather, are in relation to the harmonization of disciplines and trade facilitation, which are very difficult to calculate.

The main concerns are the development of more ambitions rules (than the multilateral standard) in areas such as intellectual property, as well as the loss of tools such as prudential measures for capital flow controls or commitments in areas like the environment, both of which could slow down the actual dynamics of local economies.

Today, Chile is waiting for the final package because, as was stated earlier, the TPP is considered a worthy project but with unknown results, especially considering the lack of US trade promotion authority.

NOTES

1. World Bank statistics.

2. (Exports + Imports) / GDP.

3. General Directorate of Economic Relations, Ministry of Foreign Affairs, Chile.

5

How Far Away Is China from the TPP?

Zhang Jianping, Director, Institute for International Economic Research
at the National Development and Reform Commission

INTRODUCTION

China's attitude toward the TPP has undergone a fundamental change since 2013, but despite the "seven misunderstandings" of the TPP before 2013 or the "get involved immediately" theory that followed, both attempts failed to be objective and realistic. There is still a great distance between China and the TPP. Big differences exist on issues such as rules of trade in goods, service market access, and investment rules, while behind-the-border issues—standards and certification, environmental protection, intellectual property rights, labor standards, and government procurement—constitute severe challenges to China's current management systems and mechanisms. In the short term, China is not qualified to enter the TPP negotiations. However, there might be practical ways for China to integrate the TPP pathway with the RCEP pathway in the future, which could push China to seek reform and adjustment when the time is right. It should be emphasized that transparent mechanisms play a significant role in the Asia-Pacific integration strategy, and that they are promoted by China, the United States, and other TPP members. It is strongly recommended that TPP negotiation members consider a more transparent information communication mechanism in their FTA negotiations.

The United States is pushing its "one body with two wings" FTA strategy globally, with NAFTA as the body and the TPP and TTIP as the wings. Simultaneously, the EU-Japan FTA negotiations are beginning to accelerate. The developed economies are in the process of formulating systems of new international trade and investment rules. Since the end of 2011, when TPP negotiations suddenly accelerated, until now, the TPP has not been just an ordinary FTA, but has embodied an early form of new, twenty-first century international trade and investment rules. As such, the TPP has aroused extensive attention and close follow-up studies among China's top officials and academic circles. There is still no clear consensus on whether China should join the TPP negotiations and, if so, when to join. However, starting in 2013, China changed course and deepened its understanding of the TPP, and it is gradually developing a relatively objective and realistic picture, together with making its own choices about strategy and policy toward the TPP.

CHINA'S ATTITUDE TOWARD THE TPP HAS CHANGED FUNDAMENTALLY SINCE 2013

At the 2011 APEC annual meeting held in Honolulu, Hawai'i, China began to pay more attention and conduct more relevant studies due to the TPP's rapid expansion and the acceleration of the negotiation progress. But with regard to its understanding of the TPP, different views and perspectives prevailed among China's academics, government officials, and the media. Prior to June 2013, China's academics mostly criticized the TPP. Their arguments can be categorized as six objections, including the conspiracy theory, pessimism theory, standby theory, spoiler theory, rival theory, and the US-dominate theory.[1] Two further objections were added soon afterward: the exclusive theory and the "get involved immediately" theory. The scholars who hold the exclusive theory maintain that the developed economies, led by the United States, took advantage of the TPP to exclude China on purpose, a position that does not tally with the fact that government and academic circles in the United States, Japan, and other states maintain a positive attitude about the TPP.[2]

With the declaration by the Chinese Ministry of Foreign Affairs that the "TPP, ASEAN-Plus-Three, and ASEAN-Plus-Six are all possible paths for Asia-Pacific regional integration" in June 2013, and the public comment by the spokesperson of China's Ministry of Commerce that "China will study the TPP's influence on China's economy and the possibility of China's entry into TPP positively," many scholars in China decided that it should enter TPP negotiations immediately. This sharp turn of perspective, which can be called the "get involved immediately" theory, has made many Asia-Pacific economies, especially the United States and Japan, puzzled. This shift in perspective is totally unacceptable because it ignores the gap between China and the TPP standards, and it does not consider practical ways to ease China's entry into the TPP. What China needs to do now is to strengthen its follow-up studies on the TPP. China needs to carry out a new round of reforms and open up in many fields in order to bridge the gap between its own rules and the TPP rules. In a word, it is not realistic to enter TPP negotiations now. China's current policy of pushing forward the China–South Korea FTA and the China-Japan-Korea FTA (CJK FTA) negotiations, accelerating the process of the RCEP, and constructing the integration of East Asia's economy should be priorities.

HOW FAR AWAY IS CHINA FROM THE TPP?

Already, 19 rounds of TPP negotiations have been actively carried out. According to the consensus reached by members of the ministerial-level conferences and leaders' conferences during APEC, the economies negotiating the TPP hoped to conclude in 2013. The negotiations involve 21 fields, and the framework agreements have been expanded from 26 chapters to 29 chapters. Until now, consensus has been reached on half of the chapters; however, for issues such as market access, intellectual property protection, state-owned enterprises, and environmental protection and labor standards, no consensus has been reached yet. Even if preliminary agreements can be reached before the end of 2013, which would probably constitute partial or early-stage agreements, the overall liberalization levels and requirements for high standards would not satisfy US expectations.

If China declares its intention to enter the TPP now, issues from a variety of fields need to be taken into consideration, including lowering tariff and nontariff barriers, and solving both on-the-border issues and behind-the-border issues. Given that China has signed regional trade agreements (RTAs) with many economies, China has accumulated abundant experience that enables it to solve on-the-border issues. For behind-the-border issues, however, China faces tough challenges.

ON-THE-BORDER ISSUES

Trade in Goods: China Is Mainly Faced with the Challenge of Rules
The TPP will promote 100 percent zero tariffs for trade in goods, and 10–15 years of transitional period for those sensitive products, without exception. For Japan, immunity was won for a few agriculture products, such as rice, corn, beef, cane sugar, and dairy products, which can retain tariffs to a certain degree. Given the FTA that China signed, there is still a significant gap between China and the developed economies on the liberalization level of trade in goods. For the middle- and high-end manufacturing industry, China might be somewhat impacted by the United States, Canada, Australia, Japan, and South Korea, while for the rules of trade in goods, the challenge is more severe. For example, for the textile and clothing industry, the TPP sets a strict rule of origin, which means that the Vietnam textile industry can enjoy tariff-free status only if the fabric originates in Vietnam. As such, that tariff-free status could be jeopardized in the future due to the fact that 50 percent of its fabric now comes from China. Some textile enterprises are moving from China to Vietnam, which will lead to the investment division effect.

Trade in Service: Market Access Is the Challenge
In service trade, the TPP has set higher-standard rules than the WTO. In terms of commitment, the TPP requires an overall opening of service

sectors and the carrying out of the "negative list." With regard to the service provision models, the "Mode 3" (commercial presence) and rules of trade in service are established separately. This means that both commercial presence and trade in service will be affected by the constraint of investment rules. In the financial and telecommunications sectors, the United States strongly requires that the two sectors be set up in independent chapters, and that each fully eliminate ration requirements of stock shares. In addition, operators must be allowed to choose service providers independently. The United States has also asked Japan to reform their postal and social insurance systems, so as not to slow things down in TPP negotiations. For China, its commitment to open up levels of trade in service when entering the WTO is the minimal requirement of the TPP as well, However, that opening process has not been completed, and there are still restrictions on the proportion of shares in a number of service subsectors. Moreover, China has just joined the negotiations of the Trade in Services Agreement (TISA), so it lacks experience in opening up trade in service. Given the high entry threshold and powerful groups of vested interests in China's service industries, such as finance and telecommunications, expanding the level of openness in trade in service is proving to be very difficult.

Investment: The Issue of National Treatment Before Market Access and the "Negative List" Barrier

Since 2000, China has signed 34 bilateral investment treaties (BIT). However, for the establishment, acquisition, and expansion of foreign direct investment (FDI) enterprises, national treatment before market access and negative list management have not been committed. It remains to be seen whether the TPP or ASEAN's agreements with Japan, South Korea, Australia, Singapore, and India will carry out national treatment before market access and negative list management, which will directly challenge China's current FDI management system and mode.

China is currently negotiating a BIT with the United States. Previously, the two economies had exchanged notes on investment agreements, which included eight terms that established US investment interests in China. US bilateral investment treaties are based on the US national security bill, whose template is very complex; on the minimum standard of national treatment issues; and on its requirements for justice, equity, and comprehensive safety measures. Because China and the United States have no established BIT in terms of investment, the United States has conducted a sweeping security censorship of Chinese investors, and many Chinese enterprises felt the obvious discrimination, including the China Investment Corporation and Huawei. National treatment before market access and negative list management have brought challenges for China as it attempts to reform and open up its domestic investment management system, along with the government's economic management. This is caused because the management mode of foreign enterprises should be applied to the domestic investors, which forces China to reform its domestic investment system in turn. Reform is also highly relevant to China's industrial restructuring, as well as foreign exchange management reform and financial reform. The Shanghai FTA is making an effort in this regard. But from the Shanghai FTA negative list that was released, very limited breakthroughs have happened in comparison with the positive list. The negative list is currently under study. How to promote reforms in this field will be a daunting task for China, which will require time to accomplish them.

BEHIND-THE-BORDER ISSUES

A series of behind-the-border issues constitute an even bigger challenge for China, including the unification of standards, the governance of state-owned enterprises, environmental protection, labor standards, government procurement, and intellectual property protection. All of these issues are independent chapters in the TPP agreement, and all require intensive consideration and arrangement.[3]

The Unification of Standards

There is a huge gap between China and the United States on the understanding of standards, together with the formulating and implementing mechanisms for these standards. For the United States, the position is that the standards should be formulated by the enterprises or the organizations within the industry, and the government should not be involved. For China, the position is that national standards should be formulated by the National Standardization Administration, based on the "Standardization Law," and certificated by the National Certification and Accreditation Administration. However, the fact is that the US government–backed Energy Star program has greatly impacted China's products. The establishment of new US rules on food safety has also led to stricter regulations on food that emphasize the producers' responsibilities and obligations, and that require a process of certification from agriculture product to dining table and whole chain regulation. This certification is required to be carried out by third-party checking and certification authorities. But in China, the third-party certification process is rather weak. Given the above facts, Chinese enterprises need to adjust their quality management systems, which would lead to a cost increase of more than 20 percent.

Environmental Protection

Drawn from its experience with NAFTA, the United States spares no effort in promoting environmental standards and labor standards, and it requires that any FTA signed by United States cover these fields. Until now, it has successfully promoted these standards to Chile, Peru, and other economies. In addition, the United States exerts influence on developing economies like China. For example, when Chile and Peru negotiated FTAs with China, they also required negotiations on environmental and labor issues. The TPP now has a special environment chapter requiring that environmental protection should take priority in foreign investment decisions. The areas of biodiversity conservation and marine fishing also require high transparency and administrative and judicial procedures. In China's FTA with Switzerland, the environmental protection chapter is provided. Among all the FTAs signed by China and another economy, this is the first time the environmental issue has become an independent chapter. But in the formulation and implementation of environmental protection standards, environmental data monitoring and transparency, and the participation of nongovernmental organizations, there is a still a long way to go before meeting the requirements of the TPP and the United States. This gap is due to weak institutional mechanisms, which cannot be solved in the short term.

Labor Standard Protection

The TPP is trying to fulfill the International Labour Organization's (ILO) fundamental commitment to basic rights, including freedom of association, prohibition of forced labor, elimination of child labor, gender discrimination, and so on. However, of the ILO's eight core conventions, a few have not been approved by China, including the freedom of association and collective bargaining of wages. These rules are very sensitive in China's existing system, which struggles to achieve systematic transformation. China cannot make external promises that it cannot keep in the short term.

State-owned Enterprises Governance

The TPP is promoting new rules for the governance of relevant state-owned enterprises. These rules specify that the share of government capital in state-owned enterprises should be below 20 percent. State-owned enterprises should not give preferential treatment and favorable financing to each other. Affiliated enterprises should not carry out affiliate transactions. State-owned enterprises should not pursue unfair competition. Subsidies and financing should be no different from nonstate enterprises, etc. China's state-owned enterprises have carried out joint-stock system reform. However, as most of their state-owned shares are rather high, these shares have surpassed 50 percent—even 80 percent in many cases—which far exceeds the TPP requirements, but cannot be changed immediately.

Government Procurement

The TPP's standard for government procurement is supposed to be higher than the WTO's Agreement on Government Procurement (GPA) and build-operate-transfer agreements (BOTs). China is currently carrying out a bilateral procurement agreement with the EU, but there has been no marked improvement in four or five rounds of negotiations in a past few years. China has domestically formulated its government procurement laws and carried out procurement processes, including the detailed environmental list. But there is still a huge gap between opening up to foreign enterprises, transparency, and third-party monitoring of China's government procurement and the normative and transparent international conventions. Issues such as high costs, tedious procedures, and inadequate supervision continue to exist.

Intellectual Property Protection

In the TPP negotiations on intellectual property, the United States strongly promotes TRIPS-Plus. This aligns with its national interest, given that the United States holds two-thirds of the world's core patents. Although Australia and New Zealand consider TRIPS to be enough, US domestic law is multilateralized and rises to international conventions. In addition, the United States proposes to expand the range of intellectual protection and extend the protection period, such as extending the terms of copyright protection to 70 years. For China, the term is 50 years. The US pharmaceutical industry advocates that if the contracting parties get generic drugs, the intellectual property rights should be extended for longer periods. For China, the pharmaceutical industry will be heavily reliant on generic drugs if TRIPS-Plus is accepted. China's pharmaceutical industry and social and medical security systems will be impacted seriously.[4]

E-commerce and Internet Freedom

The TPP agreement promotes the free flow of data across borders and Internet freedom with no restrictive measures, as well as no restrictions on outside messages. Digital products should enjoy nondiscriminatory treatment, tariffs must not be imposed on online music, legitimate free downloads are promoted, and so on. China is currently experiencing economic and social transition, where various social contradictions have become increasingly apparent and social instability has increased. In order to maintain a stable environment for development, China needs to take necessary restrictive measures on new media like the Internet. The revelations contained in Edward Snowden's leaks and examples of wiretapping make it more difficult for China to accept Internet freedom in the short term.

TIME WINDOW AND COOPERATION FOR CHINA'S ENTRY INTO THE TPP

Given the above arguments, even if China decides to participate in TPP negotiations during the bilateral pre-negotiation process with the 13 member economies, it will be confronted with the preconditions and commitments that developed economies such as the United States and Japan have put forward. Putting aside the intense issues of national treatment before investment access, the negative list, and expanding market access of service industries, other issues will create new challenges for China's existing management systems. These challenges include behind-the-border issues, government procurement, state-owned enterprises, environmental protection, labor standards, intellectual property protection, and product standards.

Considering the congressional procedures of the United States and Japan, even if China pursues pre-negotiations in 2014, it would only be part of the negotiations after two or three years. Moreover, in China, every reform of behind-the-border issues needs to be solved in medium- and long-term frameworks, instead of only in the short term. Thus, China is not yet qualified to be a party of the TPP negotiations. In the future, China can positively participate and promote the RCEP negotiations, and seek the integration of the RCEP pathway and the TPP pathway, which may be a practicable course for China. In this way, China can seek to make reforms and adjustments at the right time.[5]

At the same time, China is extremely worried that it will lose the right to help formulate the trade and investment rules of the twenty-first century if it is excluded from the TPP negotiations. For Japan and South Korea, the economic benefits of entering TPP negotiations are rather limited, but entering allows them to be involved in the formulation of new rules. At the same time, involvement in the TPP helps them promote domestic reforms. For these economies, the "rules effect" is more pronounced than the "market effect." China is pushing forward a new round of reforms and is in the process of opening up. Although China cannot be a party to the TPP negotiations in the short term, it can be a key positive force for global and Asian trade and investment liberalization and facilitation. China should conduct a close follow-up study on the TPP's development and direction, identifying the realistic gap between China and the TPP's new rules, and ultimately seeking a possible way to integrate with the TPP member economies in the future.

Currently, the TPP's transparency is very limited, which is also one of the primary reasons that China misunderstands the TPP. In fact, transparent mechanisms for communication would be very beneficial for China, the United States, and other TPP members, as well as being very important for promoting the Asia-Pacific integration strategy. Therefore, I strongly recommend that TPP negotiation members consider a more transparent communication mechanism, one which would further help the Asia-Pacific economies become a larger Asia-Pacific economic community.

Finally, the TPP's applicability for developing economies remains to be seen, even if it represents the direction that international economic development and social progress is taking. Using Malaysia as an example, the TPP will impact the health care system and rights of indigenous people, but the protection of indigenous people's rights have been enshrined in the constitution of Malaysia. The question becomes, is it necessary for Malaysia to revise its constitution for the TPP? For Vietnam, there are issues such as government procurement, state-owned enterprise reform, labor issues, environmental protection, etc. Given the conditions, the question of how to build systems and mechanisms that meet the TPP requirements in the near future looms for Vietnam. China will be paying close attention to how these issues are tackled. China's current preference is, undoubtedly, to build an East Asia mechanism, with the integration of the China–South Korea FTA, the CJK FTA, and the RCEP.[6]

NOTES

1. Zhang Jianping, "The Problems and Challenges of TPP from the Angle of Negotiators' Conflicts," in *Situation and Suggestion on Economic Integration in Asia Pacific and East Asia* (Beijing: World Affairs Press, December 2013): Chapter 2.

2. Liu Zhongwei and Shen Jiawen, "The Review of Research Frontier and Frameworks of Trans-Pacific Partnership Agreement (TPP)," *Journal of Contemporary Asia-Pacific Studies* 1 (2012): 36–59.

3. Rao Yunyan, "Template, Springboard, and Baffle: The Trinity Functions of the TPP from a Point of View of American Strategy," *World Economy Study* 8 (2013): 9–15.

4. Kang Meiling and Chen Anjun, "Protection of the Intellectual Property Right in the TPP and China's Countermeasures." *Asia-Pacific Economic Review* 6 (2013): 56–59.

5. Wang Jinqiang, "TPP vs RCEP: A Study on the Political Game behind the Regional Cooperation in the Asia-Pacific," *Asia-Pacific Economic Review* 3 (2013): 15–20.

6. Peng Zhiwei and Zhang Bowei, "The Economic Effects of TPP and FTAAP and the Implications for China," *Journal of International Trade* 4 (2013): 83–95.

6

The TPP, China, and FTAAP

The Case for Convergence

Peter A. Petri, Professor of International Finance,
Brandeis International Business School

Michael G. Plummer, Eni Professor of International Economics,
The Johns Hopkins University, SAIS

Fan Zhai, Managing Director and Head of the Asset Allocation and
Strategic Research Department, China Investment Corporation

Asia-Pacific trade negotiations are evolving more fitfully than expected a few years ago. The Trans-Pacific Partnership (TPP) negotiations are nearing the endgame, but divisions remain and political opposition is intense. The Regional Comprehensive Economic Partnership (RCEP) negotiations are at an earlier stage, but progress also appears to be slow due to the region's diversity and geopolitical strains. Further impeding progress, macroeconomic conditions—turning less favorable now in East Asia and not yet sufficiently improved in the Americas and Europe—are not especially conducive to new agreements. None of these factors is likely to prove fatal to large trade initiatives, but each adds uncertainty on what can be accomplished and when.

These challenges have a silver lining: slow negotiations offer an opportunity to reexamine fundamental, long-term goals, including region-wide free trade through a Free Trade Area of the Asia-Pacific (FTAAP). Work on these goals in the Asia-Pacific Economic Cooperation (APEC) forum and related venues has been episodic; it moved quickly with the Bogor Declaration, and later with the negotiation of the P4 trade agreement among Brunei, Chile, New Zealand, and Singapore, but forward movement has also stagnated at times. Institutions have lagged behind in facilitating market-led integration. This suggests that innovations such as an FTAAP have to be debated and nurtured well in advance of when they become feasible. This paper explores several such options, among them the expansion of the TPP to include China.[1]

WHY THE ASIA PACIFIC?

Asia-Pacific trade is a logical setting for new agreements due to its scale and dynamism. First, the region's trade is immense. Of the world's US$14 trillion in trade in 2010, US$9 trillion involve APEC economies—a useful, though synthetic definition of the region—as either an exporter or importer or both. Within the APEC region, trade in the Americas amounted to US$1 trillion, in Asia and Oceania US$2 trillion, and across the Pacific also US$2 trillion. The region comprises not only the world's "factory floor," but also its most important sources of services, technology, investment, and final goods markets.

Second, Asia-Pacific trade is dynamic—it has changed the pattern of international economic relations through innovations such as modern supply chains. The region's diverse resource endowments and development levels give rise to varied specialization advantages. These are connected by dense transport and communication links for exchanging products, people, and resources cheaply.

Third, the region's interest in formal linkages is clearly rising, spurred in part by the challenges of global negotiations. Before 2000, there were only four major trade agreements among APEC economies— the ASEAN Free Trade Area, the Canada-US Free Trade Area, the North American Free Trade Agreement, and the Australia–New Zealand Closer Economic Relations accord—while today they number in the thirties, with others in the works (Figure 1). An especially strong

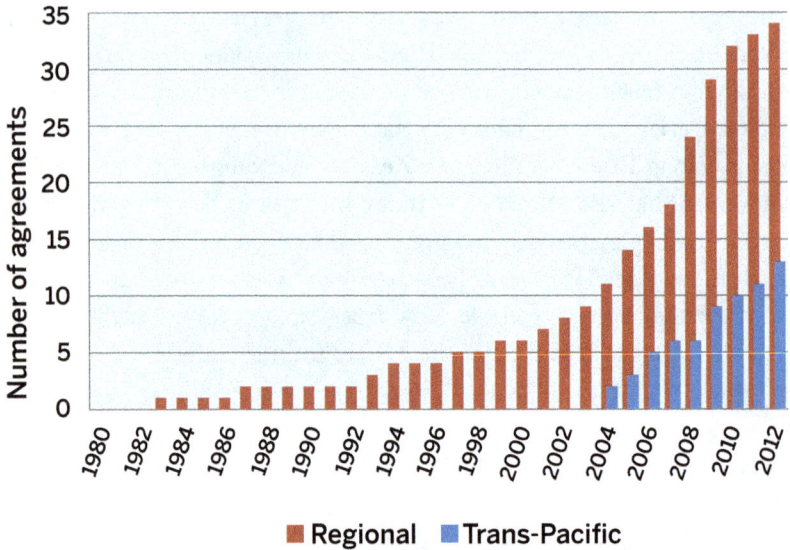

Note: *Among APEC members.*
Source: *United Nations ESCAP database.*

FIGURE 1   *Trends in Asia-Pacific Trade Agreements*

uptick is now evident in agreements that connect the Pacific's eastern and western subregions.

UNEVEN PROGRESS

Despite the importance of the Asia-Pacific trading system, the task of building regional institutions has been arduous. An Asian track for drafting new rules has proceeded slowly because the region's economies have widely differing interests, and some of its members have tense political relations. The Association of Southeast Asian Nations (ASEAN), the convener of the negotiations, is itself often divided on trade issues. Thus, even if a RCEP agreement is achieved in 2015, it may not go much beyond the bilateral deals that already crisscross the region.

Meanwhile, a trans-Pacific track has laid out an ambitious agenda of negotiations since the United States made the TPP a priority in 2009.

The group of negotiating partners has expanded from four in the initial P4 agreement to now 12. These partners are in principle "like-minded," but their negotiations have been contentious. In addition, the leadership expected from the United States has been undermined by its domestic politics. In the run-up to the US elections, special interests from directly affected sectors in business, labor, and civil society have assumed disproportionate voices in the trade debate. These disagreements feed into much suspicion of globalization in the United States, and some public interest groups portray trade agreements as serving only corporate interests. As a recent Pew-Bertelsmann trade policy poll noted, there is a double deficit: "lack of understanding and a lack of trust" (Pew Research Center and Bertelsmann Foundation 2014). Hopes for an agreement in 2014 have faded.

None of this makes region-wide trade rules less urgent. The backlog of issues accumulated since the Uruguay Round was completed 20 years ago continues to expand, and the growth of world trade is slowing. The mega-regional negotiations offer potential answers to these issues, but they will need to be supported by strong arguments from leaders, as well as policies that ensure that the benefits are widely shared. Given improvements in macroeconomic conditions and reduced geopolitical tensions, the logic of region-wide trade rules should reemerge. In the meantime, there is good reason to search for pathways to full regional integration. China's year as the host of APEC creates excellent opportunities for this work.

BENEFITS FROM THE TPP AND ITS ENLARGEMENT

The gains from Asia-Pacific free trade agreements cannot be predicted with precision—for one thing, their terms are in flux. In recent studies, we nevertheless applied an advanced general equilibrium model to estimate rough benefits for several potential agreements, including the 12-member TPP, the 16-member RCEP, and the 21-member FTAAP. These studies found, as reported below, that the greatest economic benefits were associated with agreements that spanned China and the United States.

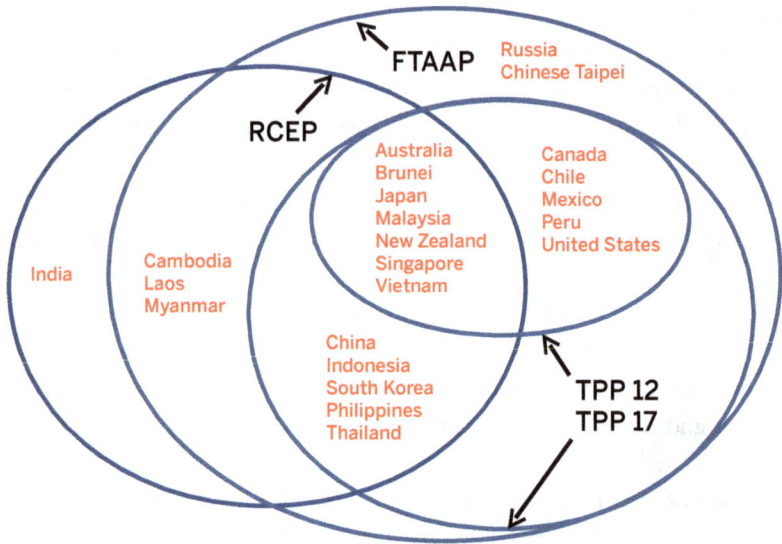

Source: Authors.

FIGURE 2   *Schematic View of Asian and Trans-Pacific Tracks*

In this paper, we add a new variant to previous simulations, an enlargement of the TPP to include China. Specifically, we hypothesize that the TPP will be eventually expanded to 17 members to include China, Indonesia, South Korea, the Philippines, and Thailand (see Figure 2). All five have expressed some interest in such an expansion and, as we shall see, the results suggest compelling benefits for them.

The modeling approach is explained in Petri, Plummer, and Zhai (2012) and on the website asiapacifictrade.org. We use a novel computable general equilibrium (CGE) framework developed by Zhai (2008) that incorporates firm-level differences in productivity. The version we use has 24 regions and 18 sectors, and also includes special detail on trade agreements and trade policy provisions in the Asia-Pacific region.

We assume that future agreements will be based on templates similar to those of past agreements. Thus, the TPP's template is assumed to be similar to the Korea-US (KORUS) free trade agreement (FTA), and the RCEP's template to those of agreements recently concluded by ASEAN. The TPP and RCEP templates differ on issues such as government procurement, intellectual property rights, investment, and competition, as well as the depth of liberalization of tariff and nontariff barriers. These differences are not accidental; US agreements seek market access for leading sectors such as services and intellectual property, while Asian agreements focus on goods, consistent with their comparative advantages. We assume an FTAAP that would bridge these objectives with an intermediate template. Pairs of economies covered by more than one agreement are assumed to use—and benefit from—the one with the strongest provisions.

The results of these simulations are summarized in Table 1. These results should be viewed as mainly qualitative (they indicate relative gains), rather than precisely quantitative (since they are subject to many uncertainties and errors). In particular, three main conclusions of the comparisons remain reasonably robust in the face of alternative formulations and estimates.

First, the benefits of Asia-Pacific integration are large; for the most comprehensive agreements, income gains could approach US$2 trillion, or nearly 2 percent of world GDP in 2025. But even the current negotiations on the TPP-12 and the RCEP would generate substantial gains. The RCEP shows larger benefits than the TPP, mainly due to our optimistic assumption that it will liberalize economic relations among China, India, Japan, and South Korea.

Second, the results suggest divergences among the interests of economies. The TPP-12 favors economies that do not yet have an FTA with the United States, such as Vietnam and Japan. The RCEP favors China, India, Japan, and South Korea, assuming that trade among them would be effectively covered by an FTA. ASEAN economies, however, would gain modestly from the RCEP, assuming that the agreement does not substantially improve the FTAs that already cover all of the region's trade flows. Finally, the TPP-17 would offer large benefits to China, the United States, and others that gain access to *both* TPP and RCEP preferences.

Third, potential gains increase sharply with the scale of integration. For example, expanding the TPP from 12 to 17 members would triple global benefits from US$285 billion to US$893 billion in 2025. Since that expansion would include most large economies in the FTAAP, overall gains would be similar.[2] Moreover, gains will depend on the

TABLE 1 *Income Gains Under Alternative Scenarios*

Template quality	GDP 2025 ($2007 bill)	Income gain ($2007 bill)				% Baseline GDP2013			
		TPP-12 High	TPP-17 High	RCEP Moderate	FTAAP Intermediate	TPP-12 High	TPP-17 High	RCEP Moderate	FTAAP Intermediate
Americas	24,867	101.7	468.0	2.5	373.3	0.4	1.9	0.0	1.5
Canada	1,978	8.7	33.2	-0.1	26.2	0.4	1.7	0.0	1.3
Chile	292	2.5	7.8	0.0	6.5	0.9	2.7	0.0	2.2
Mexico	2,004	9.9	91.1	2.8	67.7	0.5	4.5	0.1	3.4
Peru	320	3.9	8.4	0.0	6.3	1.2	2.6	0.0	2.0
United States	20,273	76.6	327.6	-0.1	266.5	0.4	1.6	0.0	1.3
Asia	34,901	125.2	1442.1	627.0	1354.3	0.4	4.1	1.8	3.88
Brunei	20	0.2	1.7	1.2	1.1	0.9	8.4	5.8	5.5
China	17,249	-34.8	808.6	249.7	678.1	-0.2	4.7	1.4	3.9
Hong Kong	406	-0.5	-1.9	46.8	84.9	-0.1	-0.5	11.5	20.9
India	5,233	-2.7	-29.3	91.3	-29.5	-0.1	-0.6	1.7	-0.6
Indonesia	1,549	-2.2	82.0	17.7	38.0	-0.1	5.3	1.1	2.5
Japan	5,338	104.6	237.3	95.8	228.1	2.0	4.4	1.8	4.3
South Korea	2,117	-2.8	136.3	82.0	129.3	-0.1	6.4	3.9	6.1
Malaysia	431	24.2	45.4	14.2	38.4	5.6	10.5	3.3	8.9
Philippines	322	-0.8	30.6	7.6	15.9	-0.2	9.5	2.3	5.0

Singapore	415	7.9	27.1	2.4	13.6	1.9	6.5	0.6	3.3
Chinese Taipei	840	-1.0	-31.5	-16.1	53.0	-0.1	-3.8	-1.9	6.3
Thailand	558	-2.4	64.9	15.5	27.4	-0.4	11.6	2.8	4.9
Vietnam	340	35.7	71.9	17.3	72.9	10.5	21.2	5.1	21.5
Other ASEAN	83	-0.4	-1.1	1.6	3.1	-0.4	-1.3	1.9	3.74
Oceania	1,634	10.7	41.3	21.7	32.1	0.7	2.5	1.3	2.0
Australia	1,433	6.6	34.1	19.8	26.4	0.5	2.4	1.4	1.8
New Zealand	201	4.1	7.2	1.9	5.8	2.0	3.6	0.9	2.9
Others	41,820	-14.1	-43.4	-6.8	162.0	0.0	-0.1	0.0	0.4
Europe	22,714	-3.7	0.9	5.1	-32.6	0.0	0.0	0.0	-0.1
Russia	2,865	-1.4	-8.8	-5.3	265.9	0.0	-0.3	-0.2	9.3
ROW	16,241	-9.0	-35.5	-6.6	-71.4	-0.1	-0.2	0.0	-0.4
WORLD	103,223	223.4	1908.0	644.4	1921.7	0.2	1.8	0.6	1.9
Memorandum									
TPP-12	33,045	285.0	892.8	155.1	759.5	0.9	2.7	0.5	2.3
RCEP	36,535	137.4	1516.8	617.9	1248.5	0.4	4.3	1.8	3.5
APEC	58,951	239.2	1973.0	553.0	2052.0	0.4	3.3	0.9	3.5

Notes: From scenarios reported on asiapacifictrade.org. The template used to represent the TPP-17 is more rigorous than the one used to simulate the FTAAP agreement. Thus, the difference between the two scenarios is partly explained by differences in membership and partly by the more extensive liberalization assumed under the TPP process. For further explanation, see endnote 2.

quality of the template; in other work, we show that global FTAAP benefits would be US$2.4 trillion with a TPP-style template versus US$1.9 trillion with the intermediate template of Table 1. The vast majority of gains in all cases would reflect trade creation, rather than the diversion of benefits from excluded economies.

POSSIBLE PATHWAYS

Regardless of the potential gains, large agreements that include both China and the United States face formidable challenges in terms of negotiations, as well as politics. They will not emerge quickly and will require ample preparation through reforms, innovative cooperation, and greater mutual trust. It is therefore important to consider pathways that could lead to convergence in the longer term. Two broad alternatives are considered below.

First, either the TPP or the RCEP could emerge as a pathway to region-wide free trade. The TPP is at this time the most probable pathway. It might initially expand to 17 members, as discussed above. Such enlargement would yield very positive outcomes for old and new members. China and the United States would reap the largest benefits, providing incentives for their joint leadership. Of course, many difficulties would be involved; China would have to accept provisions that were not included in its previous FTAs, and the United States would face large domestic adjustments that require careful implementation and confident leadership. Nevertheless, this path offers major political and economic opportunities for both economies, and some high-level attention is already directed toward it.[3] Whether the RCEP will emerge as an alternative pathway is still open to question; much will depend on whether it achieves the high standards expected by advanced economies.

Second, the TPP and the RCEP could develop in parallel, with an eventual "umbrella agreement" built around them. That agreement, often envisioned as the FTAAP, would impose new requirements that are intermediate to those of the TPP and the RCEP. For example, it could specify intermediate tariff reductions, service commitments, and intellectual property rules. It would, in turn, offer benefits more modest than those offered by the TPP. This approach would yield an initially multi-tiered system, with economies choosing whether to accept RCEP, FTAAP, or TPP standards, but with the expectation that each economy would eventually converge to high standards. This is most likely to happen by adding economies gradually to the TPP. Another possibility is that the FTAAP becomes a living agreement that is upgraded over time. Precedents for an evolutionary approach are offered by ASEAN's experience with combining "plus one" agreements and bilateral agreements with external partners, and with its upgrading of the ASEAN Free Trade Area and some ASEAN-Plus-One partnerships. Unfortunately, the US political process offers no similar precedents.

An effective multi-tiered system would require its several agreements to be reasonably compatible. There is some evidence that recent trade agreements by the United States and Asian economies are more similar than earlier ones, and that agreements increasingly borrow language from each other. The guidelines for the RCEP, for example, overlap with the structure of the TPP. In any case, the attitudes of China and the United States will be crucial. Much of the incremental gains from a region-wide agreement would accrue to these economies, and their cooperation and leadership will be essential for bridging the Asian and trans-Pacific tracks. More work is needed to analyze the details of these alternatives, but APEC provides an ideal venue for such dialogue.

CONCLUSIONS

Asian and trans-Pacific regional negotiations are moving forward, despite business cycles, elections, geopolitics, and political controversy. Estimates suggest that they could generate large economic benefits, especially if they ultimately encompass the entire region.

The gains from Asia-Pacific integration will depend on the quality and regional reach of the templates used. There is tension between these objectives. A rigorous template, as is emerging in the trans-Pacific negotiations, yields greater gains, but will also impede region-wide participation. But there are ways to bridge these alternatives, such as through the multi-track, multi-tiered process sketched above.

Detailed policy recommendations are well beyond the scope of this short paper, but three issues merit attention:

- APEC could use the current lull in negotiations to intensify work on region-wide integration, including the FTAAP. New policy dialogues and research efforts might be directed, for example, toward minimizing divergences between emerging agreements.
- The TPP and RCEP agreements could develop "mutual accession" clauses—that is, commitments to consider expeditiously applications from each other's members. They could also identify future windows for enlargement. These provisions need not guarantee accession, but making the timetables explicit would motivate planning.
- China and the United States could follow a "third track" of discussions through bilateral efforts; they have the most to gain from, and contribute to, regional integration. Their steps could range from concluding an early bilateral investment agreement to other policy changes required for joint participation in a region-wide free trade agreement.

Region-wide agreements could produce compelling economic benefits and a more cooperative political environment. Yet achieving such agreements is difficult. Lengthy and complex negotiations will be required, which—amplified by the Internet—invite opposition from numerous special interests. The case for Asia-Pacific integration will have to be made effectively by governments, especially in the largest economies, if its benefits are to be realized.

NOTES

1. This possibility has been raised in recent commentary by Ma and Shi (2013) and Gordon (2014), among others.

2. The TPP-17 and FTAAP simulations differ, both in terms of their template (the TPP-17 template is assumed to be more rigorous) and membership (the FTAAP has 21 members). These differences complicate direct comparisons of the results. For China, for example, the gains are greater under the high standards of the TPP-17 than under the wider coverage

of the FTAAP. The same is true for the United States. For Chinese Taipei, however, gains are greater under the FTAAP than the TPP-17 because it is not assumed to be part of the latter.

3. These possibilities were explicitly noted, for example, by Wang Shouwen, Assistant Commerce Minister, and Lin Yifu, Vice Chairman of the All-China Federation of Industry and Commerce, speaking at the Boao Forum on April 9, 2014 (originally http://www.bruneitimes.com.bn /business-asia/2014/04/10/china-says-it-watching-trans-pacific-trade-pact-great-interest but now at http://www.aastocks.com/en/stocks /analysis/china-hot-topic-content.aspx?id=200000331986&type=18& catg=3).

SOURCES

Gordon, Bernard. 2014. "China Belongs in the Pacific Trade Pact." *Wall Street Journal,* April 24.

Kehoe, Timothy J. 2005. "An Evaluation of the Performance of Applied General Equilibrium Models on the Impact of NAFTA." In *Frontiers in Applied General Equilibrium Modeling: In Honor of Herbert Scarf,* edited by T.J. Kehoe, T.N. Srinivasan, and J. Whalley, 341–77. Cambridge: Cambridge University Press.

Li, Chunding, and John Whalley. 2012. "China and the TPP: A Numerical Simulation Assessment of the Effects Involved." National Bureau of Economic Research, NBER Working Paper No. 18090, May.

Ma, Jun, and Audrey Shi. 2013. *Economic Benefits of TPP Entry for China.* Deutsche Bank, Hong Kong.

Petri, Peter A., Michael G. Plummer, and Fan Zhai. 2012. *The Trans-Pacific Partnership and Asia-Pacific Integration: A Quantitative Assessment.* Policy Analysis in International Economics No. 98. Washington, DC: Peterson Institute for International Economics and East-West Center.

Pew Research Center and Bertelsmann Foundation. 2014. *Creating a Transatlantic Marketplace: German and American Views.* Washington, DC.

Zhai, Fan. 2008. "Armington Meets Melitz: Introducing Firm Heterogeneity in a Global CGE Model of Trade." *Journal of Economic Integration* 23 (issue 3, September): 575–604.

The Regional Comprehensive Economic Partnership Negotiation

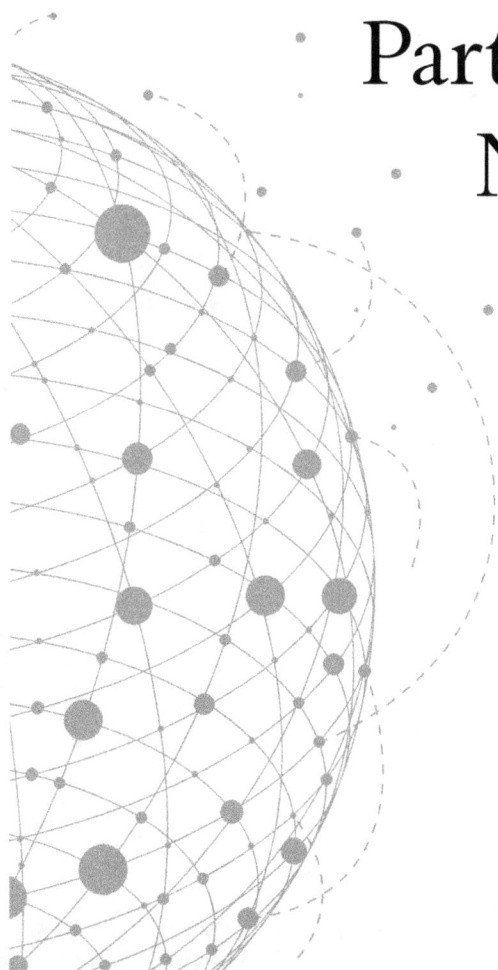

7

The Regional Comprehensive Economic Partnership

An Initial Assessment

Ganeshan Wignaraja, Director of Research,
Asian Development Bank Institute[1]

INTRODUCTION

Mega-regional trade deals are emerging as a key feature of the world trading system in the post–global financial crisis era. This trend has been motivated by the need to reduce regulatory barriers to global supply chain trade, a loss of credibility in the negotiating function of the World Trade Organization (WTO), and geopolitics (Baldwin 2012). The international spotlight is on negotiations for the US-led Trans-Pacific Partnership (TPP) and the US-EU Transatlantic Trade and Investment Partnership (TTIP). Meanwhile, Asia's own mega-regional trade deal—the Regional Comprehensive Economic Partnership (RCEP)—is quietly being negotiated. But it merits more economic analysis: the RCEP could create the world's largest trading bloc and have significant implications for the world economy.

This essay provides an initial assessment of the RCEP and explores its policy implications. It focusses on four important questions in contemporary policy debates: (1) What is the framework for the RCEP negotiations, particularly its aim, scope, and timeline? (2) How will the RCEP impact economies and sectors? (3) What does joining the RCEP imply for India, which some argue is hesitant to liberalize its trade further and could be a stumbling block to the negotiations? (4) What are the main challenges to the success of the RCEP during the negotiations and afterwards?

THE FRAMEWORK FOR THE RCEP NEGOTIATIONS

The RCEP was launched at the East Asia Summit in November 2012 in Phnom Penh, Cambodia (Basu Das 2012). While the partnership would expand ASEAN's role in coordinating regional trade, the RCEP's key aim is to reconcile two long-standing proposals into a large, region-wide trade agreement. The two proposals being joined are: (1) the East Asian Free Trade Agreement, which includes ASEAN, China, Japan, and South Korea; and (2) the Comprehensive Economic Partnership, which has added Australia, New Zealand, and India. The first was backed by China, and the second by Japan. The RCEP neatly bridges the two proposals by adopting an open accession scheme so that any party that meets the template can join. Furthermore, ASEAN is accorded the coordinating role for the RCEP process, which means better inclusion of the interests of smaller ASEAN economies.

A relatively short time frame for the RCEP negotiations was planned at the outset. Negotiations began in early 2013 and are scheduled to conclude by the end of 2015. Four rounds of negotiations have been completed to date, with the most recent held in Nanning, China, from March 31 to April 4, 2014.

The parties have stated that their goal is to achieve a modern and comprehensive trade agreement, and the negotiations are supposed to be guided by several key principles (RCEP Ministers 2012), including:

- maintaining consistency with WTO rules, such as GATT Article XXIV and GATS Article V;
- providing improvements over existing ASEAN-Plus-One FTAs;
- reflecting different levels of development of participating economies, and allowing for special and differential treatment for least-developed economies; and
- ensuring an open accession clause to enable participation of any ASEAN FTA partner, as well as other external economic partners, at a future date.

The core of the RCEP negotiating agenda will cover trade in goods, services trade, investment, economic and technical cooperation, and dispute settlement. More specifically, the RCEP seeks to achieve the following:

- gradually reduce tariff and nontariff barriers on most trade in goods to create a free trade area;
- largely eliminate restrictions and discriminatory measures on trade in services for all sectors and modes of services;
- create an open and facilitative climate for investment;
- address the special needs of less-developed ASEAN economies through early elimination of tariffs on products of interest to them, and through the provision of development assistance to narrow development gaps; and
- provide for a dispute settlement mechanism to effectively resolve trade disputes.

The TPP is often portrayed as an ambitious, twenty-first century trade agreement dealing with complex behind-the-border regulatory issues (Schott, Kotschwar, and Muir 2013). It is possible that an eventual TPP agreement will be deeper than the RCEP in two respects. First, in core issues covered by both the RCEP and TPP, the TPP will have deeper commitments (e.g., faster and more comprehensive liberalization of goods trade). Second, the TPP will cover more areas than the RCEP (by as much as 29 chapters) that aim to substantially reduce barriers to trade, as well as expand the rules on trade.

There is a lack of official information on the current state of the RCEP negotiations, which are being conducted behind closed doors. The early signs are that progress has been made in the negotiations in the areas of goods trade and trade facilitation. The parties are said to have reached preliminary agreements on tariff reduction schedules, rules of origin, customs procedures, and other trade facilitation measures (See *China Daily*, March 31, 2014). Negotiations on services and investment, however, may take some time due to differences in levels of development of the parties, the negotiation positions of the parties, and the influence of business lobbies.

Nonetheless, the RCEP is less ambitious than the TPP in terms of trade issues covered, and the prospect of development assistance for adjustment means that developing economies will find it easier to join the RCEP. Thus, an RCEP deal has a reasonable chance of success. Additionally, the RCEP, along with the TPP, will influence the emerging regional trade architecture toward achieving a free trade area of the Asia Pacific.

ECONOMIC IMPACT OF THE RCEP

Disparities in per capita income and trade policy are key differences among RCEP members. Table 1 shows per capita GDP in purchasing power parity, MFN tariff levels, and number of concluded FTAs of RCEP members. The grouping includes high-income developed economies (e.g., Singapore, Australia, Japan, South Korea, and New Zealand) as well as poor developing economies (e.g., India, Cambodia, Laos, Vietnam, and Myanmar). There are wide variations in levels of trade opening, with some economies exhibiting double-digit MFN tariffs and others having low tariffs. Differences also exist in the emphasis given to FTAs as trade policy instruments, with very active FTA-strategy economies existing alongside more passive FTA-strategy economies.

These differences, however, mask the striking collective economic importance of the RCEP trade bloc. Table 2 provides information on the RCEP members' world shares of population, GDP, trade, and investment. The grouping covers 48.8 percent of the world's population and accounts for 28.7 percent of world GDP. It also makes up 27 percent

TABLE I   *Per Capita Income and Trade Policy in Asia*

	Per capita gross domestic product based on purchasing power parity (PPP)		Simple mean, MFN tariff rate (%)[a]		Concluded FTAs	
	(Current international dollars)				(No. of FTAs)	
	2000	2013	2000	2012	2000	2013
Northeast Asia						
Japan	25,709	36,899	3.3	3	0	13
China	2,382	9,844	17	2.5	1	14
South Korea	16,528	33,189	9.2	12.1	1	11
ASEAN						
Brunei	43,386	53,431	2.6	2.5	1	8
Cambodia	909	2,576	16.4	14.2	1	6
Indonesia	2,433	5,214	8.4	6.7	1	9
Laos	1,185	3,068	9.5	9.7	3	8
Malaysia	9,102	17,748	10.2	7	1	13
Myanmar	530	1,740	5.5	5.6	1	6
Philippines	2,446	4,682	7.6	6.3	1	7
Singapore	33,195	64,584	0	0	1	21
Thailand	5,015	9,875	18.5	9.7	2	12
Vietnam	1,426	4,012	16.5	9.8	1	8
Other						
India	1,561	4,077	32.9	12.4	1	13
Australia	27,581	43,073	4.5	2.8	1	8
New Zealand	19,884	30,493	2.6	2.1	1	9

Notes: [a] *The tariffs reported are the simple average MFN tariffs across all commodities. Where data is not available, the most recent year within a five-year window (on either side) is used. Sources: IMF, World Economic Outlook Database; World Bank, World Integrated Solutions Database; ADB, Asia Regional Integration Center.*

of world trade, 24.4 percent of world FDI inflows, and 23.3 percent of world FDI outflows.

There are several *a priori* reasons why the implementation of the RCEP can generate economic gains for Asia. First, the RCEP can

TABLE 2 *Importance of RCEP in Global Economy*

Measure	Magnitude	Share of world
Population	3.4 billion people	48.8% (2013)
GDP (Current)	US$21.3 trillion	28.7% (2013)
Trade (Goods and services exports and imports)	US$12.1 trillion	27.0% (2012)
FDI inflow	US$329.4 billion	24.4% (2012)

Notes: Figures for population and GDP are IMF estimates.
Sources: IMF World Economic Outlook Database; World Bank World Development Indicators; UNCTAD, (all accessed February 20, 2013).

help regionalize sophisticated global supply chains that make Asia the world's factory. If a comprehensive agreement can be reached, trade barriers impacting goods and services in Asia will fall. Market size will expand beyond national borders, and a larger regional market will facilitate the realization of economies of scale in production.

Second, if the new regional rules align with WTO agreements on goods and services, the RCEP can help further insure against the emergence of protectionist sentiments in the global economy, particularly murky nontariff measures.

Third, in the area of investment rules—where there exists only a rather basic WTO agreement (the Trade Related Investment Measures, or TRIMs)—the RCEP promotes easier FDI flows and technology transfers by multinational corporations. Reducing barriers to investment and supporting a regional, rules-based FDI regime will further facilitate regional supply chain trade.

Fourth, by simplifying trade rules, the RCEP will also reduce the overlap among Asian FTAs and the risk of an Asian "noodle bowl" of multiple trade rules (Kawai and Wignaraja 2013). Rules of origin, in particular, could be rationalized, made more flexible, and better administered through electronic means. This would reduce transaction costs for businesses, particularly for small- and medium-sized enterprises (SMEs).

Fifth, falling trade barriers will make available cheaper imports of food and consumer goods, which will benefit consumers and low-income households.

Simulation modeling using computable general equilibrium (CGE) models is useful in quantifying the income effects of eliminating import tariffs on the trade in goods, and liberalizing cross-border trade in services through the formation of trade agreements. CGE models can trace economy-wide effects of policy changes and point to unintended economic consequences. CGE studies typically show that significant gains can arise from the RCEP.

A recent study (Kawai and Wignaraja, forthcoming) showed that the RCEP can offer large income gains to the world economy, reaching $260 billion (or a 0.54 percent change from baseline income). Furthermore, all economies that are party to the RCEP agreement are projected to achieve gains (see Figure 1). For ASEAN's dynamic members, projected gains are significant: Thailand (12.8 percent), Vietnam (7.6 percent), Malaysia (6.3 percent), and Singapore (5.4 percent). For the rest of ASEAN— Cambodia, Indonesia, the Philippines, and the remaining ASEAN economies—the gains are less than 3 percent. Among the economies of Northeast Asia, South Korea is projected to experience the largest gain under the RCEP (6.4 percent), while gains for Japan and China are less than 2 percent. Meanwhile, the gains for India are 2.4 percent, the gains for Australia are 3.9 percent, and those for New Zealand are 5.2 percent. As expected, economies that are not members of the RCEP experience losses, and the magnitude of these losses differ by economy.

The study also shows that the implementation of the RCEP scenario is likely to result in significant structural changes toward manufactures and services (and away from agriculture and other primary products) in Asia. There are also shifts within manufacturing. Among ASEAN's dynamic members, Thailand is projected to experience gains in electrical machinery and electronics, motor vehicles, and services; Vietnam in textiles and clothing; and Malaysia in metals and metal products. In the rest of ASEAN, Cambodia sees losses in a key sector (textiles and clothing), and the Philippines sees losses in motor vehicles. Meanwhile, China achieves gains in electrical machinery and electronics, and India in services and metals. Japan and South Korea see gains in most manufacturing sectors. Strikingly, seven economies see declines in agriculture, and the others see negligible gains.

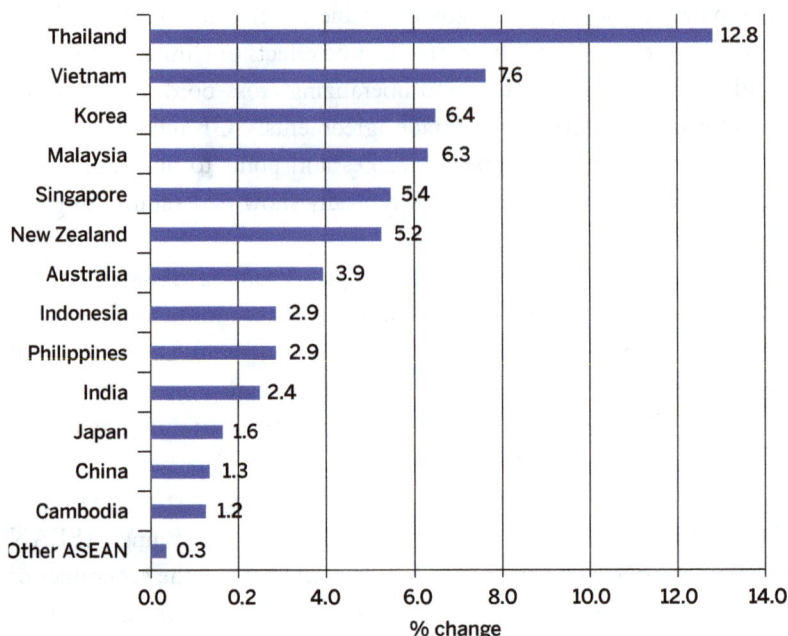

FIGURE I   *Percentage Change in Income, Compared to a 2017 Baseline*

IMPLICATIONS OF THE RCEP FOR INDIA

India's Look East Policy of 1991 signaled the intent of South Asia's giant economy to revitalize its cultural, defense, and economic ties with globally important East Asia. Over time, India has operationalized its Look East Policy by concluding FTAs with East Asian economies, including a plurilateral agreement with ASEAN in 2010, as well as bilateral agreements with Singapore in 2005, South Korea in 2010, Japan in 2011, and Malaysia in 2011. By providing for India-China trade and India–Australia/New Zealand trade, the RCEP fills in crucial, missing FTA links between India and other RCEP members. This will give the Indian business sector greater opportunities to access a larger regional market and to integrate into regional production networks. None of the other South Asian economies have expressed a desire to join the RCEP, but this may change if they become concerned about being left out of the large regional integration group (Wignaraja 2014).

Trade preferences and regional, rules-based India-China trade offer important advantages for India. However, there have been concerns among some business sectors in India, particularly in the import substituting manufacturing sector, about expanding India-China trade (e.g., Mishra 2013). Cheap imports of manufactured goods from China are thought to have adversely affected Indian businesses. Some argue that Chinese firms appear to have price and quality standards that few Indian firms can match. Concerns have also been expressed about opening up sensitive economic sectors and infrastructure to inward investment from China, particularly by state-owned enterprises that unfairly benefit from government subsidies.

But a preoccupation with the absolute advantage of Chinese firms as traders or investors is misplaced. The CGE projections mentioned above show that India can achieve potential income gains of 2.4 percent from the implementation of the RCEP. The RCEP provides inroads for Indian services to China and the rest of East Asia, where India has achieved a comparative advantage on world markets (see Wignaraja 2011). These advantages include the areas of information and communication technology, professional services, law, banking, and educational services. Moreover, India has emerged as an important destination for tourists from the Asia-Pacific region, and tourism services offer further opportunities for Indian businesses. Accordingly, India should make the case for lower barriers to services trade and more transparent investment rules in the RCEP negotiations. India has also shown growth in some manufacturing sectors in world markets (including pharmaceuticals, the automotive sector, textiles, and food processing), and this trend is likely to continue under the RCEP.

Thus, the RCEP is a major opportunity for Indian businesses in services and manufacturing, including large and small firms within these sectors. Lobbying for exemptions for sensitive sectors or more protection for declining manufacturing sectors would be an unproductive, defensive approach to the RCEP. Instead, Indian businesses should prepare for gradual market opening under the RCEP by investing in price, quality, and delivery systems that meet international standards. Above all,

Indian businesses need to invest in new technology, quality management systems, just-in-time procurement systems, research and development, relationships with overseas buyers of output, and technical training. The Indian government can support business process reengineering by Indian firms through investing more in transport and energy infrastructure, implementing second-generation structural reforms, providing access to competitive industrial finance, investing in tertiary-level technical education, and strengthening science and technology institutions.

It seems that India has adopted a generally positive approach to the RCEP negotiations. The good thing about the RCEP is that it is a step-by-step process, so any economy that meets the template can join. The RCEP should be relatively easy for India because it has concluded the more ambitious India-Japan and India–South Korea FTAs. Indian businesses, then, should embrace the RCEP, as it includes all the ASEAN economies, as well as others.

Furthermore, Indian elections in Mid-May 2014 have ushered in a more pro-business administration. The new government led by Narendra Modi has said it will adopt new economic reforms (including liberalization of regulations on the entry of foreign investment and strict labor laws). Sweeping domestic reforms in India over the next few years will make it easier for India to lock in the gains from trade by concluding a RCEP agreement.

CHALLENGES FACED BY THE RCEP

Realizing the benefits of the RCEP will depend on how effectively several challenges are addressed during the negotiations and afterwards (Basu Das 2012, Hiebert and Hanlon 2012, Kawai and Wignaraja 2013). First is the political challenge of respecting the central role of ASEAN in the RCEP negotiations, amidst the presence of major regional economies (such as Japan, China, South Korea, and India). The second challenge arises from negotiating partners having different levels of development and interests. The RCEP must overcome the risk that granting exclusions to protect sensitive sectors will ultimately limit trade and investment liberalization. The third challenge is for the

RCEP to gradually improve its coverage of new trade issues (such as competition policy, the environment, and labor standards), which are increasingly a feature in the most comprehensive FTAs in Asia and internationally. Fourth is the risk that firms, particularly small- and medium-sized enterprises, may underuse RCEP tariff preferences due to limited international competitiveness, as well as poor understanding of its legal provisions. Fifth, implementation of the RCEP will bring gains and losses at sector level within countries. With wages and jobs at risk, adjustment costs may be high in declining economic sectors. Sixth, there is the possibility that the RCEP and other mega-regional FTAs may exacerbate the divergence between regional and WTO trade rules, with the continuing erosion of WTO's central role in global trade governance.

CONCLUSIONS

This essay conducted an initial assessment of the RCEP. This is a difficult exercise as the negotiations only began in early 2013, and official information is lacking on the current state of the RCEP talks. Several points emerge from the analysis.

First, a lower level of ambition than other mega-regionals, such as the TPP, and the prospect of development assistance for adjustment suggest that the RCEP stands a reasonable chance of getting concluded. The addition of a built-in agenda to the RCEP negotiating text would permit more difficult trade issues concerning regulatory barriers to be added in the future.

Second, the RCEP is globally important as a trading bloc, and CGE simulation studies suggest that it will generate notable income gains for the global economy. All members of the RCEP will gain, but the magnitude of gains varies among economies. Structural changes will shift economic activity toward manufactures and services, and adjustments at sectoral levels will also result from the RCEP.

Third, concerns expressed by the Indian business community about increased competition arising from the implementation of the RCEP may be overstated. India has achieved a comparative advantage on world

markets in services and in some areas of manufacturing. A renewed partnership between Indian businesses and government can help the business sector prepare for market openings under the RCEP. Assistance can
take the form of investments in manufacturing capabilities and improvements in the policy environment for businesses.

Fourth, realizing the benefits from the RCEP depends on addressing
challenges during the negotiations and afterwards. Key policy challenges
are likely to arise about how to ensure ASEAN centrality in the RCEP
process, how to achieve a reasonable level of ambition in an eventual
RCEP, how to ensure optimal use of RCEP preferences, how to support
declining economic sectors, and how to enhance the role of the WTO in
global-trade governance.

The way forward for the RCEP negotiations should be to take the
best features of existing Asian FTAs (including existing ASEAN-Plus-
One FTAs), and to use them as a basis for negotiations to maximize the
quality of the RCEP, adhere to the timetable for concluding the RCEP
negotiations, and actively involve the private sector in the negotiations.
Afterwards, significant outreach and business services would be needed
for small- and medium-sized businesses to improve their international
competitiveness and lower the costs of using the RCEP. Enhancing domestic structural reforms, investing in cross-border infrastructure, and
streamlining trade facilitation would also help elicit a private sector response to the RCEP. Furthermore, adjustment assistance and social safety nets can help mitigate the negative effects of trade liberalization under
RCEP on affected sectors and jobs. Finally, a WTO agenda on global
supply chains and regionalism will facilitate greater coherence between
mega-regionals like RCEP and WTO rules.

NOTES

1. The views expressed here are solely mine and do not reflect the views of
   the Asian Development Bank or the Asian Development Bank Institute.

SOURCES

Baldwin, Richard. 2012. "WTO 2.0: Global Governance of Supply Chain Trade." Center for Economic Policy Research, CEPR Policy Insight No. 64, December.

Basu Das, Sanchita. 2012. "RCEP: Going Beyond ASEAN+1 FTAs." Institute of Southeast Asian Studies, *ISEAS Perspective*, August 17. http://www.iseas. edu.sg/documents/publication/ISEAS%20Perspective_4_17aug12.pdf.

Hiebert, Murray, and Liam Hanlon. 2012. "ASEAN and Partners Launch Regional Comprehensive Economic Partnership." Center for Strategic and International Studies website, December 7. http://csis.org/publication/ asean-and-partners-launch-regional-comprehensive-economic-partnership.

Kawai, Masahiro, and Ganeshan Wignaraja. 2013. *Patterns of Free Trade Areas in Asia: A Review of Recent Evidence.* East-West Center Policy Studies No. 65. Honolulu: East-West Center. http://www.eastwestcenter.org/ publications/patterns-free-trade-areas-in-asia.

———. Forthcoming. "Policy Challenges Posed by Asian FTAs: A Review of the Evidence." In *A WTO for the 21st Century: The Asian Perspective*, edited by R. Baldwin, M. Kawai, and G. Wignaraja. Cheltenham, UK: Edward Elgar.

Mishra, Rahul. 2013. "RCEP: Challenges and Opportunities for India." S. Rajaratnam School of International Studies, RSIS Commentaries No. 140/2013, July 25.

RCEP Ministers. 2012. "Guiding Principles and Objectives for Negotiating the Regional Comprehensive Economic Partnership." Available at www. dfat.gov.au/fta/rcep.

Schott, Jeffrey J., Barbara Kotschwar, and Julia Muir. 2013. *Understanding the Trans-Pacific Partnership.* Policy Analyses in International Economics. Washington, DC: Peterson Institute for International Economics.

Wignaraja, Ganeshan. 2011. *Economic Reforms, Regionalism and Exports: Comparing China and India.* East-West Center Policy Studies No. 60. Honolulu: East-West Center.

———. 2014. "Assessing the Experience of South Asia–East Asia Integration and India's Role." Asian Development Bank Institute, ADBI Working Paper No. 465, February 27.

8

East Asian Multi-Track Regional Partnership

Djisman Simandjuntak, Senior Economist and Chairman of the Board of Directors, Center for Strategic and International Studies Foundation

DIMENSIONS OF A GRADUAL PROGRESSION

Recognizing the practical ways in which regional integration and cooperation have evolved in the last three decades or so in East Asia (EA), it increasingly makes sense to look at EA as a region that consists of the Association of Southeast Asian Nations (ASEAN) or Southeast Asia, Northeast Asia, and Australia, India, and New Zealand. This definition has very little to do with physical geography and social geography. It is a practical decision that recognizes deepening interdependence between ASEAN, Northeast Asia, Australia, New Zealand, and India in terms of trade, investment, and migration flows. It also captures how the rest of the world relates to this region, rather than focusing on its smaller geographical parts. The world may one day mutate into a single region. For the time being, however, regionalism does open incremental opportunities for economic and social advancement, depending on the density of connectivity that has been wired into it, be it physical connectivity, peope-to-people connectivity, or—also very important—institutional connectivity. A dense connectivity transforms a physical region into a formidable economic geography (Giulani 2010, Morris 2010).

Generally speaking, EA as an emerging region is currently serving as the locomotive for the world economy's growth for a number of reasons. It is growing faster than the rest of the world primarily thanks to China, which admittedly is experiencing a slowdown, but still manages to grow by over 7 percent a year. Another contributor is the medium-size economy of Indonesia, which grows at approximately 6 percent a year. Future potential for growth is also promising as EA remains a "huge region of complementary opportunities." China is still evolving in the middle-income group. India, Indonesia, the Philippines, and Vietnam are at an even earlier stage, but are catching up. People from diverse walks of life, such as commerce, professional employment, policymaking, and academia have discovered that East Asia is a rewarding area for spending their time and effort. They all wish to be part of and benefit from the EA growth process.

However, EA is not a homogeneous region. The contrast starts by looking at income and economic development in general. On this score, EA occupies the entire spectrum of income and development levels. At one end, EA is home to very low-income economies, such as Myanmar, Cambodia, and Laos. On the other hand, it is also home to top-income countries of different kinds, such as Brunei, Singapore, Japan, and South Korea. In the lower middle there thrive Vietnam, India, the Philippines, and Indonesia; China, Thailand, and Malaysia occupy the upper middle. Beyond the favorable economic growth, there looms very large in East Asia different priorities concerning economic policymaking. Drawing a coherent agenda of economic community building in EA requires a fine balancing. The region's different stages of development combine with variations in geography, political systems, foreign policies, and history to make EA also a region of divergence.

The contrast extends to macroeconomic conditions and policies. Inflation is largely benign in EA (Kim and Lee 2013). Yet Vietnam and India are faced with the risk of inflation rising to double digits. Unemployment is also generally low, but India in recent times has faced an employment rate of almost 10 percent. What is more, there are important footnotes to unemployment in East Asia. In several economies, huge numbers of people engage in vulnerable employment that may disappear when an external shock strikes (ILO 2013). And while region-wide progress on poverty has been remarkable, the war against poverty is far from won. If the poverty line is defined at PPP (purchasing power parity) US$2 per day, around 68 percent of Indians, 60 percent of Laotians, 49 percent of Cambodians, 43 percent of Indonesians and Vietnamese, and 27 percent of Chinese still struggle at the edge of poverty. Healthy life expectancy (HALE) is short in the low-income and low middle-income economies of EA. Furthermore, inequality is worsening in the region, as reflected in rising Gini coefficients (Wang Feng 2011, Saez 2013).

Somewhat more disquieting is the profile of current account. After a long period of positive current account following the crisis of 1997–1998, Indonesia, for example, returned to a negative current account in 2013 and 2014. The situation is more serious in Cambodia and Laos, where the ratios have stood at around 6 percent in recent times, far above the limits of 4 percent that is widely considered to be threatening. However, these two economies can still count on development assistance when dealing with financing. In India, the current account deficit is much higher, in the neighborhood of 8 percent of GDP, though India can count on capital and financial flows for financing. However, for large economies such as India and Indonesia, high current account deficits are reasons for concern, no matter how optimistic one may be about unrequited transfer and direct investment inflow, or incoming portfolio investment.

Even foreign direct investment (FDI) is not a panacea from a current account perspective, since sooner or later it is going to lead to cumulative outflows in excess of cumulative inflows. While overall net investment positions in EA are not worrisome, there are again great variations. Australia and New Zealand exhibit a net position of –64 percent and –69 percent of GDP respectively, but they are able to mobilize capital inflows in sufficient magnitude. Next are Indonesia at –36 percent, South Korea at –18 percent, and India and the Philippines at –10 percent each. On the other hand, China enjoys a net position of +37 percent, Japan +56 percent, and Singapore a huge +224 percent. These statistics underline the importance of monetary policy cooperation. East Asia is on the right track with the strengthened Chiang Mai Initiative Multilateralization (CMIM) and the ASEAN Macroeconomic Research Organization (AMRO), which together are expected to evolve into a more comprehensive framework for macroeconomic policy cooperation.

After lagging for decades behind Europe in terms of regional integration and cooperation, EA has caught up at high speed in recent years. Not only was the reluctance to integrate and cooperate overcome by the ASEAN economies when they established the ASEAN Free Trade Area in 1992, but ASEAN has also evolved into an ASEAN Economic Community (AEC), which is scheduled to be completed by 2015. Intra-ASEAN trade, investment, and flows of people have expanded, though one has to note time and again that EA rather than ASEAN is the more proper definition of the region. Assessment by the Economic Research Institute for ASEAN and East Asia (ERIA) suggests that the agreed targets may not be attained in their fullness (ERIA 2012, 11–16). Nevertheless, the AEC is likely to deserve a "B" score, with targets in trade in goods achieved to a large extent, though the ones pertaining to services, investment, and flows of people much less so. Mention must also be made of the adoption of the ASEAN Charter in 2007. In spite of its limited ambitions in terms of extent and speed of integration and cooperation that go beyond interstate relations, the charter gives ASEAN a more solid foundation as a regional grouping. In the meantime, ASEAN is preparing for strategies and steps for the post-2015 period, which is likely to be critical for the future economic development of ASEAN and East Asia in general.

The process of branching out of ASEAN regional integration and cooperation has also progressed in EA. Bilateral FTAs or partnerships have been established or are in the making in EA. The Chiang Mai Initiative Multilateralization (CMIM) must have played a role in protecting EA from the oftentimes-wild impacts of global crises, such as the one that erupted in 2007–2009 in those economies with the most developed financial systems, though the CMIM still suffers from shortcomings (Siregar and Chabchitrchaidol 2013, 7–11). The various early attempts to pursue an EA-wide approach to regional integration and cooperation have admittedly failed to result in the desired outcomes so far, but they have now led to negotiations on the RCEP, which is scheduled to come to an agreement by the end of 2015.

It is extremely important for EA to insulate rising trade, investment, and people interactions, as well as the process of economic community building, from the impacts of resurging protectionist measures enacted after the 2007–2008 crisis. Of equal importance is shielding itself from interactions regarding disputes in other spheres of life, particularly territorial disputes in the South China Sea and East China Sea, as well as shielding against an escalating arms race. Not only is such insulation very important from the perspective of future growth, it is also one way of raising stakes in achieving good and peaceful relations, as functionalists and neo-functionalists have argued all along.

THE NEXT STAGE OF GRADUATION

Notwithstanding progressive growth in recent decades and the positive perception of EA among traders, investors, and governments as the world's most vital growth center, where a presence—direct or indirect—is considered essential, the fact remains that EA economies are scattered along the entire development ladder, as alluded to earlier. Economic growth will still continue to rank very high in EA's development agenda. Even Japan is faced with the need to revive growth to a higher level, as reflected in the "Abenomics." As the problems associated with Japan's aging population get increasingly severe, and its policy stance regarding immigration remains closed, the need for higher productivity of the working population will be felt more pressingly. This erodes even further the appeal of low-value processes in manufacturing and services, unless they are highly mechanized. Similar to Japan, South Korea will also have to raise productivity of its working population to be able to absorb the burdens that come with worsening aging. Given its very high income, Singapore may find growth increasingly difficult. Yet, Singaporeans do seek to go beyond their current level of per capita income. Brunei may have little urgency to seek alternative growth sectors outside of oil and gas, thanks to its resource abundance and small population, though these fossil fuels are bound to run dry sooner or later. It remains an open question whether the very advanced economies of EA will, in time, find the necessary growth impulses, or if they will succumb to the tyranny of life cycles and become satisfied with small, steady state growth.

For the rest of East Asia, growth will continue to rank very prominently in the development agenda. Indeed, the attainment of an escape velocity that would allow these economies to safely overcome the development traps is an imperative, if the lessons from Japan, South Korea, and China apply to the rest of EA, as they probably do. Needless to say, the challenges facing individual economies differ depending on physical geography, demography, cultures adhered to, level and diversity of competencies mastered by the population, the stage of development occupied, economic systems adhered to as they pertain to constitution of ownership, the role of the state in economic development, and openness to the rest of the world. To highlight the problems more succinctly, the following discussion is focused on the more populous economies. As long as these economies grow at healthy rates, the less populous ones will find ways to grow alongside them, or even outpace the populous economies.

The experiences of Japan, South Korea, and China show that sustaining progressive growth in manufacturing is indispensable to the attainment of the escape velocity of growth. A casual observation of recent patterns in the global production network shows, in fact, that acceleration is possible only in a few subsectors, notably information and telecommunication technologies, automotive industries, and some parts of consumer goods industries. It is in these few industries where growth of output and trade is fastest. It is also in these few industries where the division of labor can be pushed to greatest depths. A fundamental question arises as to what extent the world can accommodate the simultaneous, rapid growth of manufacturing in China, India, Indonesia, the Philippines, Myanmar, and Vietnam. However one answers the question, the populous EA economies are going to look at manufacturing as the only feasible locomotive for strong output and employment expansion. Some may push the acceleration under state leadership, along the lines of industrial targeting, though the probability of successfully pursuing such routes has diminished as manufacturing has spread more widely and protection measures become increasingly costly to maintain. The more popular route, however, is acceleration driven by foreign direct investments. In fact, the strategy of creating growth momentum through special economic zones, where speed of development can be raised and location costs reduced through special administrative provisions and economies of scale and scope, is still a popular option to boost the growth of manufacturing.

Using foreign investment as a catalyst of progressive growth in manufacturing requires a good policy in the widest sense of the word. Such policies include border measures that allow the inflow and outflow of goods and services to proceed at high speeds and lower costs across the different locations in the production network. On this score, the developing parts of EA have a lot of catching up to do in addressing non-tariff measures related to trade in goods, including setting and enforcing various standards. Of equal importance is good domestic regulation. For instance, the difficulties involved in infrastructure in general, and public-private partnerships in particular, pertain partly to land rights. In some new democracies, such as Indonesia, dealing with labor unions has turned out to be difficult, with the tendency for unit labor cost to rise progressively relative to productivity. Dealing with business permits has remained an arduous process, despite efforts on the part of governments to streamline the permitting process. Governments can also grow impatient, forcing foreign companies to transfer technologies. What is more, underinvestment in infrastructure is commonplace in the developing parts of East Asia. Routine expenditures, such as subsidies on current consumption of fuels, as in the case of Indonesia, are typically large in comparison to tax revenues. The call for private sector investment in infrastructure by way of public-private partnerships has materialized only marginally because of the difficulties involved in drawing up contracts and enforcing them. As a result, connectivity in the cases of low-income economies in EA leaves a great deal to be desired. The decision by some governments to focus on carefully selected clusters of metropolitan areas, such as Indonesia's promotion of the Indonesian Master Plan for the Acceleration of Economic Development, appears sensible. However, making these plans successful takes daring leadership, as China demonstrated in determinedly pushing its special economic zones (SEZ).

Given the tough competition between different locations, the temptation exists to engage in a "race to the bottom," or using location dumping as a way to get larger shares of foreign investments in manufacturing. The more thinly a government is equipped with resources, the greater such temptation becomes. The danger of governments engaging in zero-sum games, or even negative-sum games in cases of mutual destruction, is apparent. Interestingly, ASEAN recognized this danger early on. It was with a view to minimize such zero-sum games that the first substantive cooperation programs in ASEAN mostly took the form of "resource pooling"—for example, ASEAN Industrial Projects, ASEAN Complementation Projects, and ASEAN Industrial Joint Ventures. Market sharing was originally designed to complement the resource-pooling program, apart from a modest preferential trade agreement with a very limited margin of preferences. Unfortunately, none of the resource pooling programs turned out to be successful enough to catalyze cooperation in other industries. In the end, ASEAN also opted for the standard route of trade liberalization, in combination with unilateral trade and investment deregulation of the 1980s and 1990s.

There are certainly areas where liberalization initiatives need to constitute an important part of future ASEAN and RCEP integration and cooperation efforts, including addressing the sensitive and highly sensitive lists of the agreements that emerged out of ASEAN. But the ASEAN Economic Community (AEC) and the RCEP cannot be exclusively aimed at accelerating and sustaining growth—they must also enable less-developed members to grow faster or to catch up. While producing economic benefits, liberalization is socially flawed in that it benefits the most-prepared members and companies already operating in an area, while the less-prepared ones have to wait for their turn. The AEC and the RCEP are also focused on reducing environmental stresses, including those of immediate or long-term relevance. East Asian cities are suffering from severe shortages of fresh water, traffic jams, depleted public amenities, polluted air, greenhouse gas emissions, and many other ecological stresses. Reforestation is badly needed in EA. Concrete measures are needed to protect land and marine biodiversity, which are exposed to extreme strains stemming from commercial activities in EA. Pursuing growth while reducing environmental strain are herculean challenges to ASEAN and the RCEP, and they can only be addressed through regional cooperation.

MEASURES OF INCLUSION AND SUSTAINABILITY

Regionalism is a dynamic process. Post-war experiences clearly show the tendency of regionalism to spread across wider and wider geographical areas. New members accede to existing groupings. The European Union (EU), for example, expanded from the original six members to twenty-seven, and ASEAN from its original five members to ten. After all, "region" is a man-made term, as alluded to earlier. Interregional integration and cooperation are also conceivable. ASEAN and the EU wanted to pursue an interregional undertaking, but the possibility ended because of unbridgeable differences on human rights issues in pre-reform Myanmar. A convergence between the RCEP and the TPP is, of late, often mentioned as a possible route to the Free Trade Area of the Asia-Pacific (FTAAP), even though such a convergence looks remote for the time being.

Issues addressed in regional integration and cooperation tend to become increasingly comprehensive over time. The EU, for instance, started off as sector-based communties, and grew to become a single market and, later, a single currency. ASEAN's agenda was also originally confined to state-to-state economic cooperation, but moved to become a free trade area and then an economic community. The geographical extension and the widening issue coverage spurred by regional integration and cooperation appear to be unstoppable once they are launched. This is the reason for the recent tendency to conceive economic regionalism as a comprehensive partnership. Given this pattern, the three blocks of issues that are involved in regional comprehensive partnerships differ in the extent to which they have been addressed. The liberalization block, while not easy, has been dealt with the most intensively in the history of regional integration and cooperation. Barriers to trade in goods and, to a lesser extent, trade in services have been studied, quantified, and assessed in terms of costs and benefits, and these barriers have been reduced under regional liberalization for over six decades. Facilitation follows as a necessary condition for meaningful enforcement. The least advanced is functional cooperation, which primarily consists of capacity building that favors less-developed members. ASEAN members such as Laos, Cambodia, and Myanmar can benefit from trade liberalization only if, through functional cooperation, they are aided in producing new exportable goods and services. A similar question can, in fact, be raised in relation to the least-developed parts of an emerging economy, such as the eastern provinces of Indonesia. Here, tradable goods are typically confined to natural resources, which can only be explored, exploited, and traded with the help of significant financial capital and a well-educated and trained workforce. Such sectors are typically controlled by large multinational companies, alone or in cooperation with politically well-connected national companies. They are hardly accessible to people living in least-developed provinces of even emerging economies.

While facing complex issues, regional groupings are typically limited in terms of the human and financial resources at their disposal. The ASEAN Secretariat, for example, had a budget of less than US$16 million in 2012, which was raised according to the principle of equal contribution by each member, irrespective of its ability to contribute. Regional groupings are usually not equipped with the power to generate revenue, and ASEAN and the RCEP will face very difficult questions in developing a cooperation agenda that is meaningful enough for the immensely large region and population, on the one hand, but realistic enough in terms of resource constraints.

One criterion is to select issues that can be addressed effectively on a regional basis. Airspace and sea-lanes can perhaps be included in a group, together with industrial pollution, pre-competitive research and development (R&D), and fishery management. Other types of issues can be considered national rather than regional. These include many health issues and transportation issues, including some issues of connectivity. This classification of issues is becoming increasingly arbitrary. More and more, important issues are local, regional, and global at the same time.

Cooperation in science and technology (S&T) represents another important priority. First of all, long-term sustainability of growth greatly depends on progress in science and technology, as practiced in businesses, households, public facilities, and governments. Even during transitions from lower middle-income economies to upper middle-income economies, and from there to high-income status, durable success is only possible with the help of S&T diffusion and acquisition. Secondly, it is in respect to S&T literacy and capabilities that economies in ASEAN and the RCEP differ starkly. The statistical database of UNESCO and the UNESCO Science Report suggest that research and development capacities in most ASEAN economies are very limited compared to the leading S&T economies of the region, as well as elsewhere in the more developed world (UNESCO 2010). Given their limited R&D capacity, economies can offer very few contributions to R&D collaboration of either regional or global scopes. In the universe of international R&D collaborations, only a few economies in the RCEP, including ASEAN, have been equipped to participate, as reported by the Royal Society in its 2011 report on global scientific collaboration in the twenty-first century (Royal Society 2011). If this trend continues, there is little that one can expect in terms of development convergence of a lasting nature in East Asia, and a fall into the middle-income trap becomes highly probable.

ASEAN and the RCEP are well advised to propose a shopping list that can be put together into a regional matrix at both ASEAN and RCEP levels. Such programs should not be primarily conceived as transfer programs, in the sense of some economies playing the role of donor and others the role of recipient. Even under the tight resource constraints that each ASEAN economy faces, an active participation in S&T collaboration is possible, subject to reallocation of resources. While participation of all economies should be encouraged, the formula of ASEAN-minus-X or RCEP-minus-X should also be accepted in the interest of effective cooperation.

Finding new levers for effective cooperation is critical to success, yet ASEAN and the RCEP suffer from being largely state-driven undertakings. Change is needed on this score, as well as recognizing the power hidden in better information, which, in turn, can be attained with the help of open systems. The second element relates to institutionalization. ASEAN and the RCEP rely heavily on ASEAN centrality, however one defines it. Yet ASEAN is faced with tight limitations. ASEAN is still largely an association of nations when it comes to policy decisions, and it is also much more limited financially than its ambitious goals would suggest. Historical circumstances force East Asia to continue to rely on ASEAN as the mover of EA regionalism, as it has done over the years. Yet a more inclusive leadership appears to be increasingly needed. The CMIM arrangement, where voting is weighted by taking into account each member's contribution, provides a possible model for adapting. An exclusive reliance on the principles of one vote for one economy may not be enough to push community building in EA beyond its current levels.

The world between now and 2025 is bound to change in many important ways. The multi-polar power structure may take a clearer configuration. Wealth will probably continue to be redistributed in favor of East Asia, notably China, and to a lesser extent to India and Indonesia, to name only the most populous economies of EA. However, East Asia will still have to rely on European and North American scientific developments, while seeking to climb the difficult stages of the development ladder. What this implies is that EA regionalism should in no way be thought of as an exclusive grouping. Doing so would be swimming against globalization, which—despite heated criticisms—is bound to strengthen in the wake of technology changes and, probably, as a result of growing capabilities of governments, businesses, and societies to make globalization increasingly inclusive and respectful of the environment. East Asia economies will undoubtedly differ in the speed that they adjust to these emerging realities. It is important under such plurality to give a chance to multi-track community building, which can equip economies for achieving gradual convergence.

SOURCES

Economic Research Institute for ASEAN and East Asia (ERIA). 2012. *Mid-Term Review of the Implementation of AEC Blueprint: Executive Summary.* Jakarta: ERIA. Also available at www.eria.org/publications/key_reports/.

Giulani, Elisa. 2010. "Clusters, Networks and Economic Development: An Evolutionary Economic Perspective." In *The Handbook of Evolutionary Economic Geography*, edited by Ron Boschma and Ron Martin, chpt. 12. Cheltenham and Northampton: Edward Elgar Publishing Limited.

Kim, Jun Il, and Jungick Lee. 2013. "How Important Are Inflation Expectations in Driving Asian Inflation?" Bank for International Settlements, BIS Paper, No. 70: 41–63.

Morris, Ian. 2010. *Why the West Rules—for Now: The Patterns of History, and What They Reveal About the Future.* New York: Farrar, Straus and Giroux.

The Royal Society. 2011. *Knowledge, Networks, and Nation: Global Scientific Collaboration in the 21st Century.* London: The Royal Society.

Siregar, Reza, and Akkharaphol Chabchitrchaidol. 2013. "Enhancing the Effectiveness of CMIM and AMRO: Selected Immediate Challenges and Tasks." Asian Development Bank Institute, ADBI Working Paper No. 403, January.

Taguchi, Hiroyuki, and Chizuru Kato. 2010. "Assessing the Performance of Inflation Targeting in East Asian Economies." Policy Research Institute, Tokyo, PRI Discussion Paper Series, No. 10A-01, March.

Tong, Sarah Y., and Yao Jielu. 2010. "China's Rising Local Government Debt Sparks Concerns." *East Asian Policy* 2 (4): 38–49, Singapore.

United Nations Educational, Scientific, and Cultural Organization (UNESCO). 2010. *World Science Report 2010: The Current Status of Science around the World.* Paris: UNESCO.

Wang Feng. 2011. "The End of Growth with Equity? Economic Growth and Income Inequality in East Asia." *AsiaPacific Issues* 101, July, East-West Center, Honolulu.

9

A Stages Approach to Regional Economic Integration in Asia Pacific

The RCEP, TPP, and FTAAP

Shujiro Urata, Professor of International Economics, Waseda University

INTRODUCTION

The Asia-Pacific region has been witnessing the emergence of two mega–free trade agreements (FTAs), the Trans-Pacific Partnership (TPP) and the Regional Comprehensive Economic Partnership (RCEP). TPP negotiations began in March 2010, while RCEP negotiations began in May 2013. Negotiating members are different, although some economies are participating in both FTAs. Both are considered to be pathways toward the establishment of a Free Trade Area of the Asia-Pacific (FTAAP). Although the contents of these two FTAs have yet to be finalized as they are still in negotiations, it is important for policymakers to analyze their relationship—conflicting or complementary—in order to draw a roadmap for achieving an FTAAP, the eventual goal of regional economic integration in the Asia Pacific. An FTAAP would contribute to economic growth of the Asia Pacific, which would in turn promote economic growth of the world economy by establishing a free and open business environment. Such a business environment would lead to efficient use of labor and capital and promote innovation, thereby resulting in economic growth.

This essay analyzes the relationship between the TPP and the RCEP in the context of regional economic integration in the Asia Pacific. The second section makes some comparisons between the TPP and the RCEP in order to identify their similarities and differences. Based on the discussions in the second section, the final section proposes a two-stage approach to regional economic integration in the Asia Pacific.

THE TPP AND THE RCEP: COMPARISON

One observes both similarities and differences between the RCEP and the TPP, and summarizing these helps us examine their relationship. While very few similarities exist, there are a number of differences between the RCEP and the TPP. Let us begin with the similarities and then turn to the differences.

Pathways to an FTAAP

Both the RCEP and the TPP are free trade agreements, although their contents differ substantially. Both the RCEP and the TPP are characterized as mega-FTAs, because of their large number of negotiating members; 16 for the RCEP, and 12 for the TPP. Another similarity is that both the RCEP and the TPP are considered pathways to an FTAAP. This observation needs a qualification, as explained below.

At the APEC Leaders' Meeting in October 2010 in Yokohama, Japan, participants agreed that the eventual goal of regional economic integration in the Asia Pacific is to establish an FTAAP.[1] They also agreed that there are mainly three pathways leading to an FTAAP: the ASEAN-Plus-Three FTA (EAFTA), the ASEAN-Plus-Six FTA (CEPEA), and the TPP. The ASEAN-Plus-Three FTA and ASEAN-Plus-Six FTA initiatives have been merged to become the RCEP. Accordingly, the RCEP has come to be recognized as a pathway to an FTAAP. Similarities stop here.

Turning to the differences between the TPP and the RCEP, let us look at their membership, objectives, contents, and other issues.

Membership

The TPP negotiations began with eight economies—Singapore, New Zealand, Chile, Brunei, the United States, Australia, Peru, and Vietnam—which were later joined by four more, Malaysia, Canada, Mexico, and Japan.[2] At present, 12 economies, all of which are members of APEC, are participating in the TPP negotiations. It is worth noting that the TPP negotiations are quite unique because the number of members increased during the negotiations process. This indicates a realization on the part of new members of the TPP's importance. Indeed, that importance is likely to increase as membership grows, given that an FTA is a discriminatory arrangement, and the negative impacts of being a nonmember increase with the expansion of members.

Participants of the RCEP negotiations include 16 economies: 10 members of the Association of Southeast Asian Nations (ASEAN)—Brunei, Cambodia, Indonesia, Laos, Malaysia, Myanmar, the Philippines, Singapore, Thailand, and Vietnam—as well as China, Japan, South Korea, India, Australia, and New Zealand. Although the RCEP may accept new members, so far there have not been any.[3]

Seven economies—Brunei, Malaysia, Singapore, Vietnam, Japan, Australia, and New Zealand—are participating in both negotiations. Those RCEP participants that are not participating in the TPP negotiations are Cambodia, Indonesia, Laos, Myanmar, the Philippines, Thailand, China, South Korea, and India. Among those, Cambodia, Laos, Myanmar, and India are not members of APEC, while Indonesia, the Philippines, Thailand, China, and South Korea are members. Since the TPP is likely to be open only to APEC members, Cambodia, Laos, Myanmar, and India are not qualified to participate in the TPP.[4] It is important to note that Cambodia, Laos, and Myanmar are in the early stages of economic development compared to other RCEP economies. Those TPP negotiating members that are not participating in the RCEP negotiations are Chile, the United States, Peru, Canada, and Mexico. These economies are not located in Asia. One notices immediately that China and India, two Asian giants, are not participating in the TPP, while the United States, another giant, is not participating in the RCEP. As such, some consider the TPP and the RCEP to be in conflict, as China and India—particularly China—are trying to establish a regional framework that excludes the United States, while the United States is keen on establishing a regional framework that excludes China.

A brief comparison of the TPP and the RCEP in terms of economic indicators is in order. Table 1 shows that the RCEP members in total represent a substantially larger population, at 3.4 billion, compared to the TPP members, who total 0.8 billion. The TPP members have higher GDP at US$28 trillion, compared to the RCEP members at US$21 trillion.[5] The magnitude of total trade, or the sum of exports and imports, is similar for the TPP and the RCEP, with each amounting to around US$10 trillion. In terms of world shares, the RCEP members account for 48.3 percent of world population, 29.2 percent of world GDP, and 28.3 percent of world trade, while the corresponding shares for the TPP members are 11.3 percent, 38.8 percent, and 25.8 percent, respectively. These observations indicate that both the TPP and the RCEP are very important for the world economy, as their respective coverage in the world economy is substantial. Finally, it should be noted that the average GDP per capita is significantly larger for the TPP members (US$32,751) compared to the RCEP members (US$18,879), reflecting the fact that low-income economies are included in the RCEP.

Objectives

The objectives of the RCEP and the TPP are quite different, although both are FTAs. The objective of the TPP is to enhance trade and investment among the TPP partner economies; promote innovation, economic growth, and development; and support the creation and retention of jobs.[6] These objectives are to be achieved by constructing a free and open business environment through establishing a comprehensive, next-generation regional agreement that liberalizes trade and investment and addresses new and traditional trade issues and twenty-first century challenges.[7] It is further envisaged as an ambitious model for other free trade agreements in the future.

The objective of the RCEP is to achieve a modern, comprehensive, high-quality, and mutually beneficial economic partnership agreement

TABLE I *Economic Indicators of the TPP and RCEP Members*

		Population		GDP		GDP per capita (US$)	Trade	
		(million)	(%)	(US$ billion)	(%)	(US$)	(US$ billion)	(%)
RCEP	China	1,350.7	19.2	8,227.1	11.4	6,091.0	3,866.9	10.4
	South Korea	50.0	0.7	1,129.6	1.6	22,590.2	1,067.5	2.9
	India	1,236.7	17.6	1,841.7	2.5	1,489.2	782.6	2.1
	Camboida	14.9	0.2	14.0	0.0	944.4	19.2	0.1
	Indonesia	246.9	3.5	878.0	1.2	3,556.8	378.4	1.0
	Laos	6.6	0.1	9.4	0.0	1,417.1	5.1	0.0
	Myanmar	52.8	0.7	52.5	0.1	861.0	20.4	0.1
	Philippines	96.7	1.4	250.2	0.3	2,587.0	117.4	0.3
	Thailand	66.8	0.9	366.0	0.5	5,479.8	477.1	1.3
RCEP and TPP	Brunei	0.4	0.0	17.0	0.0	41,126.6	17.0	0.0
	Malaysia	29.2	0.4	305.0	0.4	10,432.1	424.0	1.1
	Singapore	5.3	0.1	274.7	0.4	51,709.5	788.1	2.1
	Vietnam	88.8	1.3	155.8	0.2	1,755.2	228.4	0.6
	Japan	127.6	1.8	5,959.7	8.2	46,720.4	1,684.4	4.6
	Australia	22.7	0.3	1,532.4	2.1	67,555.8	517.8	1.4
	New Zealand	4.4	0.1	167.3	0.2	37,749.4	75.6	0.2
TPP	US	313.9	4.5	16,244.6	22.4	51,748.6	3,882.7	10.5
	Canada	34.9	0.5	1,821.4	2.5	52,219.0	929.7	2.5
	Mexico	120.8	1.7	1,178.1	1.6	9,748.9	751.4	2.0
	Chile	17.5	0.2	269.9	0.4	15,452.2	158.1	0.4
	Peru	30.0	0.4	203.8	0.3	6,795.8	88.2	0.2
	RCEP	**3,400.5**	**48.3**	**21,180.6**	**29.2**	**18,879.1**	**10,469.6**	**28.3**
	TPP	**795.5**	**11.3**	**28,129.8**	**38.8**	**32,751.1**	**9,545.2**	**25.8**
	World	**7,046.4**	**100.0**	**72,440.4**	**100.0**	**10,280.5**	**37,006.6**	**100.0**

Notes: All the figures except GDP and GDP per capita for Myanmar are taken from World Bank, while GDP and GDP per capital for Myanmar are taken from the ASEAN Secretariat.
Sources: World Bank, World Development Indicators online accessed on March 30, 2014
ASEAN Secretariat, http://www.asean.org/news/item/selected-key-indicators accessed on March 30, 2014.

among the ASEAN member states and ASEAN's FTA partners, in order to support and contribute to economic integration, equitable economic development, and strengthening economic cooperation among the participants.[8]

Although both the TPP and the RCEP have aimed to establish high-quality and comprehensive trade agreements that promote economic growth and development, there are differences in how they emphasize economic growth and economic development. One of the most important elements for the RCEP is to achieve equitable economic development through economic cooperation. By contrast, the TPP does not put much emphasis on economic cooperation. It is only natural that the RCEP places emphasis on economic cooperation as membership includes least-developed economies such as Cambodia, Laos, and Myanmar, whose successful economic development is very important for the region's sustainable economic growth and social stability.

Issue Coverage

The issues covered by the TPP and the RCEP have been noted as being quite different, reflecting the differences in their objectives. Indeed, the RCEP is designed to cover trade in goods, trade in services, investment, economic and technical cooperation, intellectual property, competition, dispute settlement, and other issues. In contrast, the TPP's coverage is broad and comprehensive, and 24 working groups have been established in the following areas: market access of industrial goods, agriculture, textiles, technical barriers to trade (TBT), sanitary and phytosanitary measures (SPS), rules of origin, customs cooperation, investment, services, financial services, telecommunications, e-commerce, business mobility, government procurement, competition, intellectual property, labor, environment, capacity building, trade remedies, and legal and institutional frameworks. In addition to these issue-specific areas, crosscutting "horizontal issues" such as regulatory coherence, competitiveness, development, and small- and medium-sized enterprises are also addressed.

Unfortunately, the comparison made above is quite deceptive because the description of the issue coverage in the RCEP is very rough, with few details, compared to the TPP. If one considers the contents of the issue coverage of the RCEP in more depth, the differences between the two become much less significant. Table 2 shows that the major differences are environment, government procurement, labor, and crosscutting horizontal issues such as regulatory coherence, which are covered in the TPP but not in the RCEP. Although these are only four issue areas out of many, they are regarded as very important for developed economies such as the United States, which seeks to achieve a level playing field in competition and to achieve sustainable economic growth. For developing economies, on the other hand, these issue areas pose challenges.

LEVEL OF COMMITMENT, SPECIAL AND DIFFERENTIAL TREATMENT OF DEVELOPING ECONOMIES, AND MODE OF AGREEMENT

This section discerns differences in the level of commitment, the treatment of developing economies, and the modes of agreement between the TPP and the RCEP. The previous section identified substantial overlaps in the issue coverage of the TPP and the RCEP, despite some important differences. Looking beyond the overlaps, there are notable differences between the two frameworks in the level of commitment. One of the areas where the commitment differences can clearly be seen is the level of trade liberalization, or market access for goods. The TPP seeks complete elimination of tariffs, or 100 percent trade liberalization, although in reality trade liberalization rates (the proportion of tariff lines subject to tariff elimination, compared to the total number of tariff lines) for some members may be around 97–98 percent. This is because of political sensitivities concerning some products, such as sugar, in the United States and Japan. By contrast, the trade liberalization rate for the RCEP is likely to be substantially lower compared to the case for the TPP. Some observers predict 90 percent trade liberalization, based on the trade liberalization achieved by five ASEAN-Plus-One FTAs. ASEAN economies achieved nearly 90 percent trade liberalization in each ASEAN-Plus-One FTA, while only 73.3 percent of tariff lines were commonly eliminated vis-à-vis their ASEAN-Plus-One FTA partners.[9] Considering that common tariff concessions, rather than bilateral tariff concessions, are likely to be adopted in the RCEP negotiations, even

TABLE 2 *Comparison of Issue Coverage in the TPP and RCEP*

	TPP	RCEP
Trade in Goods	●	●
– Market Access for Goods	●	●
– Textile and Apparel	●	○
– Rules of Origin	●	○
– Customs	●	○
– Trade Facilitation		●
– TBT	●	○
– SPS	●	○
– Trade Remedies	●	○
Trade in Services	●	●
– Cross-border Services	●	●
– Financial Services	●	○
– Telecommunications	●	○
– Temporary Entry	●	
Investment	●	●
Economic and Technical Cooperation	●*	●
Intellectual Property	●	●
Competition	●	●
Dispute Settlement	●**	●
Legal and Institutional Issues	●	○
Others	●	●
– E-commerce	●	●
– Environment	●	
– Government Procurement	●	
– Labor	●	
– Crosscutting horizontal issues	●	

Note: "●" means the issue is covered. "○" for RCEP means that the issue is likely covered judging from ASEAN+1 FTAs and ASEAN Economic Community. * "Cooperation and Capacity Building." ** "Legal issues" for administration of the Agreement including dispute settlement.
Source: Adopted from the work done by Fukunaga of ERIA with some modification.

achieving 90 percent trade liberalization requires significant efforts on the part of ASEAN members. Furthermore, it should be pointed out that India has the lowest trade liberalization rate in its FTA with ASEAN—78.8 percent—indicating substantial difficulty in achieving 90 percent trade liberalization. Non-ASEAN RCEP members will also have to make enormous efforts to achieve 90 percent trade liberalization, except for Australia and New Zealand, which have achieved 100 percent trade liberalization in their FTAs with ASEAN.

One of the major differences between the TPP and the RCEP is the treatment of least-developed economies. ASEAN-Plus-Six trade ministers agreed to provide special and differential treatment to the least-developed ASEAN members in the RCEP. This treatment is to be consistent with existing ASEAN-Plus-One FTAs, which consider the different levels of development of RCEP negotiating members.[10] A specific example of special and differential treatment of least-developed ASEAN members can be found in the ASEAN-China FTA, which included the postponement of trade liberalization by new ASEAN members. The TPP does not provide special and differential treatment to least-developed members in terms of the contents of the agreements, although it may provide different schedules to least-developed economies for the implementation of the agreements. These differences in the treatment of least-developed economies seem to be attributable to the differences in the philosophy toward the role of government protection in economic development. In the United States, which is a leader in the TPP, market distortion created by government protection would retard economic development, whereas in many East Asian economies, which are participating in the RCEP, government protection is regarded as possibly beneficial to the least-developed economies.

Another important difference is the mode of agreement. Despite very comprehensive contents, as shown above, the TPP is trying to include all of these contents/components from the outset in the form of a "single undertaking." This has been a practice for comprehensive FTAs involving the United States. In contrast to the TPP, the RCEP is likely to adopt a gradual and sequential approach, where different components are negotiated and implemented under different time schedules, depending on the difficulty in reaching an agreement.[11] For example, market access in goods may be taken up first, say by 2015, while trade in services and investment might be negotiated after 2015. Having noted the different time schedules for different components, it is important for the RCEP to be completed by a certain date, such as the year 2025, 10 years after the expected conclusion of negotiations. This sequential approach has been adopted by ASEAN in its endeavor to establish the ASEAN Economic Community (AEC), and it may be practical in light of the diversity among the negotiating members in terms of economic development, structures, and systems.

TWO-STAGE APPROACH TO AN FTAAP

So far, we have found that the RCEP and the TPP are quite different in how they handle membership, objectives, contents, and other characteristics, although both are free trade agreements with comprehensive coverage. The RCEP, with its emphasis on equitable and sustainable economic development through economic cooperation, may begin with shallow integration—limited issue coverage and relatively low levels of trade liberalization—but gradually achieve deeper integration. An eventual goal of the RCEP may be to establish an East Asian Economic Community, a possible extension of the ASEAN Economic Community. The TPP, on the other hand, will establish a rule-based, free and open business environment by achieving high-level trade and investment liberalization and by setting up high-level rules on competition, intellectual property rights, government procurement, and other areas. The TPP aims to develop into an FTAAP, which may eventually turn into the WTO Mark II, or global economic rule.

Considering these differences, the RCEP and the TPP can be complementary and coexist, and they do not need to merge to become an FTAAP. Indeed, one may regard these two regional frameworks as two stages to reach an FTAAP, an eventual goal of regional integration in the Asia Pacific, while the RCEP may eventually develop into an East Asian Economic Community. Developing economies in East Asia may participate in the RCEP first, and they may join the TPP when they have grown economically and are ready to accept high-standard economic rules. In order for this approach to be realized, both the RCEP and the TPP need to accept new members that are qualified to join. Finally, the importance of a speedy conclusion and implementation of the RCEP and the TPP needs to be stressed, to promote regional economic integration in the Asia Pacific, which would contribute to the economic development and growth of the region.

NOTES

1. See http://www.apec.org/Meeting-Papers/Leaders-Declarations/2010/2010_aelm.aspx.

2. Concerning the TPP, a very good analysis concerning its contents, importance, difficult issues, and other matters can be found in Jeffrey J. Schott, Barbara Kotschwar, and Julia Muir, *Understanding the Trans-Pacific Partnership* (Washington, DC: Peterson Institute for International Economics, 2013).

3. RCEP, "Guiding Principles and Objectives for Negotiating the Regional Comprehensive Economic Partnership," 2012 states that any ASEAN FTA partner that did not participate in the RCEP negotiations at the outset would be allowed to join the negotiations, subject to terms and conditions that would be agreed upon by all other participating economies.

4. The rule on membership has not been decided for the TPP. According to the original TPP, membership is open to non-APEC members. The Trans-Pacific Strategic Economic Partnership Agreement states in Article 20.6 (Accession) that the agreement is open to accession on terms to be agreed upon among the parties, by any APEC economy or other state. See http://www.mfat.govt.nz/downloads/trade-agreement/transpacific/main-agreement.pdf.

5. All statistics are for 2012.

6. Office of the US Trade Representative (USTR) website, http://www.ustr.gov/about-us/press-office/fact-sheets/2011/november/united-states-trans-pacific-partnership.

7. TPP Leaders' Statement on November 12, 2011, http://www.ustr.gov/about-us/press-office/press-releases/2011/november/trans-pacific-partnership-leaders-statement, accessed on March 30, 2014.

8. RCEP, "Guiding Principles" 2012.

9. See Yoshifumi Fukunaga and Arata Kuno, "Toward a Consolidated Preferential Tariff Structure in East Asia: Going beyond ASEAN+1 FTAs," ERIA Policy Brief No. 2012–03, May 2012.

10. RCEP, "Guiding Principles," 2012.

11. This sequential approach is recommended by a group of experts on the RCEP. See Expert Roundtable for Regional Comprehensive Economic Partnership (RCEP), "Recommendations on the Approaches to be Adopted in the Negotiations of RCEP and Its Implementation," 2013.

10

The RCEP

A Chinese Perspective

Quan Yi, Editor-in-Chief, Asia-Pacific Economic Review

INTRODUCTION

The Regional Comprehensive Economic Partnership (RCEP) was designed and promoted by ASEAN because of at least two considerations.

In the first place, ASEAN is keen to retain a leadership position in the process of economic integration in East Asia. However, with the emergence of the Trans-Pacific Partnership (TPP), not only have the big players of the region become active negotiating parties to the TPP, but also nearly half of the ASEAN members are participating. The rapid expansion of TPP membership has shifted the center of gravity surrounding economic cooperation in East Asia toward the Asia Pacific, giving more weight to American dominance. This centrifugal tendency jeopardizes the ASEAN leadership and creates anxiety in the region.

Secondly, ASEAN feels the necessity to maintain its centrality in regional economic cooperation. As the hub of five ASEAN-Plus-One free trade agreements (FTAs), ASEAN and its regional partners feel the pinch of the Asian "noodle bowl effect." The ASEAN-Plus-One FTAs have become new obstacles to the construction of a regional production network based on free markets in East Asia. The RCEP has emerged as a tool to converge or integrate the ASEAN-Plus-One FTAs in alignment with the common aspirations of the region.

Launched in early 2013, the RCEP negotiations have undergone three rounds. On the basis of the Guiding Principles and Objectives for Negotiating the Regional Comprehensive Economic Partnership, the RECP negotiating committee has established seven working groups covering trade in goods, trade in services, investment, intellectual property, market competition, "eco-tech" (economic-technical) cooperation, and dispute settlement, as well as two subcommittees on rules of origin and on customs procedures and trade facilitation. The framework for negotiations is basically in place. Thus, negotiations have been split into groups and conducted in parallel.

THE RCEP IS A COMMON ASPIRATION OF EAST ASIA

The RCEP is of great importance to East Asia as a whole. Both now and in the foreseeable future, East Asia remains the world's most dynamic region, with the greatest potential in terms of economic development. China, India, and Indonesia are the largest developing economies with the most economic potential. All are members of the RCEP and will benefit from the RCEP much more than from the five existing ASEAN-Plus-One FTAs. China, India, Japan, and South Korea will be some of the biggest winners, as none have bilateral trade agreements with the others. Thus, the RCEP provides the driving force toward regional economic integration.

If successfully concluded, the RCEP will represent a milestone in the course of regional economic cooperation and integration in East Asia, and in the Asia-Pacific region as well. East Asia is one of the least economically integrated areas in the world. For various reasons, China, India, and Japan have struggled to strike deals on free trade, let alone make joint efforts to promote regional economic integration that covers the whole of East Asia. The RCEP presents a chance to break the impasse caused by big-power gaming and competition.

At the same time, the RCEP is about rule-making, or developing new rules that will promote the economic development of East Asia. Firstly, the new rules will facilitate the adjustment, improvement, and operation of regional and international production networks. Secondly, the new rules will facilitate trade in goods, trade in services, and investment in that the economic policies, regulations, and administration of the regional economies will be coordinated and harmonized. Thirdly, rules designed for economic cooperation, if properly implemented, will create a favorable environment for regional economic development. As Zhang Yunling indicated, the RCEP is an "East Asian version of development round." The new rules set by the RCEP will not only promote economic development in East Asia, but also provide useful experience for other areas, especially for the developing economies. The RCEP will have its own advantages and influence. Given that the RCEP counts as its members several large developing economies with great economic potential, it will have significant implications for multilateral trade negotiations, as it will represent an effective counterbalance to the new rule-making process championed by the developed economies (Zhang 2014).

THE RCEP SHOULD BE CARRIED OUT IN PRACTICAL STEPS

According to the guidelines of the RCEP, the negotiations were launched in 2013, and should be concluded by the end of 2015. Although the RCEP parties are devoted to the negotiation process, they need to take proper measures to strike a deal within the short time frame. With so many members, coordinating among them is a daunting challenge, but one that can be tackled through a series of practical steps.

The negotiations could be conducted on clusters of issues. Agreements should be concluded first on those areas where consensus can be easily reached. On difficult issues, a high-standard agreement should also be expected. Yet when it comes to implementation, differentiated approaches should be taken, with the relatively advanced members implementing as soon as possible. A phase-in period should be granted to less-advanced economies, which would open their markets at the expiration of the phase-in period.

Theoretically speaking, the five ASEAN-Plus-One FTAs differ from each other the least in the provisions on investment, and RCEP parties could reach consensus on investment first. China's current stance on pre-establishment national treatment and performance requirements constitutes the major obstacle to an RCEP agreement on investment. Now that China is prepared to grant foreign investors the pre-establishment national treatment and take a negative list approach to managing foreign direct investment, it is estimated that RCEP negotiations will progress swiftly and easily in this area.

The liberalization of trade in goods remains a top priority. It is expected that by 2018 tariffs will be reduced to low levels. The negotiations on tariffs could be oriented to two schedules, one for common products and one for sensitive products, but it is essential to control the length of the latter. Besides tariffs, harmonization of the rules of origin (ROO) is also an essential part of the negotiation of trade in goods. Currently, the ROO of the ASEAN-Plus-One FTAs follow either the 40 percent regional value content (RVC) standard, or the change in tariff classification (CTC) standard. If the RCEP is to further optimize East Asian production networks, the only choice is to simplify its ROO.

The negotiations on trade in services will be complex. It is advisable to liberalize trade in services sector by sector. For instance, tourism, e-commerce, health, and logistics transportation could be set as priority areas for liberalization, while telecommunications and finance sectors could follow later.

It may be imperative for ASEAN to exchange quality for time. According to the timeline of the RCEP, ASEAN hopes to complete negotiations by the end of 2015. At that juncture, the ASEAN Economic Community is also supposed to be established. Ideally, when ASEAN regional integration is upgraded, East Asian regional economic integration, in which ASEAN enjoys centrality, will be strengthened as well. However, as time is very pressing for completion by the target date, it is possible that ASEAN will try to make up time at the cost of quality. That is to say, the standards of the RCEP could be lowered for the sake of completion by 2015.

The "quality for time" tactics seem to be imperative given the fast development of the TPP. Both the TPP and the RCEP are mega-regional trade agreements (mega-RTAs), with a significant overlapping of membership. They may substitute each other to a certain extent. They can influence or even hijack each other in the course of development. Whichever moves faster and better will set new rules for trade and investment in the Asia-Pacific region, favoring its members with more leverage. Competition between the TPP and the RCEP is therefore inevitable. As the conclusion of the TPP talks often appears to be around the corner, the RCEP parties, spearheaded by ASEAN leadership, should assume a sense of urgency.

STRATEGIC THINKING ON CHINA'S PARTICIPATION IN THE RCEP

As an important economy in East Asia and the earliest partner to establish the ASEAN-Plus-One FTA, China remains an important driving force of economic cooperation in East Asia. However, China has experienced difficulties in promoting the regional trade agreement of East Asia over the years. China's preference for the ASEAN-Plus-Three pathway toward the economic integration of East Asia was frustrated by the structural constraints in the region. Based on the political economy of East Asia, China should support ASEAN in promoting comprehensive regional economic cooperation, with the RCEP as the major vehicle. The success of the RCEP is of strategic importance to China. RCEP will not only give China an open regional market with enormous potential for development, but also present an immediate market base to counterbalance the TPP, from which China is excluded (Zhang 2014).

An active and aggressive posture in RCEP negotiations could also help promote the opening of the domestic market and reform of the regulatory system. Compared with the advanced economies, China has a long way to go to establish a full-fledged market economic system, liberalize market access, establish the credit system, and increase the transparency of the legal system substantially. It is a common practice for today's FTA negotiators to establish fair, open, just, and transparent management and dispute settlement mechanisms for trade, investment, and intellectual property protection. The RCEP presents the

Chinese government with an opportunity to deepen reforms to both their economic and administrative systems. For instance, for the benefit of economic development, China can introduce the negative list in market access, reform the administrative review and licensing system, streamline the various procedural fees in the circulation realm, and create a better market environment and legal environment.

The RCEP should be supported by China as it will reassure ASEAN of its centrality, relieve the United States of suspicions that China is dominating East Asian affairs, and bring in Japan, which is happy with the RCEP.

The member economies are all closely connected with China economically. They are all partners or potential partners of China in its pursuit of FTAs. Therefore, the RCEP can be regarded as an ideal platform for China to realize its free trade ambitions, and to promote regional economic integration and peaceful development together with other regional players.

China should participate in the RCEP from a strategic perspective, and play the role of an active participant and constructive promoter. Indeed, of the 16 participants of the RCEP, China stays at the upper-middle level in terms of economic development. The China-ASEAN FTA (CAFTA) ranks high in terms of the degree of free trade in goods and the performance of implementation (Yuan and Wang 2010). Therefore, China is well positioned to be an active participant in the RCEP negotiations. China's attitude and offer are critical to the success of the RCEP negotiations. China should work with ASEAN economies and other partners to develop the template for the negotiations.

China could effectively use the RCEP as a test ground to unify its tracks of bilateral and multilateral economic cooperation, as well as its regional and subregional free trade and investment arrangements. Among the RCEP members, China has established FTAs with ASEAN, Singapore, and New Zealand. The China–South Korea FTA, the China-Japan-Korea (CJK) FTA, and the China-Australia FTA are undergoing negotiations, while China and India have completed a joint feasibility study on forming an FTA. China should strive to complete negotiations with South Korea and Australia, ideally prior to the conclusion of the RCEP agreement. At the same time, China should upgrade the

China-ASEAN FTA (CAFTA), while promoting the RCEP. The China–South Korea FTA and the China-Australia FTA should be of higher quality than the RCEP. Also, the China–South Korea FTA should serve as a model for the China-Japan-Korea FTA. The alignment of the FTAs with the RCEP—for example, harmonizing the ROO—will play a significant role in the reduction of business costs.

In addition, China and other RCEP members are engaged in various subregional cooperation mechanisms, such as the Greater Mekong Subregion Economic Cooperation Program (GMS), and in various cross-border economic cooperation zones and China economic cooperation (investment) zones in relevant ASEAN countries. Currently, China is promoting the Maritime Silk Road and the China-India-Myanmar-Bangladesh Economic Corridor, as well as infrastructure connectivity programs such as an Asian Infrastructure Investment Bank. These initiatives and programs have gained the endorsement and support of relevant countries. China could also help establish a new regional platform for technical cooperation by launching a regional intellectual property trading market. These subregional cooperation mechanisms will complement the regional mechanisms. Therefore, consideration should be given to these mechanisms when the eco-tech cooperation programs are developed for the RCEP.

SOURCES

Zhang Yunling. 2014. "The Institutional Split of Regional Framework: China's FTA Strategies and the Revival of APEC." *Asia Economic Review* (2): 10–13.

Yuan Bo and Wang Jinbo. 2010. "ASEAN+6 and ASEAN+3, Which One Is Easier? A Comparative Analysis Based on the Five ASEAN+1 FTAs." *International Trade* 12: 41–42.

11

South Korea's Recent FTA Policy

A Personal Viewpoint

Inkyo Cheong, Professor of Economics, Inha University

OVERVIEW OF SOUTH KOREA'S FTA POLICY

Since South Korea envisioned its "Roadmap for National FTA Strategy" in September 2003, it has implemented 10 free trade agreements (FTAs) and concluded negotiations for three FTAs as of April 2014. South Korea's FTA partners include the United States (US), the European Union (EU), the European Free Trade Association (EFTA), the Association of Southeast Asian Nations (ASEAN), India, Turkey, Singapore, Colombia, Peru, and Chile. Australia and Canada became South Korea's FTA partners upon the conclusion of FTA negotiations in late 2013 and early 2014, respectively. It is expected that South Korea will conclude negotiations for a bilateral FTA with New Zealand by the end of 2014.

South Korea, a semi-developed economy, has been successful in expanding its FTA network to more than 60 economies. It has developed one of the most extensive FTA networks in the world, following Chile and Mexico. South Korea was the first economy in the world to agree to bilateral FTAs with the United States, the European Union, India, and

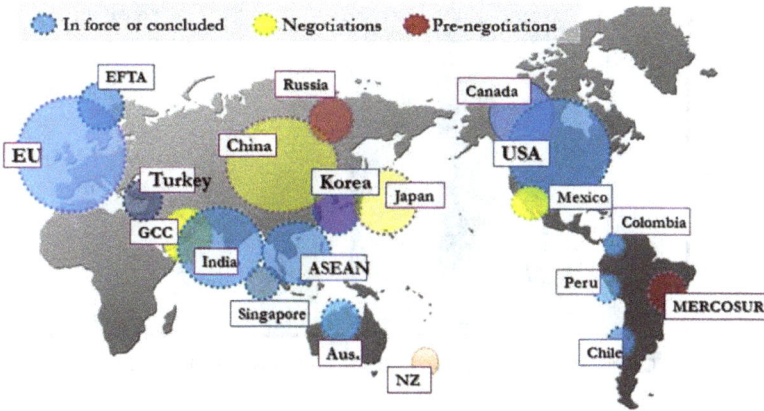

Source: Inkyo Cheong, "Korea's Policy Package for Enhancing Its FTA Utilization and Implications for Korea's Policy," ERIA Discussion Paper, forthcoming in 2014.

FIGURE 1 *South Korea's Current FTA Policy*

ASEAN, enabling free trade with more than 60 percent of the global economy. South Korea now seeks to become an FTA hub economy in East Asia. Given the current status of its FTAs (Figure 1), South Korea's free trade share will reach almost 90 percent of its total trade in the near future.

In April 2004, South Korea implemented its first FTA with Chile and began to improve its domestic environment to expand its FTA network. In spite of political disturbances, South Korea began FTA negotiations with the United States in early 2006 and concluded them one and a half years later. At this time, it opened negotiations for an FTA with the European Union. Bilateral FTAs with the United States and the European Union became the basis for its FTA platform.

The quality of the FTAs that South Korea has agreed to thus far should be noted. While early FTAs were relatively narrow, South Korea's FTAs with the United States and the European Union were its most comprehensive in terms of coverage and market access. Figure 2 shows the concession rates of South Korea and its FTA partners in terms of the tariff line. South Korea's average concession rate is 96.7 percent, and, with the exception of India, all of its FTA partners' concession rates are more than 90 percent. The Korea-US FTA (KORUS FTA)

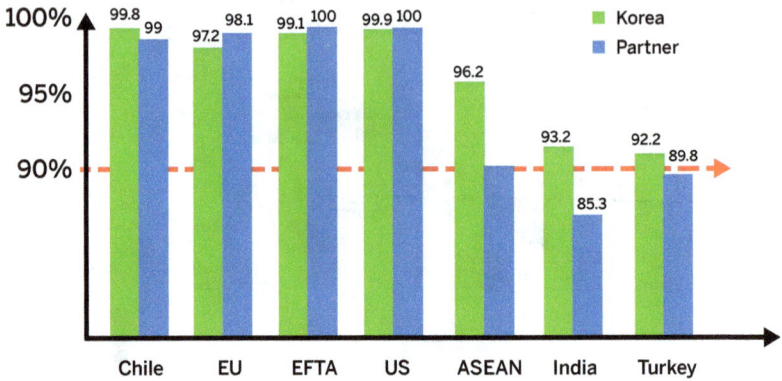

FIGURE 2 *South Korea's Tariff Liberalization Ratios*

has the highest rate of market access, with almost 100 percent tariff elimination.

South Korea has continued to expand its FTA network and currently has various negotiations in progress. However, it faces several challenges: completing the China–South Korea FTA, collecting economic gains from the improvement of its FTA hub position, participating in mega-FTAs such as the Trans-Pacific Partnership (TPP) agreement, and improving its FTA utilization ratio.

APPROACH FOR BILATERAL FTAS

Bilateral FTAs

Currently, South Korea is in negotiations for bilateral FTAs with China, Vietnam, Indonesia, and New Zealand, as well as for a China-Japan-Korea FTA (CJK FTA) and the Regional Comprehensive Economic Partnership (RCEP), as shown in Table 1. Among these economies, China seems to be the most important FTA partner for South Korea. Recognizing the importance of upgrading the ASEAN–South Korea FTA, South Korea has worked toward concluding FTAs with Vietnam and Indonesia. The Australia–South Korea FTA was concluded in

TABLE 1 *South Korea's FTA Negotiations*

	FTA partner	Beginning of talks	First round of negotiations	Recent round of negotiations	Number of rounds
Active negotiation	China	2004.9	2012.5	2014.1	9th
	Vietnam	2010.6	2012.9	2013.10	3rd
	Indonesia	2011.5	2012.7	2013.11	6th
	New Zealand	2006.12	2009.6	2014.2	5th
	CJK	2009.10	2013.3	2014.3	4th
	RCEP	2012.5	2013.5	2014.1	3rd
Slow progress	Japan	1998.11	2003.12	2004.12	6th
	Mexico	2000.5	2006.2	2007.12	4th
	GCC	2007.3	2008.7	2009.7	3rd
Official talks	Trans-Pacific Partnership (TPP), MERCOSUR (South American Common Market), Israel, Malaysia, Russia, Central America (Panama, Costa Rica, Guatemala, Honduras, El Salvador, Dominican Republic)				

Source: Prepared by the author.

December 2013, and now South Korea and New Zealand—which had been waiting to see the outcome of the FTA with Australia—are expected to complete a bilateral FTA.

Negotiations for the CJK FTA and the RCEP have been held irregularly and are not likely to be concluded in the near future. Bilateral FTAs with Japan, Mexico, and the Gulf Cooperation Council (GCC) have progressed slowly for various reasons, such as wide differences in the position for market access. The RCEP was initiated through close consultation between Japan and ASEAN. However, RCEP momentum seems to have weakened since Japan and the four member economies of ASEAN decided to negotiate the TPP.[1]

China–South Korea FTA
Since the trade ministers of China and South Korea agreed to explore a bilateral FTA between the two economies in September 2004, the FTA

has been advanced step by step over a decade.[2] Because of several factors, including differences in economic systems and economic development as well as other major concerns, it took seven years for the two parties to begin official negotiations after agreeing to organize a joint research group.

Although the government of South Korea has been interested in free trade with China, its agriculture sector has been extremely sensitive and expressed strong objections to the FTA. Because of this, both economies have agreed to two-stage negotiations: modality for market access and coverage of market access for sensitive sectors were discussed in the first stage; all remaining issues were discussed in the second stage. The first stage of negotiation was concluded in its seventh round, which took place in Weifang, China, in September 2013. The two economies agreed to pursue a mid-level FTA, including goods, services, and investment and trade rules, and to liberalize 90 percent of items and 85 percent of imported values.

Given the political and economic factors in East Asia, the China–South Korea FTA can be evaluated as more than a simple bilateral trading bloc. It should be underscored that the two economies are participants in negotiations for the CJK FTA and the RCEP, although it is uncertain whether the conclusion of the FTA will have a positive or negative effect on these larger agreements. As stated in a 2014 article in the *Journal of Korea Trade*: "The China–South Korea FTA could be a critical pillar in forming a region-wide FTA in East Asia, since the FTA between the largest economy (China) and third-largest economy (South Korea) in East Asia could produce a regional cohesiveness including Japan, Chinese Taipei, and other economies in the region."[3]

The background for the China–South Korea FTA's high priority can be found in the expectation of economic gains from the FTA. In various scenarios, South Korea can collect substantial economic gains from the FTA with China: between 1.21 percent and 2.48 percent GDP growth by 2028 (cumulative). The complete elimination of all tariffs (including those on agricultural products) brings about a 2.48 percent increase in South Korea's GDP (scenario S1 in Table 2), but lower gains (1.29 percent–1.21 percent) are expected if the elimination of agricultural tariffs

TABLE 2 *Effects of FTAs on South Korea's GDP under Various Scenarios (unit: %, accumulation)*

Scenarios/assumptions		2013	2018	2023	2028
S1	All tariffs are removed in the 1st year of implementation	0.34	0.87	1.60	2.48
S2	Manufacturing: 1st year of liberalization; primary sector: gradual elimination from the 6th year to the 15th year	0.27	0.53	0.91	1.29
S3	Manufacturing: 1st year of liberalization; primary: 100% tariff elimination from the 11th year to the 15th year	0.27	0.51	0.9	1.28
S4	Manufacturing: 1st year of liberalization; primary sector: 50% of tariffs are gradually eliminated over the period from the 11th year to the 15th year	0.27	0.51	0.86	1.21

Source: Author's calculation.

is delayed (scenarios S2 or S3) or if some part of the tariff is lowered (scenario S4).

The simulation results for the four tariff liberalization scenarios under the China–South Korea FTA are consistent with a priori expectations because if the agricultural sector is liberalized earlier and broadly, then there are greater economic gains. Here, South Korea faces a dilemma in dealing with market access for agriculture. If South Korea targets high economic gains from its FTA with China, it should choose scenario S1, but policymakers from sensitive sectors will strongly object. In this case, it will take longer to conclude negotiations for the FTA. As a compromise, South Korea has agreed to promote a mid-level FTA with China, while reducing the losses for the agricultural sector.

APPROACH FOR MEGA-FTAS

Over the last two decades, East Asian economies have discussed several formats for regional economic integration: ASEAN-Plus-One FTAs, the ASEAN-Plus-Three FTA (East Asia FTA, or EAFTA), the ASEAN-Plus-Six FTA (Comprehensive Economic Partnership in East

Asia, or CEPEA), and the RCEP. The 2012 East Asia Summit talks declared the initiation of negotiations for the RCEP and the CJK FTA. These negotiations are a challenge for China, Japan, South Korea, and the ASEAN-10 economies. Also, it is difficult to say that East Asian economies have been heading for regional economic integration. Various initiatives have been raised over time, but the general environment for regional economic integration has progressed slowly.

East Asia FTA

While ASEAN economies have taken several measures toward establishing the ASEAN Economic Community (AEC), ASEAN has faced a regional division of two groups—TPP participants and nonparticipants—that may weaken ASEAN membership. Because the four ASEAN economies are officially participating in TPP negotiations, ASEAN may have trouble dealing with the issues surrounding regional economic integration initiatives. Since it cannot force these four economies to withdraw from the TPP to consolidate the AEC, other ASEAN economies are considering TPP membership. In the vortex of raising hands for the TPP, East Asian economic integration agendas have developed into the RCEP, which includes ASEAN-Plus-Six. In addition, China, Japan, and South Korea have agreed to initiate negotiations for the CJK FTA, which the three economies have discussed for several years.

In East Asia, the AEC, the RCEP, and the CJK FTA may coexist or join forces to form a major trading bloc in the future. These various agreements may indicate the active promotion of regional integration. However, multilayered regionalism may also indicate internal disorder. Now, the question can be raised: Why the RCEP? If ASEAN promotes the RCEP as a regional integration icon, it should be a robust agreement, and ASEAN should be ready to lead negotiations for a region-wide bloc. The AEC should be established by ASEAN economies without delay. Although negotiations for the RCEP have been held intermittently, the creation of the RCEP bloc does not seem to be imminent.

If China, Japan, and South Korea appreciate the value of the RCEP, then it will be reasonable for them to avoid a trilateral FTA. ASEAN, which proposed the RCEP, has argued that ASEAN has to maintain its leadership position in regional economic integration based on the

ASEAN-Plus-One FTAs. However, if the CJK FTA is formed, it is inevitable that East Asia will focus more on the CJK FTA than on the RCEP. Although East Asian economies appear to be working together, they each have different objectives and approaches with respect to region-wide economic integration. It is difficult to determine whether they would hold one another in check, or whether most economies would participate in the RCEP under the domino effect of economic integration. In particular, ASEAN centrality and an ASEAN Free Trade Area (AFTA) may not be compatible with the CJK FTA.

Is the CJK FTA realizable within a reasonable span of time? In response to the TPP (led by the United States) and the RCEP (led by ASEAN and Japan), China has sought to initiate CJK FTA negotiations with South Korea and Japan. Japan has been concerned about the emergence of China and the weakening of its leadership in East Asia. As a result, Japan once prioritized the CEPEA (ASEAN-Plus-Six FTA) over the East Asia FTA (ASEAN-Plus-Three FTA), which was advocated by China, but has since been supportive of the RCEP in conjunction with ASEAN. However, given that Japan has joined negotiations for the TPP, it seems to be less interested in the establishment of the RCEP. Although negotiations for the CJK FTA have been held irregularly, no economies have been active in seriously driving negotiations.

The TPP

South Korea announced its concerns about negotiations for the TPP on November 29, 2013, and began preliminary bilateral consultations with TPP negotiation economies. Seven of the current 12 TPP negotiation economies, including the United States, are South Korea's FTA partners. South Korea concluded FTA negotiations with Australia in December 2013 and a bilateral FTA with Canada in March 2014. New Zealand is likely to become South Korea's FTA partner in the near future, which would make 10 TPP members as its FTA partners.

For the last three years—since the United States began to promote the TPP— South Korea's position on the agreement has been to "wait and see," since the conclusion of TPP negotiations was considered unfeasible. In addition, South Korea believed that it was more urgent to implement the FTA with the United States in 2011–2012 and to complete negotiations for the FTA with China. In line with its policy priority, the new administration, which took office in early 2013, decided to delay participation in the TPP until negotiations for the FTA with China were concluded. Moreover, US trade officials invited South Korea to TPP negotiations and indicated to South Korean counter-partners that the TPP would be concluded at the TPP trade minister meeting in Singapore in December 2013. At the end of 2013, top trade policy-makers expressed their intention for the TPP, and confirmed that this expression does not necessarily imply automatic participation in negotiations. The trade authority explained that since TPP negotiations were kept secret, consultation with TPP partners and the evaluation of each partner's participation should be made first, and that the government of South Korea would then make its decision on negotiations.

South Korea's participation in the TPP negotiations is unlikely to occur in the near future. This is largely because of the strong position the United States has taken regarding TPP participation conditions. The United States insisted upon several sensitive issues before Japan joined the TPP negotiations. If the United States raises the issues of market access for rice and beef, then negotiations will not be politically feasible for the government of South Korea. South Korea's prospects for TPP negotiations are also affected. As the TPP trade minister meeting did not conclude the agreement last year, and the end of negotiations is not imminent, South Korea may be better served making a national decision on TPP negotiations. The sizes of the circles in Figure 3 show the differences on many sensitive TPP issues. The figure summarizes the wide gaps between developed TPP members and developing ones.

Considering political events in many TPP economies, such as the United States' mid-term elections in November 2014, *The Diplomat* (2014) stated, "[The TPP] is the conundrum faced by the Obama administration, which now faces significant international and domestic opposition to two major trade initiatives: the Trans-Pacific Partnership (TPP), and the Transatlantic Economic and Trade Pact (ETP). Both are still in negotiation, but it is not too early to distinguish their relative merits."[4] As negotiations for the TPP have proceeded slowly in 2014, South Korea seems to be more cautious in expressing its intentions toward the TPP. South Korea's recent official documents state that

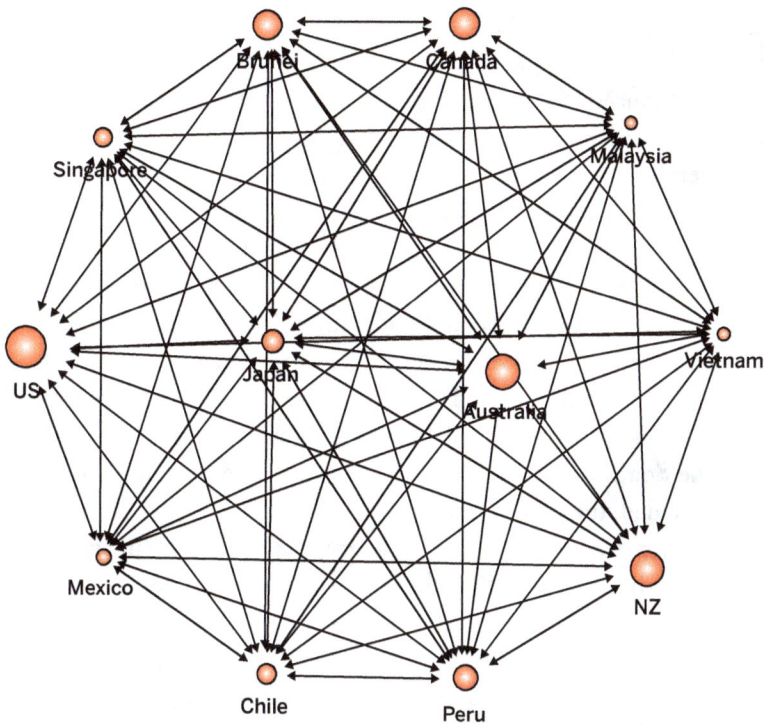

Note: Presenter's illustration using NetMiner 4.
Source: Inkyo Cheong, "The Evaluation of 2013 TPP Negotiation." Seoul: GS&J, 2014.

FIGURE 3 Dispersion of TPP Issues by Economy (for all sensitive issues)

its concerns about the TPP do not necessarily imply that it will join negotiations for a mega-FTA in the Asia-Pacific region. Moreover, it feels burdened by the preconditions that the United States' senior trade officials have established. Thus, South Korea may delay.

CONCLUSIONS

Since its first FTA with Chile was implemented in April 2004, South Korea has been active in expanding its FTA partners. Negotiations for the FTA with China have been South Korea's top priority in the last several years, and both China and South Korea are optimistic that the negotiations will be concluded successfully. However, as South Korea has expressed concern about the TPP, new issues have emerged between China and South Korea. The two economies agreed to a mid-level FTA in the seventh round of negotiations in Weifang, China, in September 2013. China seems to regard the possibility of South Korea's joining the TPP as a chance to obtain a higher market opening. China may also be concerned that South Korea will choose the TPP over the FTA with China.

In early 2014, South Korea's trade authority completed preliminary consultations with each of the 12 TPP members concerning their participation in TPP negotiations, and South Korea will decide whether to have a second round of consultations. Although the United States will welcome South Korea when negotiations with the current 12 members are concluded, the United States' preconditions for South Korea's TPP participation were confirmed in January: the sharing of financial data, nontariff barriers on cars, the certification of organic goods, and customs origin verification. Based on the estimate of its burden for joining the TPP, South Korea may decide not to seek membership. In addition to the unfavorable TPP negotiations, the unexpected confusion regarding the China–South Korea FTA seems to make South Korea neutral regarding membership. The United States has had "extremely tough" talks with Japan on opening its agricultural market, and ministerial-level talks in Singapore (February 2014) "ended with many issues still on the table, most notably Japan's protection of its farm sector."[5]

Based on the current status of TPP negotiations and the recent progress on South Korea's FTA with China, Trade Minister Yoon Sang-jick announced that "China is South Korea's most urgent FTA partner and the economy will try to conclude the negotiation for the FTA with China" on March 8, 2014.[6] Recognizing the interactions between the TPP, the China–South Korea FTA, and South Korea's FTA strategy, South Korea is expected to explore its new roadmap for FTAs and regional economic integration in the near future. Based on the performance of FTAs thus far, South Korea may place great emphasis on economic factors in deciding its new FTAs, while developing national strategies to take advantage of its extensive FTA network. Based on the weak prospects of TPP negotiations with the current 12 members, and the burden for

TPP membership, South Korea seems likely to focus on concluding the FTA with China rather than weakening its trade negotiation power by entering into negotiations for the TPP. After concluding its FTA with China, South Korea will have more options regarding the emergence of mega-FTAs.

NOTES

1. The four ASEAN economies are Brunei, Malaysia, Singapore, and Vietnam. Indonesia and Thailand are seeking to join negotiations for TPP membership.

2. This section is an extension of Inkyo Cheong, "An Analysis of the Effect of the China-Korea FTA with FTA Sequence and FTA Hub Gains," *Journal of Korea Trade* 18, no. 1 (2014): 63–84.

3. Ibid.

4. Christopher Johnston, "Trans-Pacific Partnership: Time for Some American Hustle" *The Diplomat,* March 11, 2014, http://thediplomat.com/2014/03/trans-pacific-partnership-time-for-some-american-hustle/.

5. This is based on an article by Reuters, "U.S. Readies for More 'Extremely Tough' Trade Talks with Japan," March 7, 2014.

6. For details, refer to *Daily Money Today,* "Korea's Top Trade Issue Is the FTA with China," March 18, 2014.

12

Australia's Free Trade Agreements with Japan and South Korea

Lessons for the Future

Christopher Findlay, Executive Dean of the Faculty
of the Professions, University of Adelaide

INTRODUCTION

The Australian government recently signed a free trade agreement with South Korea, announced that it had reached an agreement with Japan, and continued to work on an agreement with China. These activities were associated with a visit to Northeast Asia by Australian Prime Minister Tony Abbott in April 2014. During the 2013 national election, Abbott announced that his goal was to conclude all three agreements within 12 months of taking office—that is, by September 2014. Negotiations with South Korea, Japan, and China began in 2008, 2007, and 2005, respectively.

This recent experience provides an opportunity to reflect on the contribution of bilateral trade agreements and their link to regional economic integration. First, there is the matter of the agreements' coverage and depth, and the extent of the reforms that they encompass. Second, there is the question of the relationships between agreements of different scope, membership, and principles. As Australia and Japan negotiated their agreement, both also participated in the Trans-Pacific Partnership (TPP) negotiations, while South Korea continues to consider its options. The implications of bilateral agreements, such as those signed or agreed so far, for a complex process like the TPP and for wider regional integration is, therefore, also a topic of interest.

In this short paper, the coverage and depth of Australia's agreements with South Korea and Japan are outlined, and some of the implications of agreements of this type are discussed.

COVERAGE AND DEPTH

Key interests of Australian trade negotiators apparently include market access for agricultural exports and for services firms operating in all modes of supply in the partner economy. In turn, the partner economies request access for manufactured product imports to Australia and for new rules on inbound foreign direct investment (FDI) to Australia. The agreements with South Korea and Japan illustrate the approach to these items, which may also be applied in a future agreement with China.

The deal with Japan, for example, included a swap of access for Australian agricultural exports for access by Japan to industrial product markets in Australia. Australia will remove the 5 percent tariff (10 percent before 2010) on smaller Japanese cars, which make up the bulk of Japan's auto exports to Australia. Tariffs on all other Japanese automobiles will end in three years. Tariffs on other consumer products will also be removed. In services, there is reference in the official summary of the agreement,[1] which is called an economic partnership, to providing access to markets for funds management services, legal services, education, and telecommunications, but the details have not been specified so far.

In the case of South Korea,[2] Australia has removed tariffs on imported manufactured goods and, for some sensitive products, on schedules that are as long as eight years (e.g., some carpets that have a 5 percent tariff).

Services markets, in which Australian firms faced barriers, were reduced for legal, accounting, funds management, insurance, education, and other professional services.

Details concerning the coverage of the agreements on the treatment of imports of agricultural products into South Korea and Japan are provided in Table 1. Coverage is not universal, and the depth of tariff cuts is variable. In addition, quotas are used in some cases, and tariff cuts are often applied with safeguards. Both South Korea and Japan excluded rice. The agreement with Japan effectively excludes Australian sugar that is exported to Japan. Some dairy products are excluded in the Japan agreement. Beef tariffs are eliminated over a long period in South Korea and cut significantly in Japan. Tariffs are reduced more for frozen beef than for chilled beef, which is a closer competitor to local beef, with the reductions extending over a long period. Safeguards apply to beef in both economies.

For large FDI projects, Australia has a screening process managed by the Foreign Investment Review Board. In both agreements, the project value for screening is raised from A$248 million to A$1,078 million, which matches commitments to the United States and New Zealand. Agriculture in Australia remains a sensitive sector. The agreement with South Korea includes lower ceilings for agricultural land (A$15 million) and agribusinesses (A$53 million), and the summary of the agreement with Japan refers to "reserved policy space" to screen such proposals from Japan. This treatment is a dilemma for Australia. While seeking market access for agricultural exports, the domestic political debate has led to tighter control of foreign investment in the agricultural sector. The treatment of this issue in the case of China will be interesting to observe.

The agreement with South Korea includes a mechanism for investor-state dispute settlement (ISDS). This is significant because, previously, Australia had refused to include such a provision in a trade agreement on the grounds that it could restrict its right to regulate.[3] However, there are restrictions on its application. According to the South Korea agreement, an ISDS claim can only be made on the basis of a breach in the agreement's investment chapter, or a breach of an investment agreement between the investor and the government of the other party. It does not apply to decisions concerning investments that are subject to review under Australia's foreign investment policy, and that cannot be

TABLE 1 *Agriculture Provisions in the Korea–Australia Free Trade Agreement (KAFTA) and the Japan–Australia Economic Partnership Agreement[16]*

Item	South Korea	Japan
Beef	The 40% tariff on beef and 18% tariff on bovine offal will be eliminated over 15 years. South Korea has the right to apply a safeguard measure (initially a 40% tariff, falling to 30% and then 24% in 5-year intervals) for the next 15 years. These safeguard measures apply to volumes over a base level of imports, which is increasing by 2% a year. Australian exports to South Korea in 2012 and 2013 were about 125,000 metric tons (t), and the base volume for the safeguard measure is higher than that, at 154,584t. Australia in recent years has accounted for over half of South Korean beef imports.[17]	Japan currently imposes a 38.5% tariff on beef imports. The tariff on frozen beef will be cut to 19.5%, with an 8 percentage point cut in the first year, 2 points in the second year, and 1 in the third year (18 years). The tariff on fresh beef will be cut to 23.5%. The tariff will be cut by 6 percentage points in the first year, followed by annual 1 percentage point cuts (15 years). Japan has the right to apply a safeguard measure. On frozen beef exports, the trigger volume is 195,000 metric tons (t), with growth of 1,500t a year over 10 years. For any Australian exports above the trigger volume in the first 12 months, the tariff automatically "snaps back" to 38.5%. On chilled beef exports, the trigger volume will start at 130,000t, with 1,500t-a-year growth for 10 years. The year-one trigger levels are higher than later years—e.g., in 2013, volumes of 115,000t chilled and 173,000t frozen.[18]
Sugar	Abolish the 3% tariff on raw sugar.	The official website says that "Australian sugar exporters will benefit from tariff elimination and reduced levies for international-standard raw sugar." However, the industry report is different: "Australia has been supplying a specialized Japan-grade sugar for many years to the Japanese market, which is inherently different to the international-grade sugar supplied to its other customers. While the announced change of a tariff reduction on international-standard sugar from 184% to a 110% effective tariff is welcome, clearly this will not improve Australia's access to Japan. The tariff remains significantly higher than that of the effective tariff on the special-grade sugar that Australia supplies, which remains unchanged at 70%."[19]

Item	South Korea	Japan
Wheat	Eliminate the 1.8% tariff on wheat and 8% tariff on wheat gluten.	Not included.
Dairy	Tariffs of 36% on cheese and 89% on butter will be eliminated in 13 to 20 years. Australian dairy exporters will also benefit from growing duty-free quotas for cheese, butter, and infant formula.	Under current arrangements, Australia exports 27,000t of cheese duty-free under a global quota. Australia has gained a preferential, duty-free, Australia-only quota, growing to 20,000t (above which a tariff of 29% applies). The agreement calls for halving of the 40% tariff on processed cheese over 10 years, and immediate tariff cuts on grated and powdered cheese, and on blue-veined cheese, with no volume restrictions. Japan has granted immediate duty-free access for milk products such as protein concentrates and casein, with tariffs of up to 5.4%. For ice cream and yoghurt, a 50% reduction of a 14.9% tariff and increased quotas are specified, plus a review trigger if another economy gets a better deal on dairy.[20] Skim milk, fresh cheese, and butter are not covered.
Lamb/ goat/ pork	The 22.5% tariff on all sheep and goat meat will be eliminated over 10 years. Tariffs on key pork exports of 22.5% to 25% will be eliminated in 5 to 15 years.	Tariffs were zero for lamb, and will be bound at zero. Tariffs on pork were cut to 2.2% from 4.3%, within a quota that limits volume to 6,700t in the first year and rises to 16,700t within five years.[21]
Horti-culture	Cherries, almonds, and dried grapes will enter South Korea duty-free on entry into force. These currently face tariffs of 8% to 24%. Tariffs on macadamia nuts, fruit juices, mangoes, asparagus, and lentils, ranging from 27% to 54%, will be phased out over 3 to 10 years. Tariffs on potatoes for chipping (current tariff 304%), oranges (50%), fresh table grapes (24%), and mandarins (144%) will be eliminated during Australian exporting seasons.	A 5% tariff on macadamia nuts to be eliminated immediately; 7.8% in-season tariff and 17% off-season tariff on table grapes will be eliminated over 10 years; 16% and 17% in-season tariff on oranges and mandarins eliminated over 10 and 15 years, respectively; 10% tariff on grapefruit eliminated over 5 years.[22]

TABLE 1 *Agriculture Provisions in the Korea-Australia Free Trade Agreement (KAFTA) and the Japan-Australia Economic Partnership Agreement (continued)*

Item	South Korea	Japan
Barley	A growing duty-free quota for malt and malting barley introduced, while high out-of-quota tariffs of 269% and 513% will be eliminated over 15 years.	Barley exporters will have "increased duty-free access."
Rice	Excluded.	Excluded.
Seafood	Southern bluefin tuna (current tariff 10%) and rock lobsters (20%) will enter duty-free after 3 years.	Tariffs on shrimp and prawns, rock lobsters, abalone (fresh or preserved), oysters, crabs, yellowfin tuna, toothfish, sea urchins, fish oils, and southern bluefin tuna will be eliminated.
Wine	Immediate elimination of the 15% tariff on Australian wine.	Tariffs on bulk wine to be eliminated immediately, and those on bottled and sparkling wine will be subject to "quick tariff elimination."

Source: The primary source of this material can be found at http://www.dfat.gov.au/fta/. It is supplemented by other reporting referred to in the following endnotes.

based on a breach of commitments in other parts of the Korea-Australia Free Trade Agreement (KAFTA), such as the intellectual property and environment chapters.[4] The Australian government's position is that it considers ISDS on a case-by-case basis,[5] and that the Japan agreement does not even include an ISDS mechanism. University of Sydney Professor Luke Nottage argues that ISDS was of little value to either Japan or Australia, although he notes that its exclusion may be significant for other agreements, including the TPP.[6] US negotiators have apparently sought this provision in the TPP, although others in the United States make the case against including the provision on many grounds. [7]

IMPACTS OF THE AGREEMENTS

The agreements have been criticized for their lack of contribution to market access, their lack of ease of use, and their failure to contribute to national welfare.

Some exporter interests, for example, have been critical of the lack of market access negotiated, and the time it takes to implement the cuts in tariffs, in the agreements with South Korea or Japan. For example, the (Australian) National Farmers' Federation said that it was "disappointed" with the "overall outcomes" in the Japan agreement, although the organization recognized the benefits for sectors such as beef, wine, and seafood.[8] The dairy farmers went further to call it a "dud deal," and they worried about the message being sent as future commitments are negotiated with China.[9] The Australian trade minister reacted strongly to these responses, saying Australia "had achieved with Japan what no other country in the world had achieved, 'let alone a major agricultural exporter.'"[10]

Other Australian industry representatives have become increasingly concerned that the negotiated market access conditions are difficult to use. As illustrated with respect to agriculture, there are few commitments in common across these two agreements. Industry commentators also point to the proliferation of agreements and the different rules used in the agreements, especially concerning origin and the various procedures required to establish origin in order to make use of the negotiated changes in market access.[11]

This debate illustrates the challenge of resolving bilateral agreements in a way that produces significant results in terms of market access, especially when a timetable is imposed by domestic politics. Another example of this challenge in bilateral talks is the difficulty the United States has had in its discussions with Japan, which are regarded as the critical next step for progress in the TPP. *The Wall Street Journal* reported during President Barack Obama's visit in April 2014 that "after months of talks…significant differences remained on key issues, particularly US access to Japanese agricultural markets. Japan wants to protect its own products, including rice and beef, while the US is demanding full market access. Meanwhile, the US is apparently seeking more time to cut tariffs on Japanese vehicles."[12, 13] Likewise, while Australia has reached agreements with South Korea and Japan, its negotiations with China, which started even earlier, are still continuing.

Another criticism is that the agreements do not contribute to national welfare. The real gains from the application of new trade policy come from domestic reform, not from export market access. The question, then, is whether trade agreements now being negotiated will make contributions. Bill Carmichael of *The Australian*,[14] for example, argues that they do not, and his assessment is that pursuing the goal of market access concessions in bilateral agreements actually diminishes concern for the outcomes to the economy as a whole.

REGIONAL ECONOMIC INTEGRATION—ITS ROLE AND FEASIBILITY

One response to these criticisms is that the bilateral agreements are steps toward wider agreements that include more participants—for example, those designed to pursue regional economic integration. When undertaking the trade negotiating process in a larger group, there is more at stake. Thus, wider, deeper, and more common commitments might be found, ameliorating concerns about the impact of the smaller agreements. There might also be an effort to apply provisions that effectively multilateralize those commitments.[15]

The problem is that this outcome may not be feasible when bilateral steps were initially taken. As noted, it will always be far more difficult to achieve significant changes in market access in a bilateral agreement, since neither party can offer the other the domestic political compensation required to offset the internal reforms that created losing groups. The larger negotiation process is supposed to provide that capacity. But initiating bilateral agreements creates a new set of losers, separate from those produced by more wide-ranging reforms, which are export groups that have gained preferential market access. It will be interesting to see, for example, the reaction of some Australian agricultural exporters or services firms to a TPP that removes their position of preference. It will also be interesting to see the attitudes of South Korean and Japanese manufacturers to a TPP that removes their preferential access to the Australian market. These groups would otherwise have been supporters of region-wide and global reform. The fracturing of the free trade coalition that results from taking the bilateral road as a first step may become a significant, long-run challenge, not just for the parties to the agreements reviewed here, but for Asia-Pacific integration more generally.

NOTES

1. See http://www.dfat.gov.au/fta/jaepa/.

2. The full text is available at http://www.dfat.gov.au/fta/kafta/.

3. See page 14 of the Gillard Government Trade Policy Statement at http://www.acci.asn.au/getattachment/b9d3cfae-fc0c-4c2a-a3df-3f58228daf6d/Gillard-Government-Trade-Policy-Statement.aspx.

4. The various safeguards are discussed here: http://www.herbertsmithfreehills.com/insights/legal-briefings/text-of-korea-australia-fta-released-isds-provisions-revealed.

5. See https://www.dfat.gov.au/fta/isds-faq.html.

6. This case is argued by Luke Nottage at http://www.eastasiaforum.org/2014/04/09/why-no-investor-state-arbitration-in-the-australia-japan-fta/.

7. See http://www.cato.org/publications/free-trade-bulletin/compromise-advance-trade-agenda-purge-negotiations-investor-state.

8. See http://adf.farmonline.com.au/news/magazine/industry-news/general/robb-rejects-ags-trade-criticism/2696186.aspx.

9. See http://www.australiandairyfarmers.com.au/media-corner/australia-japan-fta-dud-deal.

10. See http://adf.farmonline.com.au/news/magazine/industry-news/general/robb-rejects-ags-trade-criticism/2696186.aspx.

11. See http://www.theaustralian.com.au/national-affairs/policy/fix-fta-fine-print-says-business/story-fn59nm2j-1226876184926.

12. See http://online.wsj.com/news/articles/SB10001424052702304518704579520694003000918 and http://www.cato.org/blog/whats-really-impeding-progress-tppwhats-really-impeding-progress-tpp-japan-united-states-have.

13. Parallels between the structure of negotiations with Australia are interesting, although US car tariffs (2.5 percent) are actually lower than those in Australia, while the United States imposes a very high 25 percent tariff on pickup truck and commercial van imports. See http://www.autonews.com/article/20130412/OEM11/304129790/u.s.-to-gradually-drop-tariffs-on-japan-vehicles-under-trade-deal

and http://www.cato.org/publications/trade-briefing-paper/ending-chicken-war-case-abolishing-25-percent-truck-tariff.

14. See http://www.theaustralian.com.au/national-affairs/opinion/trade-as-a-foreign-policy-or-driver-of-growth/story-e6frgd0x-1226878195316.

15. Continuing work on the transparency of current domestic policy and its consequences, and "winning the argument" about the value of domestic reform are also important. See http://www.theaustralian.com.au/national-affairs/opinion/trade-as-a-foreign-policy-or-driver-of-growth/story-e6frgd0x-1226878195316.

16. The primary source of this material can be found at http://www.dfat.gov.au/fta/. It is supplemented by other reporting referred to in the following endnotes.

17. See http://www.mla.com.au/Prices-and-markets/Trends-and-analysis/Beef/Forecasts/MLA-cattle-industry-projections-2013/82-beef-exports-Korea.

18. See http://www.beefcentral.com/news/article/4499.

19. See http://www.canegrowers.com.au/page/Industry_Centre/Media_Centre/Media_Releases/Japan_as_disappointing_as_04_US_free_trade_agreement_for_sugar_ASA/.

20. See http://www.abc.net.au/news/2014-04-23/andrew-robb-hits-back-at-japan-deal-criticism/5406428.

21. See http://www.agweb.com/article/japan_adds_pork_tariff_cut_to_beef_in_trade_pact_with_australia_BLMG/. According to this source, pork imports from Australia were about 700 tons in the 12 months prior to March 31, 2013. Japan imported 738,455 tons of pork worth US$3.8 billion in 2013, of which 38 percent came from the United States, the world's largest exporter.

22. See http://www.weeklytimesnow.com.au/commodities/horticulture/japan-free-trade-agreement-is-big-a-boost-to-horticulture/story-fnker6g8-1226884737630.

The Asia-Pacific
Economic
Cooperation
Forum

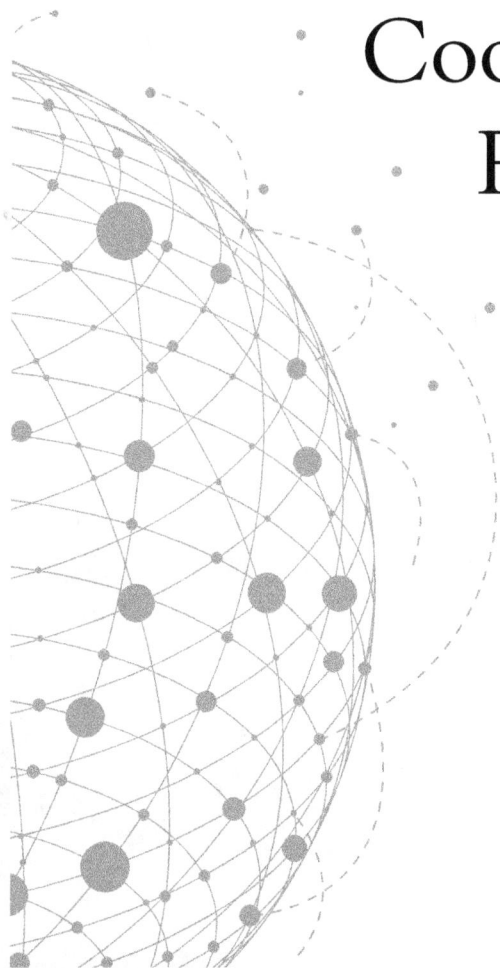

13

APEC in 2014

Meeting New Challenges

Zhang Yunling, Director of International Studies,
Chinese Academy of Social Sciences

The Asia-Pacific region represents 40 percent of the world's population, 50 percent of global GDP, and 44 percent of the world's trade, which includes the three largest global economies—the United States, China, and Japan—as well as some of the most high-potential and dynamic developing economies. The region clearly stands in the center of global economic developments and other affairs. Unlike the EU, the Asia-Pacific region finds its own way in the realm of regional community building. APEC is a unique regional grouping that brings together developing, newly industrializing, and advanced industrial economies into one regional framework. Under this framework, all members are committed to reducing barriers to trade and investment and enhancing economic and technical cooperation following the approach of concerted unilateral and collective actions.

As APEC provides a framework for bringing all members together to work on shared interests, and especially as it provides an annual meeting opportunity for leaders in the region to exchange ideas about policy concerns and pressing challenges, all members realize its importance. Although APEC faces difficult issues, it is still an irreplaceable institution for the Asia-Pacific region. APEC has been strongly backed by member governments and business communities, and it continues to be a pivotal platform to conduct policy dialogue, to initiate agendas, and even to test new ideas in economic and trade cooperation, including on various global issues.

The Asia-Pacific economies are highly integrated and interdependent, which is based on their open development strategy and supported by production networks of active trade and investment flows. The agendas of liberalization, facilitation, and cooperation under the APEC framework represent the common will of the member economies to strengthen regional integration and cooperation for sustainable economic development and prosperity. The Bogor Goals, which were set up in the early 1990s, aim at realizing an open and cooperative region in the Asia Pacific. As stated by APEC leaders at their first meeting on Blake Island, Seattle, in 1993, "The spirit of openness and partnership deepens, enabling us to find cooperative solutions to the challenges of our rapidly changing regional and global economy." Although great progress has been achieved in regional economic integration, and production networks continue to expand, the first phase of the Bogor Goals—realizing the commitments to liberalization and opening up to all APEC members by 2010—has not been achieved. In facing the new environment of emerging FTAs, the role of APEC and, especially, the means for achieving the Bogor Goals have been questioned.

APEC enters its new phase of development, and it needs to have its priorities and agendas readjusted to meet the new challenges. Currently, the Asia-Pacific region is also facing some vital challenges: the lingering impact of the 2008–2009 global financial crisis, the need to rebalance and restructure the supply-demand chains, the impact of climate change, and the need for sustainable development, as well as emerging tensions of security and international relations, among other issues. The major challenge for the Asia-Pacific region now is sustaining economic dynamism by further concerted commitments and actions in the areas of macroeconomic policy, economic restructuring, financial reforms, and the development of green economic sectors. APEC should become more active and effective in dealing with the impact of the financial crisis, reforming the international financial system, and implementing domestic reforms of both financial and economic structures. APEC should show that it values its original mission to help the member economies realize sustainable growth by improving their policies and strengthening cooperation. APEC's credibility lies in its strong role promoting change and reform that creates a more balanced economic development model and structure, while maintaining an open and integrated region.

In the face of slow progress implementing the commitments required to realize the Bogor Goals, further efforts were made by APEC to facilitate enforcement in the past years. For example, the 2001 Shanghai Accord, which aims to broaden APEC's long-term vision, sought to clarify the roadmap to the Bogor Goals and strengthen the implementation mechanism; the 2005 Busan Roadmap was set up as a midterm stocktaking of progress toward the goals; and, again, the 2006 Hanoi Plan of Action identified specific actions and milestones needed to implement the goals. However, in facing the emerging FTAs, both bilateral and subregional, APEC's role in binding the regional framework together seems very weak.

Looking back at the APEC agenda, the priority used to be one of guiding all members to keep markets open and to improve policy and business environments. APEC should continue to play this major role. As recommended by the APEC Business Advisory Council (ABAC), "a new vision is needed." In a set of recommendations for APEC trade ministers that were created in Sapporo, Japan, on June 1, 2010, the council urged APEC to build on the Bogor Goals to "reflect the changing nature of modern Asia-Pacific regional supply chains and value chains." It is clear that APEC needs to readjust the approach and roadmap of the Bogor Goals.

The diversified efforts of APEC members to develop FTAs pose major challenges to the APEC-led process of regional integration and cooperation, a process whose most significant value is to bring the region together and share prosperity. In the past, APEC has tried to coordinate the existing, complex "spaghetti bowl" of free trade agreements into a more consolidated framework. For example, in 2004, APEC adopted best practices for regional trading agreements (RTAs) and FTAs, which consisted of "model FTA/RTA chapters." APEC has also implemented many initiatives, which range from self-certification of rules of origin (ROO) and a supply chain connectivity framework (SCCF) to public-private partnerships (PPP) and capacity building.

The Trans-Pacific Partnership (TPP), led by the United States with 12 negotiation partners, has brought about serious challenges to all these efforts. The TPP was initiated by four small and open economies (Singapore, Chile, New Zealand, and Brunei). As it extended to more members and became a key strategy for the United States to achieve a high-standard FTA for the twenty-first century, APEC's principles of open regionalism and its gradual approach seem to be abandoned.

However, it is not realistic that the TPP can become an alternative to a Free Trade Area of the Asia-Pacific (FTAAP), or to upend the Bogor Goals. The TPP may attract more economies, but it will not include all APEC economies in the final negotiation process. APEC, on the other hand, is by nature diverse, and provides a flexible and inclusive institution for all of its members.

To keep the region integrated and dynamic, it is vital for APEC to emphasize its role as an intergovernmental dialogue and cooperation mechanism. While a region-wide FTA in the Asia Pacific is of pivotal interest to all members, APEC could readjust its approaches and priorities on other broad agendas. These include connectivity, clean energy, climate change, supply chain, and Phase II tariff reduction of green products. Functional cooperation becomes a key factor in APEC's ability to successfully promote these broad goals.

In facing a multitude of diverse FTAs, especially large groupings such as the TPP and the RCEP, APEC leaders have reemphasized the Bogor Goals in their annual declarations made since 2010. The leaders have reaffirmed their desire to realize the Bogor Goals by 2020, and to work out a blueprint for doing so. This shows that the Bogor Goals are still serious political commitments by the 21 economies of APEC. Considering that 2014 is the twentieth anniversary of the Bogor Goals, it may be a good time to establish a working group to develop a blueprint for the FTAAP. As stated in the leaders' declaration, the FTAAP will be built upon ongoing regional undertakings, such as ASEAN-Plus-Three, ASEAN-Plus-Six, and the TPP. However, if the FTAAP is an APEC-led agenda, APEC will need to change roles from being only a forum to actively urging all members to participate in the negotiations. Some members may not agree to this change. As to the approach that should be taken to create an FTAAP, simply merging the TPP and the RCEP

together seems unfeasible, given their differences. One of the more practical approaches may be to think of the FTAAP as a general framework
covering liberalization, facilitation, and cooperation, with differential
processes and arrangements.

China has actively participated in all APEC agendas, since the Asia-
Pacific region is of great importance both in economic terms and in
terms of international relations and security. APEC engagement has
been essential for China, as it provides a broad regional framework on
the one hand, and a gradual approach on the other.

China adopted an active FTA strategy after joining the WTO. FTAs
help China not only achieve market access, but also make rules and align
interests among members. FTA agreements, either bilateral or subregional, give China opportunities to forge close partnerships through
broad frameworks for market liberalization and cooperation. Immediately after joining the WTO, China took the initiative to establish the
China-ASEAN FTA (CAFTA), and then played a leading role in the
East Asia FTA (EAFTA, or ASEAN-Plus-Three) feasibility study. The
China-ASEAN FTA helps to create a comprehensive framework between China and ASEAN members, which facilitates trade and other
economic relations significantly. China now serves as the largest market for ASEAN's external trade, and many cooperative programs have
been implemented, from enhanced trade with GMS (Greater Mekong
Subregion) economies, to infrastructure connectivity, to capacity building for human development. China hopes that East Asia will establish
a region-wide FTA, initially under the framework of ASEAN-Plus-
Three (China, Japan, and South Korea). However, due to complex
factors, consensus seems difficult to achieve among the ASEAN-Plus-
Three members on how to establish a single institutional framework in
East Asia.

Actually, regional integration and cooperation in East Asia is characterized by multilayered frameworks, including ASEAN-Plus-One,
ASEAN-Plus-Three, and ASEAN-Plus-Eight (East Asia Summit). In
2011, ASEAN initiated the Regional Comprehensive Economic Partnership (RCEP) as an integrated FTA framework among the ASEAN-
Plus-Six economies (China, Japan, South Korea, India, Australia, and
New Zealand). China quickly adjusted its policy and has actively engaged

in negotiations of the RCEP, while at the same time continuing to participate in the trilateral FTA among China, Japan, and South Korea.

In general, multilayered frameworks give China more flexibility and room to maneuver. On the one hand, China is a leading exporter with special advantages in various areas of production, but on the other hand, it is still a developing economy. As such, China finds it difficult to conclude FTAs with many of its trading partners, especially with the developed economies. In fact, the TPP has presented a serious challenge to China's FTA strategy. Since the initial round of TPP negotiations excludes China, there is worry that the TPP will intentionally be designed to bypass China. This puts China in a difficult position. The exclusion creates concern that it is not playing a role in the rule-making process, and that the new rules will have negative effects on China's trade and investment with TPP members. Although China keeps an open attitude about the TPP, it was unable to surmount the difficulties of becoming an early negotiation partner, given that the TPP has been labeled a high-level FTA for the twenty-first century, with little flexibility for entering.

As China has vital interests in the Asia-Pacific region, it sees APEC as a unique platform to engage the United States and all other members of the region. China is organizing the APEC meetings in 2014, which it sees as a good opportunity to get APEC back on the right track. China hopes that the 2014 meetings might serve as a launching pad for the FTAAP process, although consensus will be difficult to reach, especially as the TPP is struggling to conclude and the RCEP is still in the early stages of negotiation.

14

US Economic Strategy in the Asia-Pacific Region

Promoting Growth, Rules, and Presence

Matthew P. Goodman, William E. Simon Chair in Political Economy, Center for Strategic and International Studies

INTRODUCTION

Economics is at the heart of US engagement in the Asia-Pacific region. This statement is as true today as it was in 1784, when the first US merchant ship set sail from New York bound for Canton; or in 1853, when Commodore Perry arrived in Tokyo Bay in his "black ships," seeking not territory but refueling rights for the American whaling fleet.

A few statistics make clear why the United States is drawn to Asia today. The 21 member economies of the Asia-Pacific Economic Cooperation group (APEC) account for roughly 55 percent of global GDP and 44 percent of world trade. [1] According to the International Monetary Fund (IMF), developing Asia is expected to grow by an average of 6.7 percent in 2014, making it the fastest-growing region in the world. [2] US exports to APEC economies totaled nearly $1.2 trillion in 2012, accounting for over half of total US exports. [3]

Economic exchange with this dynamic region makes a vital contribution to US growth and jobs. In the wake of the financial crisis of 2008–2009 and resulting shifts in the structure of the US economy, exports to the Asia-Pacific region have become an increasingly important source of demand and employment. By one estimate, roughly 2.8 million American jobs were supported by exports to Asia in 2012.[4]

With this much at stake, it is not surprising that the United States has been an active participant in Asia-Pacific economic integration efforts over the past 25 years, going back to the decision of the George H.W. Bush administration to co-found APEC in the late 1980s and seen today in the Obama administration's focus on completing a Trans-Pacific Partnership (TPP) trade agreement. Linking these efforts over the years, and the subject of this paper, are a number of common objectives and characteristics that distinguish the American approach to regional economic integration from that of other economies in the region.

US ECONOMIC POLICY OBJECTIVES IN ASIA

In designing and implementing economic policy toward the Asia-Pacific region, recent US administrations have been animated by three broad objectives: promoting growth and jobs; strengthening the global rules-based system; and underpinning America's long-term presence in the region.

The first priority is growth. As mentioned above, the Asia-Pacific region is one of the world's largest and most dynamic economic areas. It is an increasingly important source of demand for the global economy. Stronger demand and greater purchasing power in Asia mean (among other things) more US exports to the region, which are an important source of growth and jobs at home.

For more than 30 years, successive US administrations have worked to promote strong domestic-demand-led growth in the major surplus economies of Asia. Japan, then the world's second-largest economy, was the initial target of this policy in the 1970s and 1980s, but attention has broadened in recent years to other large, growing economies with persistent current-account surpluses, notably China. With US and European consumers and governments alike forced to borrow less and save more in the wake of the 2008–2009 financial crisis, Washington argues that large surplus economies need to consume and import more, or global growth will suffer. This is why the Obama administration has made "strong, sustainable, and balanced growth" the mantra of its policy engagement with China and other large Asia-Pacific economies in both the G-20 and bilateral channels.

United States trade policy has also supported the macroeconomic growth agenda. Recent administrations have pursued an active trade agenda in the region, including President George W. Bush's negotiation of a Korea-US free trade agreement (commonly known as the KORUS FTA) and the Obama administration's launch of the TPP negotiations. Enforcement of existing trade agreements has also been an increasingly important feature of trade policy in the past two administrations. A core objective of all these efforts has been to reduce barriers to US exports, enhance America's own competitiveness, and boost growth and jobs at home.

Regional trade policy also supports the second broad objective of US economic strategy in Asia: upholding and updating the rules of the international economic system. As discussed further below, the TPP (like its sister negotiation launched this year with the European Union, the Transatlantic Trade and Investment Partnership, or TTIP) is aimed at establishing "twenty-first century" trade and investment rules. These cover not only tariffs and other border measures, but also behind-the-border conditions governing trade and investment, such as intellectual property protection, regulatory transparency, labor and environmental standards, and competition.

As a region representing roughly half of global GDP and trade, the Asia Pacific is an important testing ground for developing and implementing these new rules. After a decade of failing to conclude a comprehensive, multilateral agreement under the Doha Development Round, the United States and willing trade partners have been forced to pursue other more targeted approaches, including mega-regional agreements like the TPP and the TTIP. The hope is that, if successful, these agreements will become the de facto template for a new multilateral system of rules.

The third consistent objective of US economic strategy in the Asia-Pacific region is to support a long-term American presence in the region. The United States is a Pacific power by nature (geography) and necessity (the pull of historical, security, and economic forces)—but also by design. Successive administrations since World War II have worked deliberately to embed the United States firmly in the region through an array of political, security, and economic arrangements.

The US network of alliances in the region—with Japan, South Korea, Australia, and others—and the troops and ships deployed in support of those alliances are the most visible manifestation of that policy. Binding trade arrangements like the KORUS FTA and the TPP can be seen as the economic equivalent of America's security alliances in the region. That is, they enmesh the United States in regional affairs through expanded trade and investment and give Asia-Pacific economies an increased stake in each other's prosperity and security.

REGIONAL ECONOMIC INTEGRATION: THE US APPROACH

In support of all three objectives described above—growth, rules, and presence—recent US presidents going back to George H.W. Bush have invested in Asia-Pacific regional economic integration (REI). Bush's secretary of state, James Baker, embraced his Australian counterpart's proposal to create APEC in 1989 as a venue for foreign ministers from the region to discuss trade and investment liberalization and capacity building. President Bill Clinton invited his APEC counterparts to a summit on Blake Island off Seattle in 1993, giving the forum's REI mission top-level political imprimatur. George W. Bush launched and completed the KORUS FTA negotiations and initiated the TPP at the end of his term. President Barack Obama renegotiated KORUS and passed it through Congress, then embraced and launched the TPP negotiations.

Washington's approach to REI in this region has been marked by two key characteristics that distinguish it from approaches championed by other economies: it is trans-Pacific versus Asia-centric; and it emphasizes high standards of liberalization and rule-making.

The first characteristic is driven first and foremost by the fact that the United States is a Pacific but not an Asian economy. But higher-level policy considerations also play a part. In pushing APEC to the fore, Secretary of State Baker was clearly animated by concerns about East Asian aspirations for community building that would exclude the United States; he later noted that such efforts would "draw a line down the middle of the Pacific."[5]

The second distinguishing feature of the US approach to REI is a preference for comprehensive trade and investment liberalization and high-standard rules of the road. This has inspired Washington's approach to APEC since the inception, but took on new substance with the launch of "twenty-first century" treaty negotiations with South Korea and the TPP partners. Both the George W. Bush and Obama administrations have insisted on the broadest and deepest possible liberalization and state-of-the-art disciplines on trade and investment-related policies, both at and behind the border. By contrast, Asia-only integration initiatives, including bilateral and subregional FTAs, have generally covered only border measures, with numerous exceptions to full liberalization.

Both economic and political considerations lie behind this second feature of US regional integration policy. Washington believes that removing most impediments to trade and investment and imposing tough rules of the road maximize economic efficiency and growth. It feels that the narrower and "shallower" agreements reached to date in Asia have done little to improve efficiency and may cause trade diversionary effects that outweigh their trade-creating benefits.

Of course, the persistence of its own market-access restrictions on imports of some agricultural and other sensitive items shows that Washington does not always practice what it preaches with regard to high standards. This highlights the role of domestic politics in US REI policy: to win congressional support for trade agreements it has negotiated, the White House must achieve the best possible results for US export interests, uphold US labor and environmental standards, and minimize the damage to domestic vested interests. Washington's insistence on high standards in the negotiating room to a great extent reflects these political realities back home.

THE TRANS-PACIFIC PARTNERSHIP

The priority that Washington places on negotiation of a TPP trade agreement illustrates the objectives and characteristics of US economic strategy enumerated above. The TPP's three-part purpose is to stimulate American growth and jobs, strengthen the rules of the regional (and global) trading system, and lock the United States more deeply into regional affairs. As its name and membership suggest, it is trans-Pacific in nature, incorporating most of the Pacific-facing economies of the Western Hemisphere, as well as a number of Asian economies. And it is explicitly designed to produce, as President Obama said in announcing his embrace of the TPP in late 2009, "the high standards worthy of a twenty-first century trade agreement."[6] In addition to lowering border barriers such as tariffs, the TPP aims to establish disciplines on an array of behind-the-border measures that impede trade and investment, such as excessive or nontransparent regulation; preferences for domestic, especially state-owned, enterprises; and inadequate intellectual property protection.

As this author has argued elsewhere, a number of myths cloud regional perceptions of the TPP.[7] One is that the negotiations are "splitting Asia," since not all Asian economies are eligible to join, while those that are eligible must choose between joining the TPP, which is viewed as being led by the United States, and the Regional Comprehensive Economic Partnership (RCEP), which is preferred by China. Yet in principle, the TPP is open to any APEC economy willing to strive for high-standard rules; indeed, US strategy from the outset was to begin the negotiations with a small group of "like-minded" economies and to incentivize others to join over time—a strategy that is ostensibly working. Conceptually, there is no reason that even non-APEC economies like India and Myanmar should forever be excluded; in fact, the logic of the US-ASEAN Expanded Economic Engagement (E-3) initiative is to help all ASEAN economies meet the high standards being sought in the TPP.

As for having to "choose" between the TPP and the RCEP, the seven Asian economies participating in both tracks clearly view the two approaches as not mutually exclusive. And as discussed further below, the TPP and the RCEP could one day converge in a region-wide agreement, or at least become interoperable, with enormous potential gains to world income.

Another myth that until recently was popular in Beijing is that the TPP is part of an effort by Washington to "contain" China. Yet no Asia-Pacific economy—including the United States—wants to exclude China from regional economic integration; on the contrary, all want to deepen their economic ties with that economy. True, one goal of the TPP is to create a level playing field that, among other things, allows other economies to better compete with China, but this is a far cry from "containment." Over the past few months, elite opinion in Beijing has shifted noticeably from rejecting the TPP outright to seeking a better understanding of it; indeed, there are some signs—such as Beijing's embrace of a comprehensive bilateral investment treaty (BIT) with the United States and its launch of the Shanghai Free Trade Zone—that China's leadership is preparing the ground for eventual membership in a high-standard regional agreement.

A third myth is that the high standards that Washington is espousing in the TPP are too ambitious for Asia. Yet all participants—including less-advanced members like Vietnam—have made clear that they believe there are substantial welfare gains to be had from a high-standard agreement that opens up new market opportunities and helps each economy address structural impediments in its own system. Moreover, participating economies understand the political dynamics in Washington that, alongside the economic benefits, drive US ambition in the talks. And most welcome an active US role in championing high-standard rules and norms in the region.

The prospect of an early conclusion of the TPP negotiations remains very much in doubt. Although most of the agreement's 29 chapters have been closed, by all accounts significant differences remain on a number of challenging issues, notably intellectual property, competition, and environmental standards, as well as the market-access provisions.

One of the greatest sources of uncertainty is whether the Obama administration will be able to persuade the US Congress to support a final agreement without so-called trade promotion (formerly "fast track") authority, which is traditionally required to provide the political clarity US negotiators need to close trade deals. Although there is a clear majority in favor of trade liberalization in Congress—including among "Tea Party" members—there is concern that not even broadly supported legislation could pass Congress in the current environment of mutual distrust and dysfunction.

However, negotiators in the talks themselves report a shared sense of urgency and determination among all participating economies to complete the agreement quickly, and a basic accord in the next few months remains possible. Trade negotiations are always darkest before the dawn, as differences are narrowed to the most politically difficult issues. But insofar as they involve political rather than technical decisions, the final deals can be done quickly if the will is there.

The stakes could not be higher for the Obama White House. Conclusion of the TPP is the sine qua non of success not only for the administration's regional economic policy, but also, arguably, for the broader strategy of "rebalancing" toward the Asia-Pacific region. In addition to its economic benefits, a successful agreement would anchor the United States more firmly in the Asia Pacific and bolster American leadership there. Without the TPP, the rebalancing strategy would contain little of substance that is new.

THE PATH TO FTAAP

The parallel negotiation of two major regional trade agreements in the Asia-Pacific region—the TPP and the RCEP—raises the prospect of harmful trade diversion and a patchwork of inconsistent rules that could hamper rather than facilitate regional economic integration. This concern is heightened by the plethora of other arrangements being negotiated in the region, including the trilateral China-Japan-Korea FTA.[8] Competition between the different tracks could also accentuate geopolitical strains in the region as economies line up in one economic camp or another.

A more benign interpretation of these trends is that the various trade agreements under negotiation are not mutually exclusive and may eventually converge at the broader APEC vision of a Free Trade Area of the Asia-Pacific (FTAAP). Petri et al. have shown that the potential economic benefits of such a region-wide agreement are enormous, with annual global income gains on the order of $1.3 to $2.4 trillion by 2025.[9]

Full convergence of the TPP and the RCEP may be impossible given their different scope and the varying standards each will produce. However, there may be ways to harmonize important parts of the two agreements that would make them interoperable in practice.

As argued in a recent Center for Strategic and International Studies (CSIS) report, common rules on value-chain management would be one promising place to begin.[10] The emergence of global value chains as the defining feature of twenty-first century trade and investment patterns—in which a product idea is conceived in one economy, inputs are procured and produced in others, assembly occurs in yet another, and the final product is shipped and marketed around the world—has fundamentally altered the stakes in trade negotiations. Rather than bargaining primarily for market access for their goods and services exports, economies must also ensure unrestricted value chains, i.e., the smooth flow of investment, technology, and inputs across and behind borders.

All of the regional arrangements under negotiation, including the TPP and the RCEP, will likely cover an array of value-chain disciplines, including logistics procedures, services and investment liberalization, and information/communications technology facilitation. Consistency and high standards across these efforts would facilitate regional integration and promote better economic outcomes. One major report has estimated that, were all countries to reduce value-chain barriers in a few key areas even halfway to established best practices, it could boost global GDP by $2.6 trillion.[11]

As the oldest and arguably most successful forum for trade and investment integration in the Asia-Pacific region, and one that works by nonbinding consensus, APEC could serve an important role in facilitating value-chain harmonization. Since adopting the Bogor Goals of free trade and investment in 1994 and in its more recent FTAAP vision, APEC has served for a quarter century as an incubator for regional integration efforts. As host in 2014, China has a unique opportunity to launch a process aimed at making the value-chain provisions of the region's numerous trade arrangements interoperable at a high standard.

APEC has so far focused specifically on key cross-border logistics issues in work programs on "supply-chain connectivity." For instance, APEC economies set a goal in 2010 of achieving a 10 percent reduction in the time, cost, and uncertainty of cross-border transactions by 2015. This has been important—and little heralded—work. The CSIS report recommends that China lead a broader initiative on value chains, building on APEC's existing work but incorporating a number of other policy issues along the value chain, including investment, data flows, and regulatory coherence.

CONCLUSIONS

From Washington's perspective, a successful economic strategy in the Asia-Pacific region is essential to sustaining American growth and jobs in the twenty-first century. It is also central to Washington's efforts to remain a champion of the international rules-based order. And it underpins America's long-term presence in the region, which in turn contributes importantly to the region's security and prosperity, and thus to America's own. For all these reasons, the United States is likely to remain an active—even impatient—participant in regional economic integration efforts, through APEC, the TPP, and other regional arrangements.

NOTES

1. US Department of State, "21st Annual APEC Economic Leaders' Meeting Fact Sheet," October 8, 2013.

2. International Monetary Fund, "World Economic Outlook Update," January 2014.

3. US Department of State, op. cit.

4. Scot Marciel, "Economic Aspects of the Asia Rebalance," Statement before the US Senate Committee on Foreign Relations Subcommittee on East Asia and Pacific Affairs, December 18, 2013.

5. Cited in Claude Barfield and Philip I. Levy, "Tales of the South Pacific: President Obama and the Transpacific Partnership," American Enterprise Institute, December 2009.

6. White House, "Remarks by President Barack Obama at Suntory Hall," news release, November 14, 2009.

7. Matthew P. Goodman, "Five Myths about TPP," CSIS, April 30, 2013.

8. According to the Asian Development Bank's Asia Regional Integration Center, there were 75 FTAs involving at least one ADB member under negotiation, and another 51 either proposed or under consultation and study, as of October 2013.

9. Peter Petri, Michael G. Plummer, and Fan Zhai, "The Trans-Pacific Partnership and Asia-Pacific Integration: A Quantitative Assessment," Peterson Institute for International Economics, November 2012.

10. Matthew P. Goodman, Scott Miller, and David A. Parker, "Enhancing Value Chains: An Agenda for APEC," CSIS, November 2013.

11. World Economic Forum, Bain and Company, the World Bank, "Enabling Trade: Valuing Growth Opportunities," Geneva, 2013.

15

Where to with Cooperation Across Asia and the Pacific Now?

Peter Drysdale, Emeritus Professor of Economics,
The Australian National University

China's hosting of the APEC Summit in November 2014 is a timely opportunity to provide new direction to economic integration across Asia and the Pacific. In the past five years, the launch of the Trans-Pacific Partnership (TPP) negotiations (organized in APEC's backyard by the United States) and the Regional Comprehensive Economic Partnership (RCEP) (organized under the umbrella of ASEAN) have dominated thinking about regional integration. In APEC, some still believe that these initiatives might provide the foundations for a broader regional free trade agreement, a Free Trade Area of the Asia-Pacific (FTAAP). This is a pipe dream that diverts policy energy and attention away from a more important agenda for APEC: to encourage national reforms behind the border and build connectivity and deeper integration among the Asia-Pacific economies. Transregional free trade agreements like the proposed TPP may be small steps along the way, but they are incidental to the main APEC game and what needs to be done to achieve free trade and integration across Asia and the Pacific.

THE MAIN GAME FOR APEC

There are three big goals that APEC can achieve in Beijing in November. The overarching APEC objective for 2014 is to raise the vision of economic cooperation in the Asia-Pacific region beyond the preoccupation with a narrowly defined concept of free trade, and to work toward realizing the full potential of the region. APEC needs to pursue three vital, interrelated dimensions of cooperation:

- ensuring the global environment needed for sustained growth;
- encouraging the efficient structural transformation of Asia-Pacific economies;
- fostering regional economic integration.

Right now, the most important threats to realizing the potential of Asia-Pacific economies are global threats—including the still weak and uncertain recovery from the global financial crisis and global warming. The Asia-Pacific economies need to work to overcome these threats. Other important threats to continued growth and rising living standards are weaknesses in the structures, regulations and institutions of all APEC economies. The region has experienced steady growth and dynamism, which requires continuous structural change and adjustment.

The region's future is threatened by the erosion of respect for the core principles of the multilateral regime that underpin the successful management of trade and other international commerce. APEC, as well as the RCEP, should work to restore the centrality of the WTO, rather than try to replace it.

The Asian economies are already highly integrated. Their interdependence has grown under the global trading regime, not through bilateral or regional trading arrangements. Deeper regional economic integration remains a worthwhile first objective, but it involves more than pursuing mega-regional trade deals. The RCEP governments, for example, should not be content with negotiating a "single undertaking" for a trade deal, along the lines of the TPP. A comprehensive RCEP can aspire to be a model for an ultimately global set of principles-based rules for managing trade and many other forms of international commerce in the twenty-first century. These rules should take account of the interests of all emerging economies, not just the currently most powerful. A first objective should be for APEC to lead the definition of those principles and rules.

A second objective is to ensure an effective follow-up of the 2013 commitment to the APEC Framework on Connectivity. Accelerating investment in the economic infrastructure needed to boost connectivity can contribute to all of the three dimensions of economic cooperation identified above. Driven by a determination to improve infrastructure, APEC can seize the opportunity created by the establishment of the Asian Infrastructure Investment Bank (AIIB). China's welcome decision to contribute to better regional infrastructure through the AIIB will more likely lead to success if the proposed multilateral development bank is positioned to reinforce the efforts of Asia-Pacific economies, which are implementing structural reforms in an effort to mobilize new external and internal funds for infrastructure development. It can also promote APEC's connectivity agenda. The participation of APEC members in establishing the facility and its mode of operation will also ensure that the AIIB's work achieves international best practice, that its funding is productively disbursed, and that there is a sense of regional and international ownership and participation.

There is a third goal, one that is a corollary to the infrastructure initiative. The time has also come to connect the economic architecture that has developed in APEC to the economic architecture that has emerged around the ASEAN-Plus-Six economies. The ASEAN-Plus arrangements in East Asia include both India and economies in Asia that are not members of APEC but are critical to enhancing Asia-Pacific integration, connectivity, and infrastructure across the region. It is important that these economies now be routinely engaged in dialogue with APEC leaders to build broader regional cooperation outcomes in a positive geopolitical environment. The organizational infrastructure and engagement that has been developed in APEC over the past 25 years will facilitate that. The question is how to achieve this objective, given the constraints on the expansion of APEC membership and the risks of undermining the value and centrality of the ASEAN-Plus arrangements. A way forward that can achieve this objective is set out below.

THE REGIONAL INTEGRATION AGENDA

Currently, the regional integration agenda is focused on transregional FTAs, and APEC's explicit goal is to ultimately achieve an FTAAP. This is a serious misdirection of APEC efforts and energy. Even if a region-wide trade deal could be achieved, after years of politically painful negotiations, it would not lead to the investments in infrastructure that can deliver greater gains in terms of regional economic integration. A 2013 study by the World Economic Forum (WEF) points to the huge potential gains of investment to improve connectivity, explaining that supply chain barriers to international trade are far more significant impediments to trade than tariffs. In fact, reducing supply chain barriers could increase world GDP over six times more than removing all tariffs.

The large number of bilateral FTAs signed to date have been useful at the margin, but they have not brought significant commercial or domestic reform in the region and, with the difficulties in concluding the Doha round, the hiatus in trade reform puts weight on making the most of region-wide trade initiatives. Region-wide trade initiatives should be used to pursue regional economic and political cooperation and to build a stronger global economic system.

In the field of geopolitical cooperation, tensions in Northeast and Southeast Asia over territorial and other issues threaten constructive cooperation and regional stability.

The rapid growth of trade and investment in East Asia was driven by unilateral trade and investment liberalization and opening up. This was the foundation for the deep integration that has emerged in Asia around the development of production networks and value chains. APEC was a leader in this. It was the forum that promoted concerted unilateral liberalization, including the massive liberalization by China in the lead-up to its accession to the WTO at the APEC Summit in Osaka in 1995. APEC also took leadership in laying the foundation for the Information Technology Agreement, and more recently, the Environmental Goods Agreement. These developments built the foundations of comprehensive Asian and trans-Pacific economic integration, and the beginnings of multilateral political cooperation that was no longer based on old hub-and-spokes security relationships.

Until recently, China was not ready or willing to take an active leadership role on issues at a regional or global level, but now appears able and ready to join a coalition for trade reform. While China should remain open to eventual participation in the TPP, a more effective way forward immediately will be through the ASEAN-Plus arrangements, which provide a framework for mobilizing middle powers to affect real change in regional institutions.

No single nation can significantly influence regional political or economic outcomes in bilateral dealings with any of the principal parties, though China has potentially more sway than any other. There is a greater prospect of shaping regional outcomes positively by mobilizing efforts at building regional political and economic cooperation among a coalition of players. Initiatives that seek to build an open Asian economic community through the RCEP could be encouraged, particularly those that entrench the rules and commitments that will sensibly need to be incorporated in the TPP, while also reinforcing its own goals through those mechanisms. A comprehensive regional cooperation initiative at this time would also encompass much broader strategic interests.

For the RCEP to effectively complement the TPP in this way, the overriding interest must be to shape the RCEP, over time, so that it sets sound principles-based rules for managing contemporary trade and other international commerce. If emerging economies in other regions see the merit of sound rules agreed upon by China, India, Indonesia, and other RCEP economies, those rules could form the basis for a global regime, rather than standard rules or rules set under other arrangements, including those under the proposed TPP.

The goal of a high-standard agreement would be to have developing economies commit to standards they aspire to reach in reasonable time frames, and not to exclude them and punish them for not starting with developed-economy standards immediately. China and other RCEP economies are absolutely integral parts of Asian supply chains, which are driving economic integration and growth in East Asia and globally. It is through these supply chains that the newer emerging economies in Southeast Asia and South Asia can join the globalization process and embrace the rules of an open trade and investment regime.

The RCEP involves more participants than the TPP, including all of Asia's main economies, such as China, Indonesia, and India. The RCEP is a way forward with economic cooperation, underpinned by the ASE-AN-Plus framework, despite all the region's political problems. Bringing together the ASEAN-Plus-One trade agreements with Japan, China, South Korea, Australia and New Zealand, and India will be difficult even with ASEAN as the fulcrum. Pursuing negotiations in the same manner as the TPP or traditional FTAs would mean a long, drawn-out negotiating process. There is growing recognition that consolidating the Plus-One FTAs may be politically and technically very difficult. There is a palpable appetite in the region and beyond for new ideas on how to move forward with the many overlapping FTAs and the regional agreements that seem destined to become bogged down in low-productivity negotiations.

The RCEP is also a strategic opportunity to create a more favorable geopolitical environment in the region. It will need re-branding to engage high-level political efforts to that end, and it will need ramping up quickly around the ASEAN Economic Community (AEC) and Asian economic community conceptions of the RCEP.

A productive strategy is to see a streamlined economic cooperation agreement as one of several steps needed for ultimately achieving a RCEP that embraces a comprehensive agenda of regional economic integration, development, and political cooperation. This would parallel the strategy for creating the AEC. Upgrading of the ASEAN Free Trade Area (AFTA) of the 1990s to the more comprehensive ASEAN Trade in Goods Agreement (ATIGA) was one of the first steps taken to implement the AEC, alongside a broader program that included work to implement the Master Plan for ASEAN Connectivity. Negotiating an innovative umbrella FTA among RCEP participants could be pursued in parallel with the other steps needed to achieve deeper economic integration, regional development, and political goals.

RCEP participants should not have to wait until a "single undertaking" on trade liberalization, with a whole set of new rules, is agreed upon before seeking other opportunities for beneficial economic integration. It can strive to achieve significant initial commitments on trade liberalization and lock in progress toward ambitious end-point goals.

Institutional support for the several dimensions of economic integration to be pursued under the RCEP should be created as soon as possible. The thinking about how to do this has been well developed by ASEAN as it progresses toward the AEC, and is also consistent with the achievement of APEC's Bogor Goals.

In this conception, the most effective strategy to achieve these ambitions on the determined timeline will be a creative combination of agreed and binding targets for 2025; initial commitments (the down payment) negotiated by 2015; and further cooperation and negotiations to implement these targets by all members, starting from 2015 onward and conducted within the newly established institutional framework.

A strategy along these lines would address economic and political worries that are widely shared across the region. It would make it easier to involve India and other less-developed economies in Southeast Asia, contribute to connecting South Asia with East Asia, and deliver a major and successful mega-regional cooperation initiative. Ramping up the process would itself deliver significant improvements in the regional political environment. The achievement of real economic integration and cooperation across East Asia and South Asia, and its WTO principle-led delivery, can also present a way forward for dialogue (in the G-20, for example) on WTO reform.

The experience with the TPP and the RCEP prompts the question of how these and other regional and transregional trade and investment arrangements impact the global trade and investment regime. Whichever conception of progress on regional integration through negotiation prevails—through the RCEP or TPP—it is clear that the idea of the FTAAP, as traditionally conceived, will be irrelevant to the outcome. The FTAAP cannot be superimposed on what is already evolving across Asia and the Pacific through the TPP and RCEP efforts. These arrangements will be difficult, if not impossible, to unravel; they will determine the future shape of trade and economic cooperation throughout the Asia-Pacific region.

How should APEC, then, help shape the global outcome and the global regime? APEC, with its proud history of open regionalism and its vital interest in the WTO-based multilateral trading rules, should lead the way in answering that question.

What APEC could most usefully do is work to define the principles that should dominate the conclusion of transregional arrangements and shape reform of the WTO and the international investment regime. This will not be easy since APEC includes all the vested interests against change and reform of the international economic system. This reality, however, has not blocked creative policy innovation in the past. The formation of an APEC task force or eminent persons group to articulate a *global* strategy on trade and investment reform would be both timely and welcome and better secure free trade in Asia and the Pacific in its broadest sense.

THE INFRASTRUCTURE AGENDA

Promoting infrastructure investment is a priority in Asia and the Pacific for two reasons. The steady but fragile recovery of the global economy needs a boost of investment demand that will sustain productive growth in the longer term. Meeting the large deficit in infrastructure demand in the region is critical to the continuing growth and development of regional economies through deeper regional integration and connectivity.

Currently, very low rates of interest globally provide an excellent opportunity to invest in economic infrastructure that raises long-term productivity and serves to integrate economies with that objective. Members of both APEC and the G-20 are trying to accelerate investment in economic infrastructure for these reasons, but it will not be easy to go beyond declarations of good intentions and studies to actually achieve a significant boost in infrastructure investment.

Finance is not the immediate constraint. Economies with a sound, enabling environment for investment can mobilize financing for well-prepared projects that are expected to earn adequate economic rates of return. There are many viable projects, including ones that have been identified by the multilateral development banks, but the institutional and regulatory weaknesses in many economies delay bringing projects to fruition, if they get up at all.

Of course, the governments of individual economies bear the principal responsibility for improving policy environments and the capacity to prepare viable projects. But there is scope for cooperation by coordination between groups such as APEC and the G-20, which can assist with infrastructure delivery. APEC is beginning to help regional governments to develop the necessary human capital and institutional capacity, and to overcome the policy and administrative obstacles to accelerating investments.

Improving the enabling environment and capacity to manage investments in infrastructure is essential, but it is not sufficient to guarantee success. A strategy to accelerate investments in economic infrastructure needs to complement policy development. Decisions to implement well-conceived infrastructure initiatives must be backed by a political commitment to solve problems in implementation. Experience is the most effective means of underlining the policy changes and institutional upgrading needed to expedite investment in subsequent projects.

The best example in the Asia-Pacific region is ASEAN's determination to create an ASEAN Economic Community. Southeast Asian governments are beginning to invest in the necessary transport, communications, and energy networks, with support from the ASEAN Infrastructure Fund.

APEC officials are drawing up a blueprint for a comprehensive upgrading of physical, institutional, and people-to-people connectivity among Asia-Pacific economies in line with their commitment to the APEC Framework on Connectivity approved by APEC leaders at their 2013 meeting. The next step might be to draw up an APEC Master Plan on Connectivity to translate the hopes set out in the blueprint into a pipeline of investments, backed by a serious, long-term process for working together to create essential skills and institutional capacity.

APEC is not, and should not become, a financing or implementing agency, so there is no established procedure for financing work in the APEC Master Plan on Connectivity, or for conducting feasibility studies for any regional initiative to achieve better connectivity. This problem could be overcome by support from the new Asian Infrastructure Investment Bank (AIIB), which is expected to be formally launched by China to coincide with its hosting of the APEC annual meeting in 2014. This work might be done in tandem with the Asian Development Bank (ADB) and the World Bank.

The new AIIB, open to shareholding by any government and by private investors, is designed to narrow gaps in the region's economic infrastructure. Helping to finance some of the investments needed to achieve the aims of the APEC Framework on Connectivity fits neatly into this mandate. It would be appropriate to commit a very small part of the AIIB's expected capital base to finance the preparation of the APEC Master Plan on Connectivity and feasibility studies of some pilot projects.

Short-term support would make it possible to launch the decades of capacity building and investment needed to create and sustain adequate transport, communications, and energy networks, as well as build institutional links among the Asia-Pacific economies. G-20 leaders could welcome these Asia-Pacific initiatives and draw them to the attention of others.

The G-20 can also lead the way to ensure that financing does not become a constraint to investment in economic infrastructure once more governments improve their ability to prepare and implement projects. G-20 leaders have already set up a working group, backed by expertise from several international organizations, to look for ways to tap global capital markets for investment in infrastructure on a much larger scale than now.

This working group will study alternative means to attract private savings, including public-private partnerships, bond issues, and lending for individual infrastructure projects, either directly to governments or intermediated through international financial institutions. This policy-oriented research is likely to raise new issues and policy challenges.

It is necessary to boost the capacity to attract investment by reducing the actual, and then the perceived, risk of investment in infrastructure in various economies. The most important determinant of that risk is the track record of governments—that is, the quality and predictability of their policy and institutional frameworks, combined with their willingness to invest public resources and to work with the private sector to anticipate and/or respond to the inevitable practical problems of upgrading infrastructure.

The share of private financing of investment in infrastructure will need to increase, but public sector investment will remain dominant and essential to leveraging finance from global capital markets. Policy development to encourage private sector investment, therefore, needs to be complemented by work to identify when public investment in infrastructure is justified, and to ensure that the capacity of governments to borrow is assessed as objectively as possible. An announcement at the APEC Summit that the AIIB would help to embed public-private partnership (PPP) centres throughout Asia, including in China, would be a positive way of providing reassurance of this.

Individual or institutional private investors cannot be expected to acquire the expertise needed to estimate the potential benefits and risks of many specific infrastructure projects. The existing multilateral development banks were created to reduce the transaction costs of making these assessments, as well as to reduce the risks of these investments. But, at present, they are not making a significant contribution to the commercial financing of investment to upgrade or extend essential economic infrastructure, partly due to their limited financial capacity.

The establishment of the AIIB will spur existing development banks to consider expanding the financing capacity. The AIIB will create new competition for existing development banks. At the same time, the new bank will have a strong incentive to cooperate with them. Tapping into the expertise of banks that have accumulated knowledge and experience is the most effective way to build up the capacity of new international financial institutions. The APEC Summit is an excellent opportunity to launch the AIIB.

At their 2014 meeting, G-20 leaders can welcome the initiative to create the AIIB and encourage existing multilateral development banks to share information, experience, and expertise to help them succeed. Leaders can also ask the World Bank and other multilateral development banks to prepare strategy papers during 2015. These papers would set out how international financial institutions can step up their capacity for leveraging private sector finance for infrastructure, and how they could increase their own commercial lending to meet a much larger share of the financing needed to narrow gaps in economic infrastructure. These strategies should also recommend ways in which G-20 governments could help to overcome the current constraints facing multilateral development banks.

EVOLVING REGIONAL ARCHITECTURE

China's leadership of APEC in 2014 presents the opportunity to shape the evolution of more effective regional architecture. There is no quick fix to this, and there will need to be creative adaptations of the present regional architecture. The challenge will be to use established regional arrangements, within which there is a great deal of flexibility, to entrench gradual but purposeful change.

The first step would be simple. China can convene a high-level dialogue to connect the APEC forum to the East Asia Summit (EAS) membership around the APEC Summit. It is important to connect the premier regional economic dialogue (in APEC) to the political dialogue (that has been the character of the EAS). Bringing together economies in the ASEAN-Plus process that are not APEC members with APEC leaders is an initiative the APEC chair can take without broaching vexed membership questions. The rationale in organizing such a meeting around the Beijing summit would justifiably be the trans-Asian interest in China's infrastructure initiative and ASEAN centrality to regional cooperation principles.

The two economies in APEC most easily capable of affecting this kind of de facto architectural extension without fuss are the United States and China. China would obviously have to clear the way with the United States and explain the value of the initiative to other APEC and EAS members.

At the Vladivostok summit in 2012, the Russian Presidential Executive Office invited the Eurasian Economic Commission to join related meetings. What was important about this invitation was that the chairman of the Council of the Eurasian Economic Commission (the Customs Union's governing body) was given the opportunity to participate in APEC ministerial meetings, as well as others, during the summit week to explain the vision of a Eurasian Economic Union. This was a perfectly sensible and very strategic move, totally consistent with the spirit of APEC's open regionalism. And it helpfully opened the way to doing things rather differently in APEC. APEC's open and flexible framework can be routinely used in this way to connect with the EAS.

Some have argued that eventually there will need to be a choice made between APEC and EAS as to which venue the Asia-Pacific leaders would in future "strut their stuff." As a recent US Congressional Research Service report observes: "The Obama administration frequently has portrayed APEC as the premier economic and trade organization in the Asia-Pacific region, and views the EAS as the main geopolitical association in the region. This view is not shared by all of the other members of these two associations." But the Russians, without anyone much noticing, have opened an innovative new play. APEC can be transformed into a platform on which anyone with anything to contribute on economic cooperation can be invited to join.

As host in 2014, China can invite India, Myanmar, and other non-APEC members of the EAS to the APEC party to do important regional business, especially if it is connected to the summit's infrastructure agenda. Connecting India and Myanmar, this year's ASEAN chair, to such a meeting around the APEC Summit would be an important step forward in architectural evolution. This way of thinking about the APEC process is an effective game changer for welding the APEC and EAS processes together, and avoids the unnecessary choice of downgrading one or the other regional arrangement.

16

Placing Increased Priority on Services in APEC

Sherry Stephenson, Senior Fellow, International Centre for Trade and Sustainable Development

INTRODUCTION

Services sectors have a tremendous weight in modern economies. They account for two-thirds of world GDP, employment, and inward foreign direct investment (FDI), on average. Formerly, it was understood that services accounted for only 22 percent of world trade; however, when measuring trade in value-added terms, services constitute nearly 50 percent of global trade in goods and services since they are incorporated as inputs into the production of primary and manufacturing products, adding significant value.

In APEC, services have reached 67 percent of the region's GDP and 52 percent of its employment. Nevertheless, there is still high potential for increasing trade in services in APEC, as well as for diversification of the services that are traded.

Achieving this will depend upon enhanced services liberalization at the global level and, of course, at the APEC level. This paper argues that services should be a key priority for APEC members in order to promote connectivity and regional economic integration. There are several reasons for prioritizing services. First, services are still the most restricted sector in APEC economies, which means that services liberalization would achieve the biggest trade gains for the region. Second, it is well known that efficient services account for the greatest productivity increases, with spillovers for all other economic sectors. Finally, services and investment are the two main areas that still constitute unfinished business from the Bogor Goals. Treating these issues at the regional level would be a plus, moving the region a step forward.

IMPORTANCE OF SERVICES AT THE GLOBAL LEVEL

Under traditional measurements of cross-border services trade, services are shown to account for around 22 percent of global trade. However, this percentage share does not take into account the share of services that goes into the production of goods, agricultural products, and natural resource products, and which are incorporated into the final value of these exports. A new understanding of the importance of services in international trade—and probably a more accurate one—is now available with the publication of the new WTO-OECD trade in value-added (TiVA) database. This takes into account the contribution of services as intermediate inputs, and can measure the value of intermediate goods and services as they cross borders before final products are completed, through the operation of global value chains (GVCs). The services that are both "embodied" and "embedded" in the production of the primary sector and manufacturing, as well as other services sectors, add much of their value. This is shown in Figure 1, where the weight of services in global exports is measured in both gross and value-added terms, and with the contribution varying from 22 percent to 46 percent. The actual importance of services in global trade in value-added terms is, therefore, more than double that of the traditional estimate. And services constitute fully two-thirds of the inward stock of foreign direct investment (FDI), a figure that continues to increase dynamically. This is particularly notable given the tendency of FDI to lead trade flows in modern economies.

This new way of understanding the role of services underscores its importance in goods trade as well, and highlights the fact that economies wishing to strengthen their competitiveness in goods must also improve the productivity of their services sector, including liberalizing services trade and emphasizing regulatory reform.

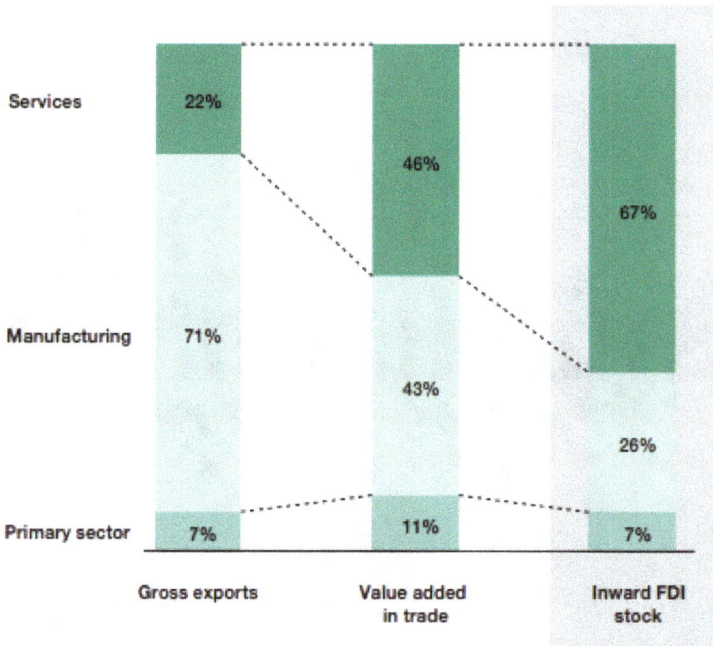

Source: *UNCTAD-Eora GVC Database, UNCTAD FDI Database.*
Graph taken from UNCTAD, World Investment Report 2013.[1]

FIGURE 1 *Contribution of Services to Gross Exports, Value-Added in Trade, and Inward FDI Stock*

IMPORTANCE OF SERVICES IN APEC

Services are of great importance for APEC, accounting for 67 percent of GDP on average. Many APEC member economies demonstrate a much larger proportion of services in GDP, with Hong Kong and Singapore as the most services-intensive APEC economies (approaching 90 percent of GDP), followed closely by the United States and Australia at almost 80 percent of GDP. Services accounted for 52 percent of total employment in APEC in 2012, and are estimated to be the largest driver of job creation over the next decade.[2]

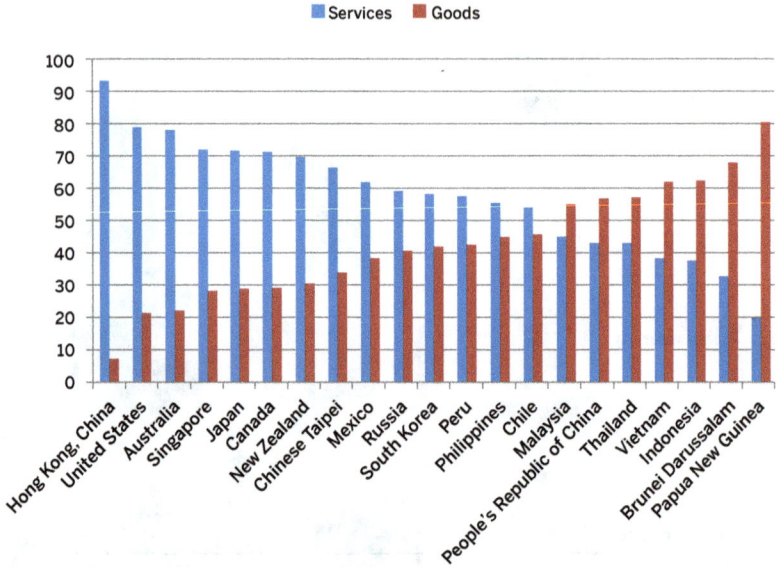

Source: USC and APEC, Trade in Services in the APEC Region, 2012.[3]

FIGURE 2 *Composition of GDP (Services/Goods) in APEC Economies*

It is interesting to note that there is a correlation between the contribution of services to GDP and the GDP per capita in APEC economies, as shown in Figures 2 and 3, with the more developed APEC economies showing higher services intensity. It has been noted by many trade analysts that increasing the density of services activities toward a greater "servicification" of the economic structure is associated with higher rates of economic development.

A greater services intensity, as measured by services as a percentage of GDP, can be shown to be positively correlated with GDP per capita of time, as shown in Figure 3. APEC economies have been moving toward greater services intensity in their productive structures over the past two decades.

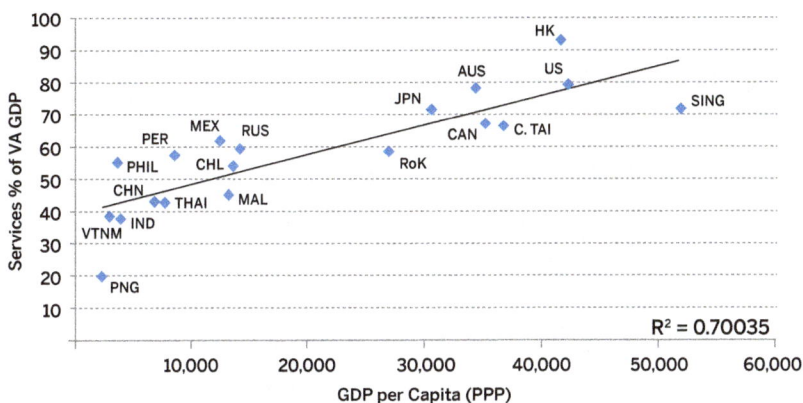

Source: USC and APEC, Trade in Services in the APEC Region, 2012.[4]

FIGURE 3   GDP per Capita and Services Contribution to GDP

Although individual APEC members have achieved high levels of services intensity in their economies, intra-APEC trade in services remains low in comparison with trade in goods. In 2010, only 6 percent of total services produced within APEC were exported, while 63 percent of total goods were exported.

Figure 4 shows that the majority of intra-APEC services trade tends to be in transport and in business services. All other services sectors (communication, finance, insurance, construction, recreation, etc.) show very modest amounts of intra-APEC trade and, therefore, still have a high potential for expansion.

The following figure presents APEC services exports in gross terms and in services value-added terms, showing that services exports have increased at a much faster rate than services output since 2002. This tendency underlines the fact that the region is highly involved in the operation of global value chains (GVCs).

The new WTO-OECD trade in value-added (TiVA) database mentioned earlier divides the share of services in gross exports into three contributing sources: (1) direct domestic services industry, (2) indirect domestic services content, (3) services that were embodied in imported

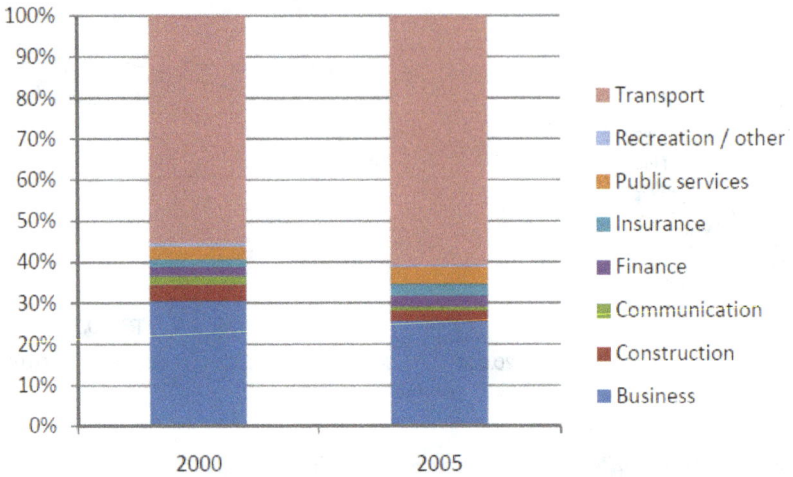

Source: Trade in services database developed by Joseph Francois, 2009 and author's calculations. Graph taken from APEC Policy Support Unit, Trade in Services in the APEC Region, 2010.[5]

FIGURE 4 *Intra-APEC Trade in Services by Sectors*

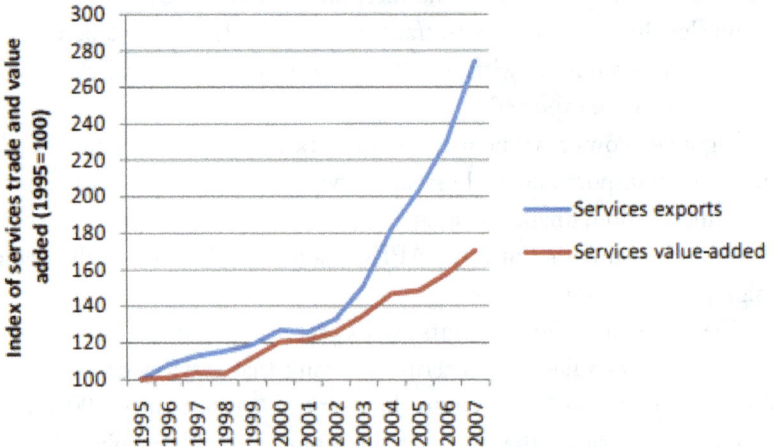

Source: World Development Indicators and author's calculations. Graphic taken from APEC, Trade in Services in the APEC Region, 2010.[6]

FIGURE 5 *APEC Services Exports and Value-Added (1995 = 100)*

intermediate goods, which can be either re-imported domestic services or foreign services content.

As shown in Figure 6, more than 20 percent of the services component of APEC exports comes from imported services that originate abroad, 30 percent from direct domestic services input, and almost 50 percent from indirect domestic services inputs that originate from intermediates. The value of re-imported domestic services value-added content of gross exports is extremely small.

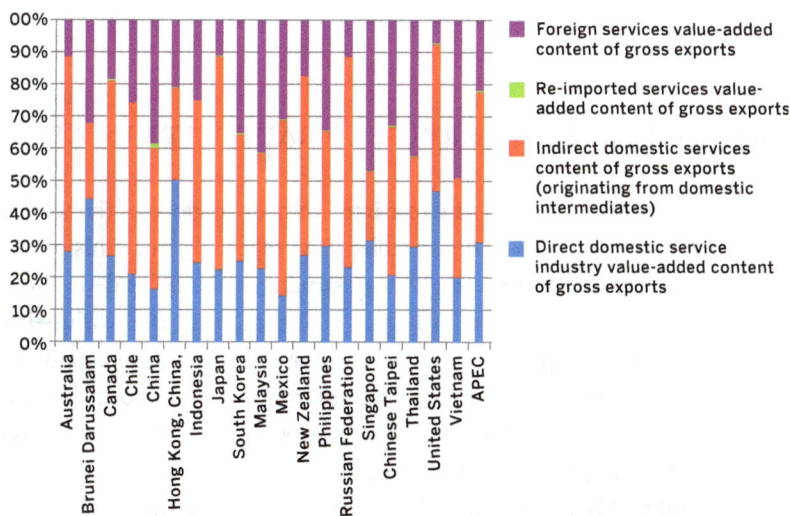

Source: PSU computation based on WTO-OECD TiVA database. Data is for 2009, and APEC total does not include Papua New Guinea.
Graph taken from Pasadilla, "Taking Stock of Services-Related Activities in APEC," 2014.[7]

FIGURE 6 Services Value-Added Component of Gross Exports

On the services value-added spectrum, there are wide-ranging positions within APEC. The United States has the least amount of foreign content in its services exports, at less than 10 percent. In contrast, Singapore has the largest foreign content in its services exports, accounting for nearly 50 percent. The large share of domestic services content could be explained in different ways. This is partly a result of the remaining and still significant barriers to services trade in many sectors, as well as to the fact that many services still require proximity between seller and buyer, giving preference for local service providers.[8]

Similar to what has been occurring in trade, or perhaps accounting for the change in trade patterns, FDI inflows in APEC have also increasingly shifted from manufacturing to services. Figure 7 shows that this is clearly the case for Japan, China, Thailand, and Singapore. Increased services FDI flows to APEC economies underline the growth of producer services that support global value chains, as services are the fastest area of growth for FDI flows in APEC.

IMPEDIMENTS TO SERVICES TRADE WITHIN APEC

Services trade tends to be highly restricted in many regions of the world. Liberalization of services trade is challenging, especially since this often has to do with the reform of regulatory structures and behind-the-border discrimination. As shown in Figure 8, all regions in the world—including the APEC region of East Asia and the Pacific—show relatively high indexes of protection in services, according to the World Bank's services trade restrictiveness index. This is especially the case for professional services and transportation. In East Asia and the Pacific, services trade is still highly restricted, with barriers to services trade much more significant in the five sectors canvassed than in OECD economies.

Behind-the-border barriers and impediments are the most significant problems for trade in services. Domestic regulations, industry standards, professional requirements, and efficiency of government agencies have a larger impact than market-access barriers. As Figure 9 from the USC Marshall School of Business report shows, the market-access restrictiveness index varies for the four services sectors that were canvassed in the study (retail and distribution, transportation, professional services, and financial services). However, the market-access restrictiveness on the whole tends to be less important than the other three barriers, which are of a regulatory nature. This information was obtained through interviews and a survey conducted by USC researchers.

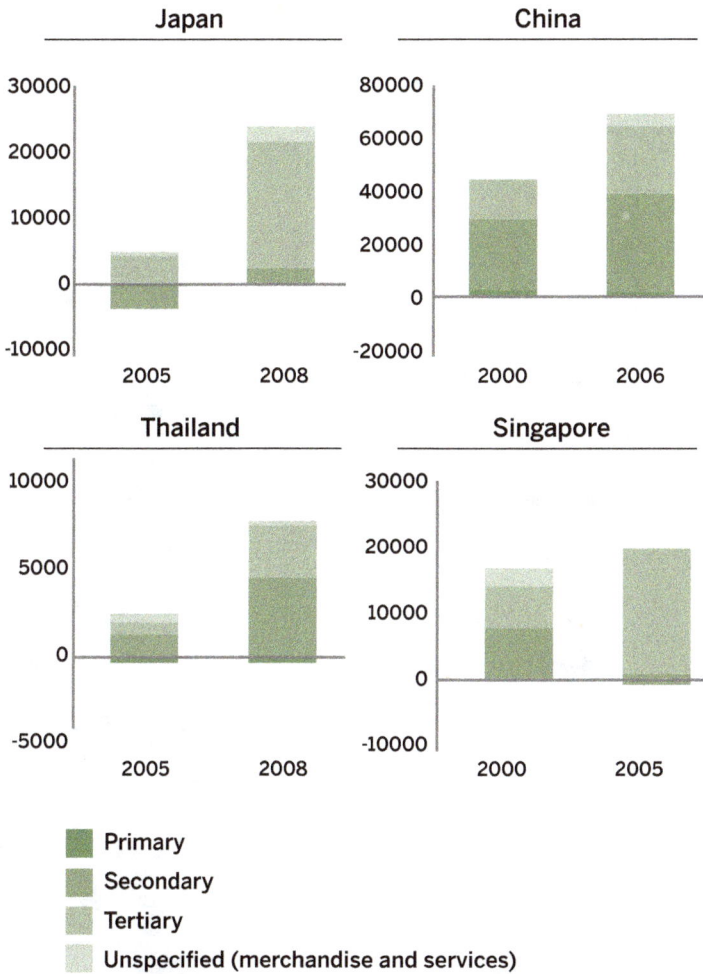

Source: WTO and IDE-JETRO, Trade Patterns and Global Value Chains in East Asia, 2011.[9]

FIGURE 7 *FDI Inflows in Some APEC Member Economies by Sector (2005; 2008)*

Among APEC member economies, Singapore, Hong Kong, and New Zealand are the most open to trade in services; Indonesia, Vietnam, and the Philippines are currently among the least open APEC economies to services trade.[12] There appears to be a general correlation between

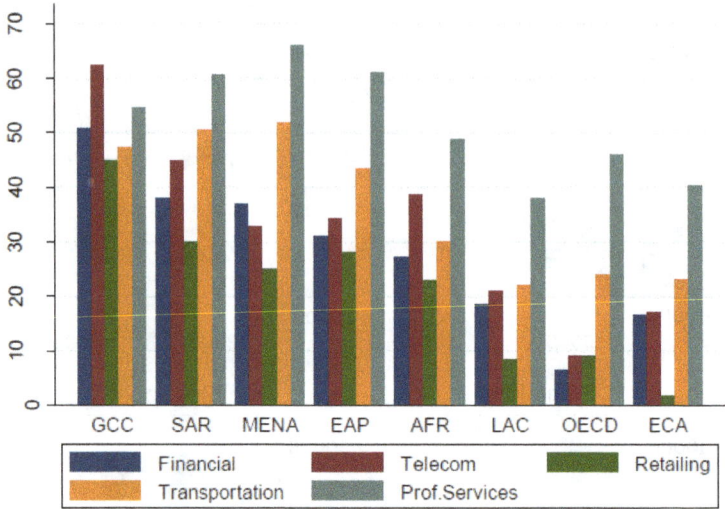

Note: The services trade restrictions index (STRI) at the regional level is calculated as a simple average of individual country's STRIs. The STRI in the cross-border air passenger transportation sub sector comes from the QUASAR database of WTO (2007). Regional abbreviations: HNO – High income non-OECD, SAR – South Asia, EAP – East Asia Pacific, MENA – Middle East and North Africa, AFR – Sub-Saharan Africa, LAC – Latin America and Caribbean, ECA – Europe and Central Asia, OECD - High income OECD. Source: Borchert et al., Policy Barriers to International Trade in Services. 2012.[10]

FIGURE 8   *Services Trade Restrictiveness Index (STRI) by Region*

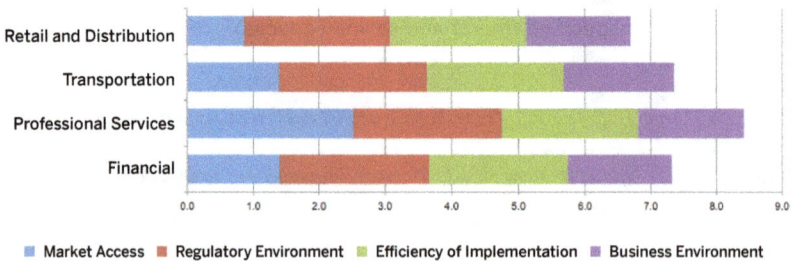

Source: USC and APEC, Trade in Services in the APEC Region, 2012.[11]

FIGURE 9   *Impediments by Services Sectors in APEC*

services exports and the level of restrictiveness of the sector in APEC economies. The largest services exporters in the region (United States, Singapore, Hong Kong, and Malaysia) show a relatively open regulatory environment for trade in services.[13]

GAINS FROM LIBERALIZING SERVICES TRADE WITHIN APEC

Since services sectors are among the most restricted components of APEC economies, the potential for their contribution to economic growth through liberalization is significant. Several studies have shown that far greater benefits can be derived from trade liberalization in services rather than in goods. According to the World Economic Forum's 2013 report *Enabling Trade*, improving supply chain operations and services barriers even halfway to the world's best practices could increase global GDP up to six times more than removing tariffs.[14]

Liberalization of trade in services in APEC also has huge potential. It is estimated that a 10 percent reduction in trade costs could result in US$100 billion of additional services-related GDP within APEC.[15] Furthermore, studies on reforms in services sectors by the APEC Policy Support Unit[16] show that restrictions in key services sectors such as transportation, telecommunications, and energy considerably drag down economic growth and trade within the region. Structural reforms in just these sectors could generate about US$175 billion in annual savings for APEC.

PLACING INCREASED PRIORITY ON SERVICES IN APEC

Although services are economically important for the region, there is still much work that must be done to strengthen policy focus and policy initiatives in the services area in APEC. Between 2006 and 2012, 38 percent of APEC-funded projects—just over one-third—were related to services. From these initiatives, around 64 percent of the spending was on workshops and capacity-building seminars, while the rest involved research studies or survey and database projects.[17] Given that services represent on average nearly half of world trade in value-added terms, there is a strong argument for increasing spending on APEC-funded projects to match this relative importance.

Among the challenges that APEC faces, similar to economies in all regions, is the scarcity of data on trade in services. Differences in definitions and measurements, and the lack of detailed services trade statistics for all economies, make it difficult to identify trends in trade patterns, as well as to measure the effectiveness of services-oriented policies. Another challenge has to do with the lack of focus on regulations that affect services while negotiating trade agreements. From the FTAs concluded by APEC members, 80 percent of the services provisions in these agreements focus on market-access barriers, while only 20 percent have to do with behind-the-border issues such as regulatory heterogeneity between economies.[18] Working on the liberalization of trade in services with the intent of harmonizing regulations and reducing behind-the-border impediments should be complementary and equal in importance to scheduling market-access obligations.

More efficient services sectors could generate many spillovers in APEC economies since services are embodied in the output of all economic sectors. Hence, better services lead to better competitiveness. Therefore, policies focused on improving services are also indirectly addressing issues such as the capacity to export, as well as the possibility of participating in global value chains. More efficient services would also contribute to:

- more inclusive growth, through employment effects and gender opportunities for women;
- greener growth, reducing the natural resource and material content of the economic growth path through services innovation. A focus on services within APEC can help to leverage energy from ongoing domestic reforms and generate momentum for the entire region (e.g., China, Latin American APEC economies);
- greater participation in global value chains, especially for small- and medium-sized enterprises (SMEs), which constitute the large majority of services exporters.[19]

This paper advocates for services to be given a higher profile within APEC. Services should be elevated in importance in APEC's agenda, and efforts made to reorient the prominence of services in its work. Specifically, the following is recommended for APEC:

First, discussion of services should be elevated to the Senior Officials level within APEC for examination of crosscutting key issues to raise awareness and understanding. Senior Officials should produce statements annually that recognize the importance of services. This could be done through maintaining an annual public-private dialogue on services, which could ideally be organized in proximity to the meeting of APEC Trade Ministers. This would reinforce the fact that APEC is treating services as a priority issue. It would also facilitate addressing crosscutting issues related to trade in services, and coordinating diverse APEC working groups and committees that deal with different services-related initiatives, often at the sectoral level.

Second, the APEC Senior Officials should develop a services policy framework and a stand-alone work program on services, which could be a multi-year priority program with several components. Among the crosscutting issues of focus for the APEC services work program, the following could be considered:

- services, competitiveness, and SMEs;
- contribution of services to value-added in APEC domestic economies;
- services and productivity growth in APEC;
- examining the role of services in global value chains and services as global value chains on their own;
- services and regulatory reform (on an economy-wide basis);
- services and innovation;
- services, employment, and more inclusive growth;
- services contribution to a more sustainable growth path.

Third, a section on services should figure each year in the APEC Leaders' Declaration.

NOTES

1. United Nations Conference on Trade and Development (UNCTAD), *World Investment Report 2013: Global Value Chains—Investment and Trade for Development*, 2013. Available at http://unctad.org/en/publicationslibrary/wir2013_en.pdf.

2. The University of Southern California Marshall School of Business and APEC Business Advisory Council, *Trade in Services in the APEC Region*, 2012. Available at http://www.keidanren.or.jp/abac/report/20120918_USC_Report.pdf

3. Ibid.

4. Ibid.

5. APEC Policy Support Unit, *Trade in Services in the APEC Region: Patterns, Determinants, and Policy Implications*, 2010. Available at: http://publications.apec.org/publication-detail.php?pub_id=1070.

6. Ibid.

7. Gloria Pasadilla, "Taking Stock of Services-Related Activities in APEC," paper presented by APEC Policy Support Unit to APEC Senior Officials, February 2014.

8. Ibid.

9. World Trade Organization and IDE-JETRO, *Trade Patterns and Global Value Chains in East Asia: From Trade in Goods to Trade in Tasks*, 2011. Available at http://www.wto.org/english/res_e/booksp_e/stat_tradepat_globvalchains_e.pdf.

10. Ingo Borchert, Batshur Gootiiz, and Aaditya Mattoo, *Policy Barriers to International Trade in Services: Evidence from a New Database*, The World Bank Development Research Group, Policy Research Working Paper 6109, June 2012.

11. USC and APEC, *Trade in Services in the APEC Region*, 2012.

12. Ibid.

13. Ibid.

14. World Economic Forum, in collaboration with Bain & Company and the World Bank, *Enabling Trade: Valuing Growth Opportunities,* 2013. Available at http://www3.weforum.org/docs/WEF_SCT_Enabling-Trade_Report_2013.pdf.

15. USC and APEC, *Trade in Services in the APEC Region,* 2012.

16. APEC Policy Support Unit, *The Impacts and Benefits of Structural Reforms in the Transport, Energy and Telecommunications Sectors in the APEC Economies,* 2011.

17. Gloria Pasadilla, "Taking Stock of Services-Related Activities in APEC," 2014.

18. USC and APEC, *Trade in Services in the APEC Region,* 2012.

19. Ibid.

17

Connecting APEC Economies through Infrastructure, Governance, and Social Inclusion

Tan Khee Giap, Co-Director, Asia Competitiveness Institute,
Lee Kuan Yew School of Public Policy, National University of Singapore

Yap Xin Yi, Research Assistant, Asia Competitiveness Institute,
Lee Kuan Yew School of Public Policy, National University of Singapore

INTRODUCTION

Globalization is still the correct pathway for both developed and developing economies to promote growth, enhance regional economic integration, and raise the standard of living. Export-led growth has enriched millions of people in East Asia as manufacturing and labor-intensive industries have relocated to developing economies. This relocation has been aided by international trade and international investment, resulting in industrial restructuring and technological upgrading (Tan, Yuan, Yoong, and Yang 2013).

These processes continue today as economic power shifts among the world's major engines of growth—namely, the United States, the European Union (EU), China, and Japan. Resource-rich ASEAN is strategically located at the trading pathway between the East and the West. With a population of close to 600 million people, ASEAN has never been so important and attractive to investors and global powers.

However, as established by the Asia Competitiveness Institute (ACI) at the National University of Singapore, ASEAN economies do not trade actively with one another, except for Singapore's strong bilateral trade with Indonesia, Malaysia, and Thailand (see Table 1). Indeed, bilateral trade between China and ASEAN has risen sharply since 2000. With a moderate annual 10 percent projected growth, it would exceed US$800 billion by 2020, overtaking other major trading relationships as the biggest bilateral trading partnership in the world (Tan, Low, Tan, and Lim 2013).

It is most interesting to quantitatively observe the importance of major economic engines on the growth of ASEAN-5—Indonesia, Malaysia, the Philippines, Singapore, and Thailand. Contributions of the United States, the EU, and Japan to the growth of ASEAN have been declining relative to China over the decades. For example, in terms of trade and investment, the United States and the EU used to be 9.2 times and 4.49

TABLE 1 *Engines of Growth among ASEAN-5 for 1990–1999 and 2000–2010*

	Indonesia	Malaysia	Philippines	Singapore	Thailand
Indonesia	1.31	0.09	0.03	0.13 (0.17)	0.06
Malaysia	0.15	1.23	0.06	0.33^ (0.49^)	0.16 (0.20^)
Philippines	0.01	0.03	1.07	0.03	0.02
Singapore	0.26^ (0.16)	0.30^ (0.43^)	0.07	1.18	0.15 (0.22^)
Thailand	0.14	0.18 (0.24^)	0.07	0.21^ (0.30^)	1.27

Note: ^ Denotes stronger bilateral trade between ASEAN members; figures in brackets refer to the period 1990–1999.
Source: Tan, Yuan, Yoong and Yang, 2013.

TABLE 2 *Relative Importance of China, EU, Japan, and the US as Engines of Growth for ASEAN-5, 1980–2020*

Title	Relative Impor-tance of US vs. China as an Engine of Growth for ASEAN-5	Relative Impor-tance of China vs. Japan as an Engine of Growth for ASEAN-5	Relative Impor-tance of EU vs. China as an Engine of Growth for ASEAN-5
Period	Ratio	Ratio	Ratio
1980–89	9.17	0.31	4.49
1990–99	4.30	0.71	2.41
2000–10	1.53	1.88	1.02
2011–20	*0.65	*4.52	*0.51

Note: China's importance as a major engine of growth for ASEAN economies has been rapidly increasing over the past three decades.
*Source: *Forecasted by ACI; Tan Yuan, Yoong, and Yang, 2013.*

times more important, respectively, than China in the 1980s, but that level has declined steadily throughout the 1990s and 2000s. By 2020, the projected US and EU impact will be merely 0.65 times and 0.51 times, respectively, of China's impact. Meanwhile, the impact of China's trade and investment on the ASEAN-5 economies used to be merely 0.31 times that of Japan in the 1980s; by 2020, its impact is projected to be 4.52 times more important than Japan (see Table 2).

We can also observe a similar rise in importance of China in terms of trade and investment in disaggregate to 11 Asian economies over the past three decades. However, the United States and Japan, if taken together, would remain important engines of growth for some Asian economies (see Table 3). Compared to China, the EU still maintains its impact as an engine of growth for several Asian economies, such as India, Malaysia, the Philippines, Thailand, and Indonesia. As for recent Japanese efforts to reorganize its value-chain networks into ASEAN, coupled with the latest attempt to relocate production out of China, we can expect to see a reshuffling of trade and investment in relevant ASEAN economies by Japanese multinational corporations (see Table 3).

Because so much of ASEAN's trade is with regional partners, it will have to play a critical role in the region's newly emerging free trade

TABLE 3 *Relative Importance of China, EU, Japan, and the US as Engines of Growth for Asian Economies*

Economy	Relative Importance of US vs. China as an Engine of Growth for 11 Asian Economies, 2000–2010	Relative Importance of US plus Japan vs. China as an Engine of Growth for 10 Asian Economies, 2000–2010	Relative Importance of EU vs. China as an Engine of Growth for 11 Asian Economies, 2000–2010	Relative Importance of China vs. Japan as an Engine of Growth for 10 Asian Economies, 2000–2010
	Ratio	Ratio	Ratio	Ratio
India	1.94	2.28	1.61	2.98
Malaysia	1.69	2.18	1.03	2.04
Philippines	1.59	2.14	1.05	1.75
Thailand	1.57	2.16	1.06	1.75
Japan	1.53		0.91	
Indonesia	1.47	2.20	1.03	1.37
Singapore	1.34	1.74	0.94	2.52
Australia	1.15	1.81	0.92	1.52
South Korea	1.09	1.40	0.76	3.20
Chinese Taipei	0.99	1.26	0.63	3.73
Hong Kong	0.70	0.86	0.46	6.33

Note: Relative to China, the US and Japan, if taken together, would remain important engines of growth for quite a few Asian economies. Relative to China, the EU still maintains its impact as an engine of growth for a few Asian economies. Japan's influence, however, is rapidly declining, but will likely undergo an overhaul due to renewed Japan-ASEAN connectivity. Source: Tan, Yuan, Yoong, and Yang, 2013.

agreements. It is useful to ask how ASEAN might promote a comprehensive strategy that brings together multiple regional economic architectures, including the Regional Comprehensive Economic Partnership (RCEP), the Trans-Pacific Partnership (TPP), and the Free Trade Area of the Asia-Pacific (FTAAP). As we move toward the ASEAN Economic Community (AEC), we must also work simultaneously to further strengthen the multilateral trading system and regional economic integration.

Globalization would be further enhanced by improving ASEAN connectivity with the United States, China, and Japan. Later sections of this paper will elaborate on the connectivity and infrastructure requirements of ASEAN growth as the region considers entering wider free trade agreements. Indeed, the Asia-Pacific Economic Cooperation (APEC) forum is committed to a multi-year plan on infrastructure development, as stated in the 2013 APEC Economic Leaders' Declaration: "Under Physical Connectivity, we commit to cooperate in developing, maintaining, and renewing our physical infrastructure through a Multi-year Plan on Infrastructure Development and Investment. The plan will assist APEC economies to improve the investment climate, promote public-private partnerships, and enhance government capacity and coordination in preparing, planning, prioritizing, structuring, and executing infrastructure projects."

The paper will also discuss the urgency, principles, modality, participation, and support needed by the Asian Infrastructure Investment Bank (AIIB), an important initiative proposed by President Xi Jinping at the 2013 APEC Leaders' Meeting in Bali. The AIIB, together with the Asian Development Bank (ADB), could potentially play an instrumental role in bringing to fruition the RECP, the TPP and an FTAAP.

FREE TRADE AREA OF THE ASIA-PACIFIC: RECOMMENDATIONS

Given the social turmoil currently taking place in several ASEAN economies, the targeted objective of achieving a full ASEAN Economic Community by 2015 seems unlikely. The process of regional economic integration will also likely be delayed, as the ASEAN-Plus discussions for the RCEP is progressing more slowly than expected.

Similarly, several recent rounds of negotiations for the TPP experienced difficulties, including lack of decisive support from the US Congress and disappointing results from President Obama's April 2014 visit to Asia, which failed to secure a comprehensive solution from Japan and

Malaysia. It looks like the TPP is also unlikely to be concluded in the near future.

Yet greater globalization in trade and investment still remains the most viable pathway to sustainable, balanced, and inclusive growth and development. Renewed WTO momentum toward strengthening the multilateral trading system is crucial. Given the proliferation of free trade agreements, such as the TPP and the RCEP, which are progressing in parallel, it is important to ensure renewed WTO momentum in the multilateral trading system.

An FTAAP was first suggested in 2004 by the APEC Business Advisory Council during its meeting in Chile, and a concretized pathway to an FTAAP was outlined in Japan during the APEC Leaders' Meeting in 2010. Some thoughts on how an FTAAP can proceed, such as linking the TPP and the RECP, was suggested in Singapore in 2014, and is likely to be revisited during the APEC Leaders' Meeting in Beijing, China, later this year.

At the APEC 2013 gathering, President Xi Jinping actually stated that China welcomes the "mushrooming of regional free trade agreements as a positive sign" and that "the ocean is vast because it admits hundreds of rivers." In order to accelerate regional economic integration, some steps that might be taken to move toward an FTAAP are enumerated below.

First, all APEC members have an interest in ensuring that the commitments toward achieving the Bogor Goals are implemented, and the most likely route to that goal is achieving an FTAAP. Whether this FTAAP is "to be led" or "supported" by APEC can be discussed further among members. Pacesetters are needed to retain focus and steadily move toward the longer-term goals.

Second, APEC needs to prioritize. Some have commented that APEC is not doing enough, and have even suggested that APEC be downgraded to the ministerial level instead of the leaders' meeting level. We disagree because there is still a lot more APEC can do. APEC should work toward specifically defined objectives in a well-coordinated manner.

Implementation of the following objectives is especially important to businesses: (1) the 2012 APEC List of Environmental Goods (EG list), which aims to reduce applied tariffs to 5 percent or less on a list of 54 products by 2015; (2) the Supply Chain Connectivity Initiative (SCI), which aims to achieve a 10 percent improvement in supply chain performance by 2015, and (3) the Ease of Doing Business Initiative (EODB), which set targets of a 25 percent improvement in ease of doing business by 2015.

Third, APEC should ensure that some of its initiatives feed into the WTO's work activities. The WTO conducts much practical work that is useful to the business sector. Yet the WTO continues to struggle with decision making and implementation, despite majority desires for further trade investment. It is now imperative for platforms such as APEC to lead the way, as it has done in the past. APEC's comprehensive agenda covers trade in goods, services, and investment. Some of this can feed into the WTO's agenda. For example, APEC might extend its EG list to other sectors, or it might propose nontariff measures and improve transparency of regulations.

Finally, APEC must seek to harmonize current trade agreements such as the TPP and the RCEP. By ensuring that the highest yet still realistic standards are met, they might lead successfully to an FTAAP. In the words of Lim Hng Kiang, Singapore's minister for trade and industry: "China's 2014 chairmanship will be crucial for achieving our 2015 targets. Faltering on this means we falter in our path towards our FTAAP aspirations" (Lim 2014).

ASEAN CONNECTIVITY AND INFRASTRUCTURE REQUIREMENTS

China-ASEAN Connectivity

The rapid growth in GDP and regional development imbalances in China over the past three decades have led to factor market distortions, environmental degradation, infrastructure constraints, governance issues, and public policy contradictions. These experiences offer valuable lessons for policymakers in developing economies, and are of considerable academic interests in terms of public policy debate.

Furthermore, as China attempts to rebalance its external demand–driven, export-oriented, quantitative growth model to a more domestic-driven, consumption-led model that includes quality growth adjustments, the mammoth rebalancing task is expected to have profound impacts

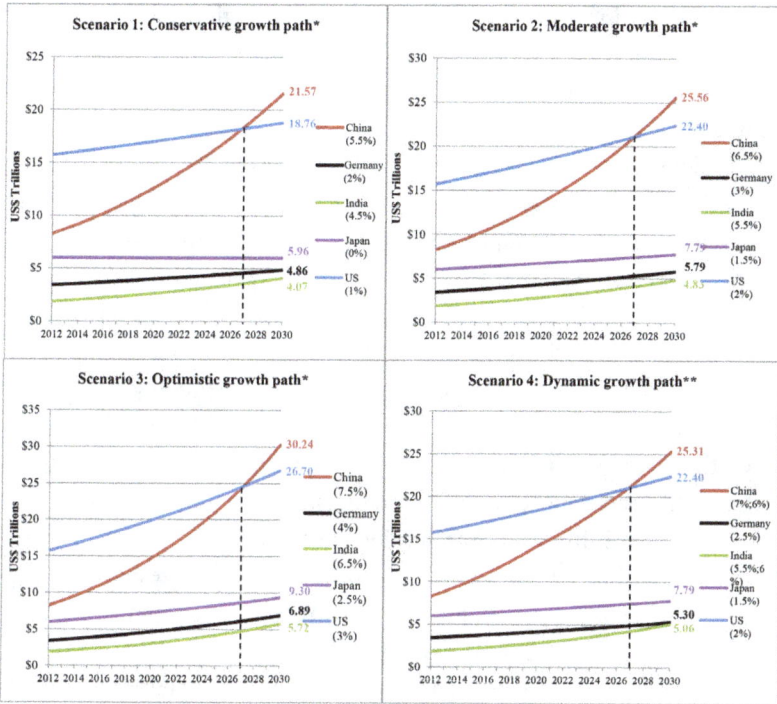

^ Projected by ACI at LKYSPP, NUS;
* Constant average growth rates for period 2012–2030; source for 2012 data: World Bank;
** For China 2012–2020, 7% per annum and 2021-2030, 6% per annum; for India 2012–2020, 5.5% per annum and 2021-2030, 6% per annum; for Germany, Japan, and the US, steady-state growth, at 2.5%, 1.5%, and 2% per annum respectively.

FIGURE 1 *Projected Nominal GDP Growth Paths for China, Germany, India, Japan, and the US: 2012–2030^*

and far-reaching implications to global trade and regional economic integration.

China's progression into the world's largest economy is projected to happen by 2027 at the latest, with stable GDP growth per annum of 6 percent to 7 percent for the next two decades or so (see Figure 1). China is fully aware of its growing economic prosperity, and is keen to share that prosperity, especially with its immediate ASEAN neighbors.

Prosperity sharing, in fact, is vital. By increasing regional economic integration and business opportunities through China-ASEAN connectivity, China's peaceful rise will become more meaningful, and its reception by people of the region more positive.

Nondemocratic systems tainted with corruption are still very much the reality in some Asian economies. These sociopolitical systems tend to create environments that value patronage over performance and connection over ability. Nevertheless, the paramount issue is the ability to govern effectively, and to formulate and execute public policies that are beneficial and inclusive to the majority of citizens. In fact, *discipline* is essential before *democracy*, which we believe will eventually come, even for China.

With closer government cooperation between China and ASEAN—along with increasing economic openness, greater market accessibility, and conducive initiatives—the resiliency of private sector business potential can be further galvanized, given the rich natural resources, abundant labor supply, and vast regional landmass. The challenge ahead is how to work toward achieving the goal of greater regional connectivity in infrastructure, institutions, and people-to-people contact.

Japan–ASEAN Connectivity

During the late 1980s and early 1990s, manufacturing activities by Japanese multinational corporations (MNCs) had been steadily moving out of ASEAN to the coastal provinces of China because of lower land costs and production facilities; an efficient infrastructure consisting of highway, air, and sea ports; and an abundant supply of relatively cheap labor, both skilled and unskilled.

Since 2010, Japan and China have been going through an increasingly difficult phase in their bilateral relationship, due to complex factors that include the decades-long stagnation of the Japanese economy, China's overtaking of Japan as the world's second-largest economy, unsettled historical baggage, and disputes over sovereignty. This strained bilateral relationship between the two Asian giants is expected to continue, remaining unresolved for decades, or at least for the medium term.

Japanese MNCs are, thus, actively planning for production relocation from China. As part of their business risk diversification process, they plan to reestablish manufacturing value chains in the new, competitive ASEAN, which has undergone transformational changes since the 1997 Asian financial crisis.

In view of the latest geopolitical developments, coupled with the implications of the United States' return to the Asia-Pacific region to balance China, ASEAN is positioned to entice foreign direct investment from the world's major economies, including Japan, China, the United States, and the EU. It is paramount for Japanese MNCs, in particular, to identify the appropriate investment destinations, regional headquarters, and manufacturing capabilities and capacities within ASEAN.

Overcoming Financing Bottlenecks: The AIIB

APEC should promote regional connectivity on three fronts. Infrastructure, financing, and human development are three bottlenecks that the APEC community currently face. Failing in any of these areas would risk the emergence of wider pockets of permanent economic underclasses, notwithstanding the great progress APEC has achieved in terms of globalization in trade and investment.

Both physical and soft infrastructure connectivity are, therefore, vital for improving connectivity, economic linkages, and social inclusivity within APEC economies. Physical connectivity should be comprehensive across the region, especially for connectivity over air, sea, and land. Connectivity of institutions in terms of good public governance, transparency, and the rule of law would lead to closer cooperation between governments. It would also serve to encourage private sector collaboration, which is crucial for enhancing economic efficiency. Connectivity among people could be promoted through social inclusivity, with the most critical needs being more equitable distribution of income, affordable public healthcare, housing, education, and transportation.

The thrust of the East Asian model for economic development is essentially infrastructure connectivity, which serves to relieve production bottlenecks and incorporate longer-term targets. The experience and success of East Asian economic development have shown that releasing production bottlenecks through investing in a comprehensively planned infrastructure program is a major prerequisite for economic takeoff, and a useful vehicle for sailing through the middle-income trap.

Due to the relatively massive capital required, the long gestation period, and the longer-term nature of returns on investment for infrastructure projects, financing costs tend to be expensive, and funding sources are often in keen competition with other funding commitments. As such, there are existing financial bottlenecks as well.

Government must play a facilitating role in harnessing and promoting infrastructure investment to ensure that regional economic and social integration is balanced, sustainable, and inclusive. Both physical and soft infrastructure provisions for greater connectivity are increasingly viewed as forms of regional public goods.

A longer-term roadmap for Asia-Pacific connectivity should be planned, and stronger economies that have comparative advantages in terms of capital, technology, and competitive skills should play an active role in meeting the pressing infrastructure bottlenecks causing growth inertia and imbalanced regional development.

President Xi Jinping proposed at the 2013 APEC Leaders' Meeting in Bali that an AIIB be established, which is an excellent idea and a proactive move that should be welcomed. In his proposal, it was stated that the AIIB initiative aims to promote interconnectivity and economic integration in the region, including—though not confined to—the ASEAN region. Therefore, it is paramount to cooperate with existing multilateral development banks (MDBs) to make full use of their advantages and to jointly promote the sustained and stable growth of Asia (Tan 2013).

The scale of infrastructure investment needs in Asia is enormous, as well as long overdue. Slow and uneven regional economic recovery adds pressure on fiscal budgets. In 2012, the total official development assistance package was about US$125 billion. Existing funds are insufficient for the region's needs. The ASEAN Infrastructure Fund (AIF) stands at US$485 million, yet according to a 2009 study by the ADB, infrastructure requirements in Asia for the period 2010 to 2020 amount to US$8 trillion! (Table 4) A lack of bankable projects is the main bottleneck. Based on anecdotal estimates from industry players and data from Project Finance International, the estimated share of bankable projects and infrastructure needs for the period 2010–2020 is shown in Figure 2.

The prime minister of Singapore, Lee Hsien Loong, commented at the China-ASEAN Summit of October 9, 2013, that Singapore

TABLE 4 *Infrastructure Needs for Asia and ASEAN Economies**

	Total	Non-bankable	Marginally bankable	Bankable
Asia	trillion^	~ 4–5 trillion	~ 2–4 trillion	~ 1 trillion
ASEAN ex Singapore	trillion^	–600bn	–450bn	–100bn
Selected ASEAN economies*	billion*	–350bn	–300bn	–60bn

Note: *Economies included are Indonesia, the Philippines, Thailand, and Vietnam. ^ Estimates by Asian Development Bank.

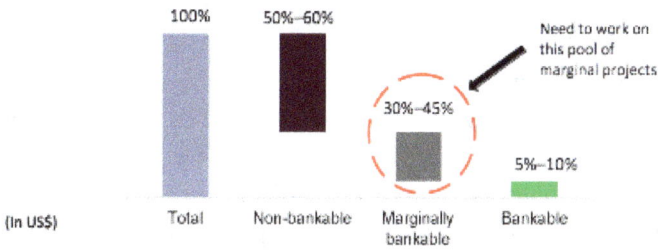

FIGURE 2 *Shares of Bankable and Non-bankable Projects for Infrastructure Needs*

welcomes the proposal to establish the AIIB. Given the enormity of infrastructure investment needs in Asia over the next decade and beyond, the World Bank, the ADB, and the newly established AIF are working with Asian economies to meet these needs. However, in view of the pressing need to resolve production and financing bottlenecks, regional governments could do more, and the AIIB can help to complement these organizations.

It would be ideal if the AIIB has an inclusive membership, covering member economies of ASEAN and enabling non-ASEAN economies to join as well. The right profile of members and major investors would ensure a strong credit rating for the new institution. An inclusive membership would also encourage participation of private sector funds. Singapore is open to participating in the AIIB, in the same way it participates in the ADB and AIF, and looks forward to studying the details in partnership with ASEAN members.

For investing in bankable projects, the ability to attract private sector investments over time is paramount. Bankable projects could be assessed on (1) macroeconomic, legal, and regulatory contexts; (2) technical and environmental viability; (3) economic and financial viability; (4) project implementation and management capacity; and (5) overall risk profile. The AIIB can facilitate improvements to the regional legal and regulatory environment. With the World Bank and the ADB already active in disbursing development grants, focusing on bankable infrastructure projects is an area where the AIIB can play a complementary and differentiated role (Tan, Tang, and Yao 2014).

The AIIB can catalyze private sector participation by lowering the risk of participation. For example, the AIIB can invest in mezzanine debt tranches or provide credit guarantees for project bonds, among other strategies. The private sector should be invited to participate in financial/technical advisory and structuring work. The AIIB could co-invest in projects directly with the private sector. The European Investment Bank (EIB), for example, only finances up to 50 percent of total project costs, leveraging its capital with funding from private sector financial institutions. AIIB capital could be leveraged by raising bonds purchased by the private sector. The AIIB could issue bonds for its own financing after it has established a successful track record.

In addition, infrastructure initiatives could be complemented by forming cooperative institutional and operational links with other multilateral development banks (MDBs). An existing network of MDBs already cooperate by exchanging information on their respective priorities and action plans, joint project appraisal missions, and co-financing projects. The AIIB can structure its involvement in particular projects jointly with other MDBs. For example, the AIIB can provide loans, while the other MDBs provide grants. In the future, the AIIB can also complement the roles of some existing regional initiatives, such as the AIF.

CONCLUSIONS

The economic impact and influence of the United States, the EU, and Japan in ASEAN economies have been overshadowed by China's rapid economic involvement since the 1980s, and have declined steeply in the new millennium. Lee Kuan Yew, the founding father of Singapore, was the first to call for economic repositioning of the United States in Asia, and in ASEAN in particular. Strategically it makes sense for ASEAN to discourage dominance by any economic heavyweight. Hence, the return of the United States, hopefully followed by the recovery of the EU and the production relocation of Japanese MNCs to ASEAN, would serve to revitalise ASEAN, which is different from containing China (Tan, Yuan, Yoong, and Yang 2013; Tan, Yoong, and Yuan 2014).

ASEAN should manage US participation in the Asian regional economic grouping. As of now, the United States is still an important engine of growth for all the Asian economies, except for Chinese Taipei and Hong Kong. The active participation of the United States—in APEC, in the East Asia Summit, and in its TPP leadership role—are critical for ensuring the ongoing engagement of this major engine of growth in Asia.

It is important for ASEAN to balance its economic interests not just with China and the United States, but also with the EU and Japan. The Asia Competitiveness Institute (ACI) has identified several new developments impacting China's position as the factory of the world: costs in China are rising, multinational corporations are considering relocations from China to ASEAN, and Chinese markets have become more accessible. The ACI feels that the window of opportunity for ASEAN is about five years. Indonesia, Malaysia, and Thailand are in good positions to capitalize on this latest development, while Singapore could serve as a regional financial center and logistic-transportation hub to service the emerging, buoyant regional trade and investments (Tan, Low, Tan, and Lim 2013; Tan and Tan 2014).

The proposed AIIB is another institution that can reinforce ASEAN's key role in the region. Asia is moving into an era of unprecedented urbanization, and there is now much interest in developing livable townships and cities. The AIIB could quickly demonstrate its ability to implement successful projects, tapping into both China's and Singapore's relevant experiences in developing comprehensive urban solutions. To support the development of the AIIB, the Pacific Economic Cooperation Council (PECC) should form a task force to conduct comparative studies of other MDBs and infrastructure funds, focusing on governance, structure of investments, and best practices that the AIIB might adopt. It is time to study the most effective approaches that the AIIB might use to tap into private sector monies and achieve a positive credit standing (Tang et al. 2014).

REFERENCES

Lim Hng Kiang. 2014. Opening Speech by Singapore's minister for trade and industry at the 2014 Pacific Economic Cooperation Council (PECC) Conference on New Priorities of Regional Economic Integration-Mandate for APEC, February 10, 2014, Singapore.

Stiglitz, Joseph E. 2002. *Globalization and Its Discontents*. New York City: W. W. Norton & Company.

Stiglitz, Joseph E. 2006. *Making Globalization Work*. New York City: W. W. Norton & Company.

Tan Khee Giap. 2013. "Infrastructure Connectivity: Urgent Needs and Long Term Targets." Presentation prepared for the APEC 2014 Symposium: Opportunities and Priorities, organized by APEC China 2014, December 9, 2013, Beijing.

Tan Khee Giap and Tan Kong Yam. 2014. "Assessing Competitiveness of ASEAN-10 Economies." *International Journal of Economics and Business Research*, United Kingdom.

Tan Khee Giap and Vittal Kartik Rao. 2014. "Sub-National Competitiveness Analysis and Simulation Studies for 35 States and Union Territories of India." *International Journal of Indian Culture and Business Management*, United Kingdom.

Tan Khee Giap, Linda Low, and Kartik Rao. 2013. *Annual Analysis of Competitiveness, Simulation Studies and Development Perspective for 35 States and Federal Territories of India: 2000–2010*. Singapore: World Scientific Publishing Co.

Tan Khee Giap, Linda Low, Tan Kong Yam, and Lim Amanda. 2013. *Annual Analysis of Competitiveness, Development Strategies and Public Policies on ASEAN-10: 2000–2010*. Singapore: Pearson Education South Asia.

Tan Khee Giap, Mulya Amri, Linda Low, and Tan Kong Yam. 2013.

Competitiveness Analysis and Development Strategies for 33 Indonesian Provinces. Singapore: World Scientific Publishing Co.

Tan Khee Giap, Tang Zhou Yan, and Yao Dong Fang. 2014. "A Case Study on Shandong-ASEAN Infrastructure Connectivity." Asia Competitiveness Institute Policy Discussion Paper, Lee Kuan Yew School of Public Policy, National University of Singapore.

Tan Kong Yam, Tilak Abeysinghe, Tan Khee Giap, and Ruby Toh. 2014. "Shifting Drivers of Growth: Policy Implications for ASEAN-5." *Asian Economic Papers*, MIT Press.

Tan Khee Giap, Yoong Sangiita Wei Cher, and Yuan Randong. 2014. "Assessing Competitiveness and Development Strategies in 34 Greater China Economies." *International Journal of Chinese Culture and Business Management*, United Kingdom.

Tan Khee Giap, Yuan Randong, Yoong Sangiita Wei Cher, and Yang Mu. 2013. *Annual Analysis of Competitiveness Simulation and Development Perspective for 34 Greater China Economies*. Singapore: World Scientific Publishing Co.

Tang Guoqiang, Ian Buchanan, and Tan Khee Giap. 2014. "An Asian Infrastructure Investment Bank—the Design Agenda—Joint Recommendations by AUSPECC, CNCPEC, and SINCPEC." Paper presented at the 2014 PECC-SINCPEC-CNCPEC Conference on New Priorities of Regional Economic Integration—Mandate for APEC, February 10–11, 2014, Singapore.

18

APEC's Role in Promoting Asia-Pacific Regional Economic Integration

Liu Chenyang, Director and Professor of APEC Study Center of China, Nankai University

The Asia-Pacific region, which approximately accounts for 40 percent of the world's population, 55 percent of world GDP, and 44 percent of world trade, has been playing an important role in the development of the world economy and international trade in recent years. The process of Asia-Pacific regional economic integration (REI), therefore, will further promote economic development and create greater prosperity not only for the region, but also the world.

As one of the world's largest regional economic cooperation entities, APEC contributes significantly in promoting the economic development, equitable growth, and shared prosperity of the Asia-Pacific region, thus manifesting itself as a highly effective mechanism to strengthen the Asia-Pacific REI process. The year 2014 marks the twenty-fifth anniversary of APEC. It means APEC is no longer a teenager, but an energetic young person who should make a new "career plan." With the changing international and regional environment, APEC is called upon to play a more active role in promoting the future process of Asia-Pacific REI.

A REVIEW OF APEC'S CONTRIBUTION TO THE PROCESS OF ASIA-PACIFIC REI

The adoption of the Bogor Goals in 1994 built a lighthouse for APEC's process of trade and investment liberalization and accelerated the voyage of Asia-Pacific REI. Through the launching of the Osaka Action Agenda in 1995, APEC set out the road map to achieve the Bogor Goals with the adoption of individual action plan (IAP) and collective action plan (CAP) mechanisms.

Meanwhile, several key factors have been taken into consideration by APEC in choosing the ways of promoting Asia-Pacific REI, including the complex regional geopolitical structure, the diversity of APEC members' economic development levels, and their aims to participate in regional cooperation. As a result, a unique APEC approach was created. While recognizing the diversity of APEC member economies, it reflects the concepts of voluntarism, consensus, openness, and inclusiveness. The APEC approach has proven to be adaptable to the development of APEC, and it has played a key role in keeping the momentum of Asia-Pacific REI.

During the past two decades, APEC has pursued its many visions with the Bogor Goals at the heart.[1] The markets of APEC member economies became more and more open, demonstrated by the significant reduction of trade and investment barriers, the gradual elimination of nontariff barriers, and the improvement of market transparency. Thus benefiting from the improvement of the business environment, a vibrant regional market for services has emerged. The APEC region has also become much more open to foreign direct investment (FDI).

Achievements have also been made in the area of trade and investment facilitation, and the implementation of the Trade Facilitation Action Plan (TFAP) has successfully reduced the costs of trading. Effective cooperation has been carried out to promote paperless trading, transparency, business mobility, alignment of standards with international standards, improved competition, and anti-corruption policies and regulatory reform.

Furthermore, the development of APEC's ECOTECH process has set up priorities for the economic and technical cooperation in the Asia-Pacific region, and has encouraged the developed and developing APEC member economies to participate in capacity building and technology assistance in a strategic way. Human resource development cooperation and related capacity-building activities have also played an important role in narrowing the economic development disparity among APEC member economies and promoting the stable economic development of the Asia-Pacific region.

APEC understands that the development of Asia-Pacific integration should be based on mutual understanding, friendship, and the sense of community among APEC member economies. In this sense, intercultural exchange is another important area in which APEC can promote the Asia-Pacific integration process. During the past two decades, APEC has made great efforts to encourage member economies with different cultural and faith backgrounds to develop social interaction and achieve mutual understanding, acceptance, and trust, which are essential to address social, legal, governance, and economic challenges and to promote a harmonious community in the region.

APEC has also been making great efforts in coordinating the development of regional trade agreements (RTAs) and free trade agreements (FTAs) in the Asia-Pacific region. To ensure that the proliferation of RTAs/FTAs does not add to the complexities of the international and regional trading environment, APEC has established best practices and model measures for RTAs/FTAs with the aim of promoting high quality, comprehensiveness, transparency, and broad consistency. They are neither mandatory nor exhaustive, but serve as a guide to the kind of provisions that might be included in a RTA/FTA, where appropriate. In addition, APEC has undertaken a range of capacity-building activities—including policy dialogues, seminars, and workshops—in order to promote broad consistency in agreements through the adoption of best practices and model measures.

INTERNAL AND EXTERNAL DRIVING FORCES FOR APEC TO FURTHER PROMOTE ASIA-PACIFIC REI

These achievements clearly demonstrate that APEC has played an active and supportive role in promoting Asia-Pacific REI since its establishment.

APEC economies, however, have acknowledged the rapidly evolving international and regional environment in the new century, as well as the opportunities and challenges ahead. Consequently, there are both internal and external forces driving APEC to play a more active role in further promoting Asia-Pacific REI.

First, APEC is expected to push for a healthy recovery of the sluggish world economy. Now, the world economy is on the whole moving forward in a positive direction, yet uncertainties and destabilizing factors have remained prominent. The structural problems of major developed economies are far from being resolved, and it has become more imperative to enhance macroeconomic policy coordination. With growing external risks and pressure, some emerging economies in the Asia-Pacific region are experiencing a slowing of economic growth. As well, trade and investment protectionism has resurfaced. Obviously, the world economy faces daunting challenges before achieving full recovery and sound growth. During the past three decades, the energetic Asia-Pacific economy has been an important engine of world economic growth. APEC, which is entrusted with the important mission to promote regional and global growth, must face the challenges head-on with courage and resolve.[2] It is undoubted that the deepening REI will pour new vigor into the Asia-Pacific economy, which will then give stronger impetus for a healthy recovery of the world economy.

Second, considering the fact that the FTAs/RTAs in this region are advancing in parallel with different rules and standards, APEC is capable of playing a more active and effective role in coordinating the development of FTAs/RTAs in the Asia-Pacific region. The rapid proliferation of FTAs/RTAs in recent years is happening amidst rapid economic growth in the Asia-Pacific region and greater interdependence among economies through trade and investment. For many economies, participation in FTAs/RTAs is not simply a second-best choice following the WTO negotiation standstill, but also an effective approach to regain or enhance their economic competitiveness. And, the influence of the "Domino Effect" has also stimulated some economies to join FTAs/RTAs as a passive corresponding activity. It should be emphasized that through participating in various Asia-Pacific economic integration mechanisms, many economies want to gain not only economic benefits, but also noneconomic benefits, such as strengthening political relations and comprehensive strategic partnerships with other economies. In this sense, an FTA or RTA is by no means just an economic agreement among the parties, but also an integral part of their overall strategy of diplomacy, security, and foreign economic relations and trade. At present, it seems that the Asia-Pacific REI process has achieved a kind of balance with a unique mutual incentive and competitive relationship among different tracks, especially the "TPP track" and the "Asian track" led by the RCEP. However, the balance is not stable but somewhat fragile. If some REI mechanisms are utilized as tools of political speculation or strategic games among regional powers, the balance will be easily broken.[3] A malignant competition among different tracks is never wanted by any economy in the region. Therefore, APEC has the responsibility to coordinate the development of FTAs/RTAs through promoting Asia-Pacific REI in a region-wide scope.

Third, APEC should strengthen its role as a strong supporter of the WTO from the plurilateral level. In fact, APEC has a tradition of leadership on WTO matters. To support the Doha Development Agenda (DDA) remains one of the top priorities of APEC in recent years. Although the future of the WTO Doha round negotiation is still uncertain, it should be emphasized that the multilateral trading regime is charged with the heavy responsibility of coordinating national trade policies, balancing international trade relations, reducing trade frictions, and promoting world economic growth, and it plays an important role in countering the effects of the international financial crisis and opposing protectionism. It should also be realized that the multilateral trade liberalization and the Asia-Pacific REI processes are complementary. The future of APEC is closely linked with a strong and energetic multilateral trading system. Likewise, a more open and liberalized international trade and investment environment will significantly promote the Asia-Pacific REI process. Therefore, it is of great significance and importance for APEC members to fulfill their commitments to firmly oppose and jointly resist protectionism of all forms, and work to make the multilateral trading regime a balanced and inclusive one that benefits all.

Fourth, APEC should further promote Asia-Pacific REI to better comply with the trend of global value chain (GVC) cooperation. In recent years, GVCs have greatly transformed international trade. To be concrete, GVCs make exports depend more and more on imports. In East Asia, for example, about 65 percent of total manufacturing exports are GVC-related. In quite a few APEC member economies, foreign value-added is about a third or even half of the total value of exports.[4] So, GVCs clearly reward open borders and nondiscrimination in trade and FDI. However, they may also trigger "systemic risk," which means that a single incident in one sector or economy will probably give rise to an obstacle or even disruption of the whole system of value chains. Both of these opposite yet interlinked scenarios intensify the necessity of APEC members to enhance GVC cooperation, which forms the internal driving force for APEC to further promote REI in the long term.

PATHWAYS FOR APEC TO FURTHER PROMOTE ASIA-PACIFIC REI

Promoting the Establishment of the FTAAP

First of all, APEC should set up a mid-term goal for the post–Bogor Goal era, which will clarify the overall direction of APEC's efforts in promoting Asia-Pacific REI in the next decade. In this regard, the establishment of a Free Trade Area of the Asia-Pacific (FTAAP) would be the most rational choice. As a matter of fact, APEC leaders have affirmed their commitment to achieve an FTAAP in several declarations during the past few years, and now it is time for APEC members to carry out their leaders' instruction. Besides, an FTAAP will be a free trade arrangement that includes all APEC member economies, and nobody would worry about membership qualifications. It should also be pointed out that an FTAAP could be realized through several approaches, such as collective negotiation, enlargement, or convergence of existing RTAs in the Asia-Pacific region, which means that it would be practical. In the short term, it is important for APEC members to embrace the principles of openness, inclusiveness, and transparency, as well as the spirit of flexibility, and to establish and launch as early as possible an information exchange mechanism for FTAs/RTAs in the Asia-Pacific region. The aim should be to improve communication and exchange of views, and to create favorable conditions for pursuing an FTAAP.

Enhancing GVC Cooperation to Foster a Big Asia-Pacific Market

With an FTAAP as an overall target, APEC should take more effective measures than before to facilitate the free flowing of goods, services, capital, and people in the region, actions that will not only deepen Asia-Pacific REI, but also significantly promote Asia-Pacific GVC cooperation. Accordingly, APEC member economies should give full play to their comparative advantages, optimize the economic resource allocation, improve the industry layout, and make joint efforts to foster a big Asia-Pacific market where benefits are shared by all. Priorities in this aspect should include, but not be limited to, enhancing trade facilitation and supply chain management, improving logistics infrastructure network construction, and facilitating cross-border movement of natural persons.

Attaching More Importance to Investment Liberalization and Facilitation

Optimizing regional industrial specialization and economic resources allocation are also of great importance for APEC if it is to achieve a high level of REI. In this aspect, FDI of transnational corporations plays a key role. Therefore, APEC should be more ambitious to promote investment liberalization. APEC could conduct a stocktaking of the achieved outcome documents on investment in recent years, such as *Non-binding Investment Principles* and *APEC Investment Facilitation Action Plan*, and use them to strengthen enforcement procedures. Effective measures could be taken to enhance capacity building of member economies to reduce investment barriers, especially behind-the-border barriers. Meanwhile, it is recommended that APEC attach more importance to investment facilitation, which is less sensitive and more easily yields results and progress. APEC should also strengthen private-public cooperation through listening to the views of business about the investment climate, and by building and maintaining effective public-private dialogues.

Promoting Connectivity and Infrastructure Development Cooperation

Connectivity and infrastructure development will help to increase trade and investment opportunities in the Asia-Pacific region, improve regional production networks, and consolidate the foundation for a big Asia-Pacific single market. Cooperation in this area will improve the quality and effectiveness of Asia-Pacific REI, substantially strengthen the implementation efficiency of the FTAs/RTAs in the region, and help to create a transparent, stable, and efficient trade and investment environment with lower transaction costs. APEC member economies are in consensus on the importance of connectivity and infrastructure development cooperation. Their resolve could be proved by the endorsement of the APEC Framework on Connectivity and the APEC Multi Year Plan on Infrastructure Development and Investment, both developed at the 21st APEC Economic Leaders' Meeting held in Bali in 2013.

At present, several Asia-Pacific regional or subregional cooperation organizations have already been formulated, or have set about to formulate, and they have identified connectivity cooperation frameworks with infrastructure development as a priority. These cooperation frameworks share a certain degree of similarity in targets, mechanisms, key areas, or memberships, which lay a foundation for the development of cross-region infrastructure networks. In this regard, APEC could play an active coordinating role. For example, APEC may consider establishing an online Asia-Pacific Connectivity Cooperation Information Platform. The platform will collect and release information on the overall plans and projects of connectivity cooperation carried out under different mechanisms of the Asia-Pacific region, aiming to enhance communication and attract more stakeholders to participate.

To sum up, APEC has not only the responsibility but also the capability to make a larger contribution to the future process of Asia-Pacific REI. Guided by the principles of openness, inclusiveness, and win-win cooperation, APEC member economies should try to foster closer partnerships and make joint efforts to meet challenges and achieve sustainable development and long-term prosperity in the Asia-Pacific region.

NOTES

1. Wang Yi, "Building on Past Achievements to Make New Progress and Shaping the Future through Asia-Pacific Partnership," remarks presented

at the APEC Informal Senior Officials' Meeting, December 10, 2013, in Beijing, China.

2. Xi Jinping, "Give Full Play to the Leading Role of the Asia-Pacific Maintain and Advance an Open World Economy," address at APEC Economic Leaders' Meeting (Session I), October 8, 2013, in Bali, Indonesia.

3. Liu Chenyang, "New Trend of Asia-Pacific Economic Integration," paper presented at the CNCPEC Seminar on TPP 2012 Progress and Challenges, December 7, 2012, in Beijing, China.

4. Razeen Sally, "Global Value Chains, Trade Policy and Asia." *East Asia Forum*, June 13, 2013, http://www.eastasiaforum.org/2013/06/13/global-value-chains-trade-policy-and-asia/.

Toward Converging Frameworks

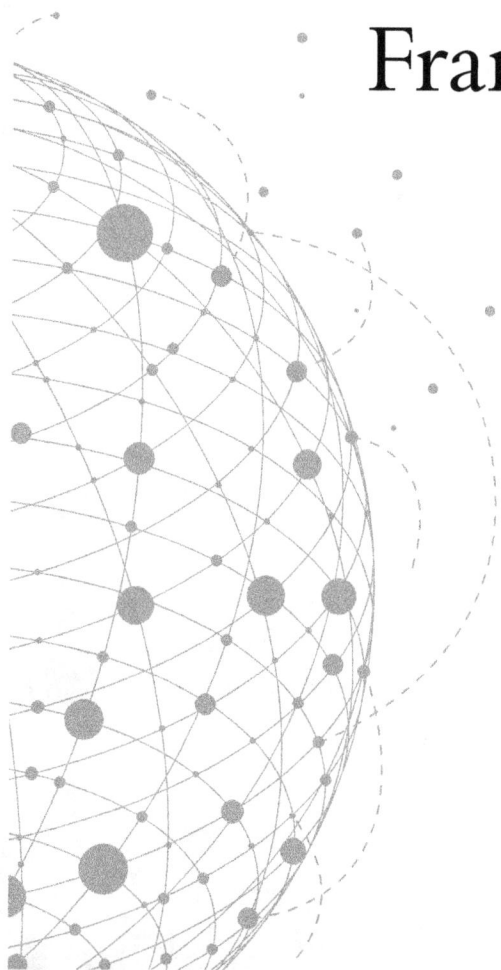

19

The TPP and RCEP

Prospects for Convergence

Robert Scollay, Director, New Zealand APEC Study Centre

In 2010, APEC leaders envisioned a process where the Free Trade Area
of the Asia-Pacific (FTAAP) would evolve from two parallel tracks. These
tracks were subsequently labeled the "trans-Pacific track," represented by
the Trans-Pacific Partnership (TPP), and an "East Asian track" (Petri,
Plummer, and Zhai 2012). At the time, the leaders had in mind that
the East Asian track would be defined by the ASEAN-Plus-Three and
ASEAN-Plus-Six processes. Today, however, the Regional Comprehensive Economic Partnership (RCEP) has been clearly established
as the most qualified process for leading the East Asian track, even if
some RCEP participants may not yet accept that it is playing such a
significant role.

An expectation that the FTAAP will evolve from the trans-Pacific
and East Asian tracks naturally implies that the two tracks will converge
at some point, although no process for such a convergence has yet been
mapped out, even in outline form, and no indication has been provided
by the leaders about how they envisaged that convergence might occur.
The purpose of this paper is to identify and consider some issues that
may influence how, when, and even if convergence might be achieved.

The paper begins by briefly summarizing the key developments that
have been reached in the TPP and RCEP negotiations, including some

comparison of the nature of the two negotiating processes and the anticipated eventual agreements as defined by the participants. It goes on to discuss the convergence challenges, which can be grouped into three areas: membership issues, issue coverage, and the level of ambition.

COMPARING PROGRESS TO DATE

The TPP evolved from the earlier Trans-Pacific Strategic Economic Partnership (TPSEP). Negotiations for the TPP began in early 2010, and by the end of 2013 there had been 19 negotiating rounds, as well as various intersessional meetings of negotiating groups and ministers. During the course of the negotiations, the number of participants gradually increased to the current 12 APEC economies. At least two additional APEC economies are pressing for admission to the TPP, and at least two non-APEC members have indicated an interest in joining when the opportunity arises. There have been reports since at least mid-2013 that a substantial number of the agreement's chapters have been finalized or are nearing finalization. On the other hand, it is clear that the most difficult and sensitive issues still remain to be agreed. An expectation was created in some quarters that the full agreement might be finalized by the end of 2013, although in retrospect it is clear that this expectation was never realistic. The question of whether the TPP can be concluded by the end of 2014 has become entangled with the question of whether the United States Congress will grant President Obama trade promotion authority (TPA), or "fast track," prior to the mid-term congressional elections in November 2014.

Negotiations for the RCEP commenced in May 2013. The RCEP was presented as a way to avoid choosing between the ASEAN-Plus-Three and ASEAN-Plus-Six as the basis for an East Asian regional trade agreement. In practice, however, participation in the RCEP is the same as the ASEAN-Plus-Six group: the 10 ASEAN members, plus China, Japan, South Korea, India, Australia, and New Zealand. Four negotiating rounds have now been held, and a ministerial meeting to be held in mid-2014 is expected to give further direction regarding the scope of the agreement and the level of ambition to be pursued. The stated intention of the participants is to conclude the agreement by the end of 2015, although this target is widely viewed as over-optimistic.

Figure 1 provides a schematic representation of the current state of participation in the TPP, the RCEP, and potentially in the FTAAP. Seven APEC members are participating in both the TPP and the RCEP. All 12 current participants in the TPP are APEC members. The Pacific Alliance is a trade agreement among four (soon to be five) Latin American economies on the Pacific seaboard that consolidates existing trade agreements among its members, and is intended to serve, among other things, as a vehicle for further integration with the Asia-Pacific region. The alliance includes a non-APEC member, Colombia, and is negotiating accession with another non-APEC acceding member, Costa Rica. Both have made clear their desire to participate in the TPP, as well as the FTAAP at some future date. Twelve of the 16 RCEP participants are APEC members. Of the remainder, Cambodia, Laos, and Myanmar are the three least-developed ASEAN members that are not APEC members, and India has never been a member of APEC. Four APEC members, Chinese Taipei, Hong Kong, Russia, and Papua New Guinea are not participating in either the TPP or the RCEP, although Chinese Taipei has made clear its desire to participate in the TPP.

TPP participants have repeatedly emphasized their intention to craft a "high-standard, twenty-first century" agreement, with a broad agenda covering the full range of important issues surrounding modern international trade regulations, and with commitments and rules that reflect this high level of ambition. There are over 20 negotiating groups working on some 29 chapters, and the agreement is being explicitly negotiated as a "single undertaking."

The Guiding Principles and Objectives for Negotiating the RCEP (ASEAN 2012) emphasize flexibility, including (but not limited to) the provision of special and differential treatment for members at lower levels of development, as well as recognition of "the individual and diverse circumstances of the participating economies." The RCEP agenda is to include "trade in goods, trade in services, investment, economic and technical cooperation, intellectual property, competition, dispute settlement, and other issues." The negotiating modality is left open. The RCEP's Guiding Principles and Objectives state that "negotiations on

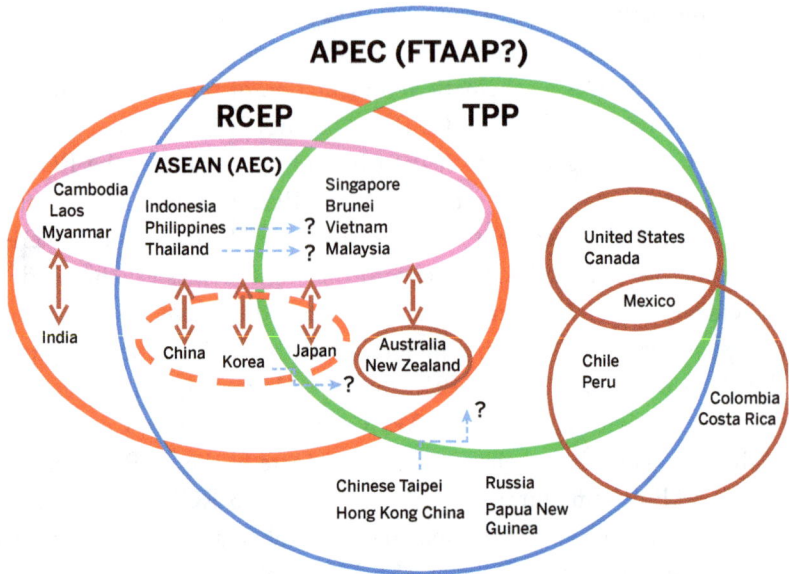

FIGURE 1 *Current Configurations of Regional Integration Initiatives*

trade in goods, trade in services, investment, and other areas will be conducted in parallel to ensure a comprehensive and balanced outcome," while the framework (ASEAN 2011) endorsed by ASEAN leaders states that the "agreement can be accomplished in a sequential manner, or single undertaking, or through any other agreed modality."

THE TPP AND THE RCEP—CONVERGENCE ISSUES

Membership Issues

There are clearly membership issues that will need to be resolved if the TPP and the RCEP are to converge into the FTAAP. For the time being, TPP participation is restricted to APEC members. It is difficult to imagine ASEAN supporting the FTAAP unless participation is open to all ASEAN members. This would imply the need for decisions to be made on whether potential future FTAAP participants, including the current non-APEC members of the RCEP and possibly Colombia and

Costa Rica, should first be admitted to APEC before being eligible for inclusion in the FTAAP. At this point in time, the position of India looms as potentially the most problematic of these issues. The RCEP's Guiding Principles and Objectives state that once it has been concluded, the RCEP will be open to accession by other "economic partners." Accessions to the RCEP by non-APEC members could further complicate APEC and FTAAP membership issues, especially if these issues have not been resolved beforehand.

Issue Coverage

Table 1 highlights the overlapping elements in the stated agendas of the RCEP and the TPP, as well as those issues that are on the TPP agenda but not on the stated agenda of the RCEP. Rules of origin and the trade facilitation issues of customs, sanitary and phytosanitary measures (SPS), and technical barriers to trade (TBT) do not appear as agenda items in the RCEP's Guiding Principles and Objectives. However, commentary from RCEP negotiators indicates that these issues, and possibly also trade remedies, will be covered under the heading of "market access for goods." In addition, telecommunications and financial services will be covered within the RCEP's services agenda (Ministry of Trade of Indonesia 2014). It is easy to envisage that temporary entry may also be covered in the RCEP within the services agenda, and textiles and apparel within the market access for goods agenda. Given the long-standing emphasis in East Asian trade policy discussions on supply chain facilitation, it is also difficult to imagine that supply chain facilitation will not be covered in some form in the RCEP agenda, even if it doesn't receive a separate chapter. Issues related to small- and medium-sized enterprises (SME) are also likely to be addressed in some form.

Government procurement and e-commerce could be viewed as natural future extensions of the RCEP's existing agenda, which will evolve to include other issues as they arise. Regulatory coherence is a "new generation" issue in the TPP agenda, one whose content and scope have yet to be clearly defined. It is likely, though, that the substantive content will overlap with concerns being addressed within the ASEAN Economic Community (AEC) initiative, and should consequently be amenable to inclusion in the RCEP agenda. The issue of state-owned enterprises

TABLE I *TPP and RCEP—Common and Differentiated Agendas*

Common Elements	TPP Only
Market Access for Goods	Government Procurement
Rules of Origin	SOEs
Trade Facilitation?	• Unless included in RCEP under
• Customs	Competition
• SPS	E-Commerce
• TBT	Environment
Services	Labor
Investment	Trade Remedies
Competition	Textiles and Apparel
Intellectual Property	Temporary Entry
Economic and Technical Cooperation	Horizontal Issues
• Development also a horizontal issue	• SMEs
in TPP	• Supply Chain Facilitation
Dispute Settlement	• Regulatory Coherence
"Other Issues" (RCEP)	Separate Chapters in TPP
	• Telecommunications
	• Financial Services

Sources: Office of the US Trade Representative (2011); ASEAN (2012).

(SOEs) is one of the most controversial in the TPP, and it is not yet clear how the issue will be treated in the final agreement. If the TPP adopts an approach to SOEs that focuses on competition-based principles, it could open the way to exploring potential convergences with the RCEP's competition section. Conversely, the TPP might adopt approaches to SOEs that are far less amenable to convergence with the RCEP.

The TPP agenda issues that most clearly lack counterparts or potential counterparts in the RCEP agenda are environment and labor. These issues are contentious within the TPP, with unofficial comments suggesting that preferences among members fall along a spectrum. At one end is the preference for legally enforceable measures, and at the other is the preference for unenforceable expressions of commitment to agreed common principles. Eventual TPP provisions may be very difficult for some RCEP participants to accept if they lie at the former end of the spectrum (legally enforceable measures), but much easier to accept if they lie at the latter end (unenforceable commitments).

Any feasible "middle ground" solution in the TPP is likely to include provisions requiring some degree of scrutiny of member policies in these areas, and the degree of acceptability of these provisions to all RCEP participants may well depend on the specific content.

Differences in agenda coverage between the TPP and the RCEP may prove to be less daunting challenges to convergence than might be suggested by an initial glance at each agenda's list of issues. Much will depend on the approach finally adopted in the TPP to developing provisions on some of the most controversial and innovative issues on its agenda.

Differences in Level of Ambition

From what is known to date—or can be deduced or inferred—about the agendas of the two initiatives, the differences in level of ambition between the TPP and the RCEP, rather than differences in coverage, are likely to be the biggest obstacle to convergence.

In the case of market access for goods, initial rhetoric surrounding the TPP suggested an intention to achieve 100 percent elimination of tariffs. Information emerging from the negotiations, however, strongly suggests that this objective will not be achieved, with some participants poised to insist on, and likely to receive, traditional "carve-outs." This would be a serious blow to the market-access ambitions of some other participants. At the same time, there is no indication that the level of tariff elimination eventually achieved will not be very high, perhaps as high as 98 percent of tariff lines.

There is no official RCEP target for the level of tariff elimination to be achieved. Based on the Economic Research Institute for ASEAN and East Asia (ERIA)'s comprehensive mapping of FTAs in the region (Lee and Okabe 2011), Fukunaga and Kuno (2012) recommend an elimination target of 95 percent on tariff lines, while pointing out that this will be challenging for some RCEP participants. Achievement of this target, however, could be a significant step toward convergence of the TPP and the RCEP into an eventual FTAAP. To an impartial observer, a gap of 3 percent in tariff elimination coverage—the gap between 98 percent and 95 percent—should not be impossible to bridge over time. Furthermore, for some economies that are participating in both the TPP and the RCEP, the remaining tariffs are likely to include traditional "carve outs."

In a comparison between the TPP and RCEP approaches to all aspects of market access, the TPP does not necessarily always emerge favorably, especially if facilitating regional economic integration is the primary criterion. In two areas, rules of origin and scheduling of commitments, the RCEP has the potential to deliver superior outcomes.

Rules of origin that facilitate comprehensive regional economic integration need to incorporate provisions for full cumulation, mandate coequality between regional value content (RVC) and change in tariff classification (CTH) rules, and develop efficient operational certification procedures (OCPs) that facilitate trade. Information emanating from the TPP negotiations suggests that the TPP rules are unlikely to meet these criteria. On the other hand, the ASEAN-Plus FTAs from which the RCEP is evolving have already experimented with rules of this kind. As Medalla (2011) points out, further steps within the RCEP to achieve harmonized rules based on these criteria will be both technically and politically challenging, but not impossible, and they would make significant contributions to regional integration.

Trade agreements that are fully supportive of regional economic integration need to incorporate common schedules of commitments from all members. Information from the TPP negotiations again suggests that the TPP approach to scheduling commitments is unlikely to meet this test. On the other hand, the RCEP still has the opportunity to agree on this approach, and it is hoped that the opportunity will be grasped.

In the case of services trade, the TPP has adopted the "negative list" approach. Difficulties for convergence will be created if the RCEP adopts the General Agreement on Trade in Services (GATS)–based approach that the ASEAN-Plus-One FTAs follow. In their summary of analysis from the ERIA mapping project, Ishido and Fukunaga (2012) also highlight the very low level of liberalization achieved in those FTAs, which often provide little advancement on GATS commitments.

On investment, there is insufficient information on the agendas or possible outcomes in the TPP and the RCEP to enable reliable comparisons to be made. One investment issue, however, that has been extremely contentious in the TPP, and is potentially equally contentious in any future convergence process, is investor-state dispute settlement (ISDS). Opposition to ISDS derives in part from legitimate concerns over the outcomes of ISDS proceedings in the past, but the case can also be made that such outcomes can be avoided if the ISDS provisions are drawn with sufficient care. In the interests of future convergence with the RCEP, the TPP negotiators need to ensure that the TPP provisions on ISDS take these concerns fully into account.

Intellectual property (IP) has been one of the most contentious issues— if not *the* most contentious issue—in the TPP, as evidenced by the draft text of the TPP intellectual property chapter leaked in late 2013. The chapter was extensively annotated with large sections of text in square brackets, indicating wide areas of disagreement. Conflicting opinions on intellectual property may well make it one of the most difficult issues to resolve in any convergence process. This is partly because of the far-reaching nature and high-level ambition of the TPP proposals, but also because the TPP negotiations, like some others concerning IP, suffer from the lack of a sound analytical framework. Proposals are often based on the premise that more IP protection is always better, a premise drawn perhaps by analogy from the analytical foundation for trade liberalization. In the case of IP, however, welfare-maximizing outcomes are achieved by optimizing rather than maximizing the level of protection. If the level of protection falls short of the optimum, society is deprived of innovation and creative output that it would be willing to pay for, and welfare is sacrificed. But welfare is also sacrificed if IP protection exceeds the optimum. This is because the value of additional innovation is outweighed by the costs to society, in the form of excessive monopoly rents and limitations on the flow of information and ideas. If they wish to avoid creating unnecessary barriers to convergence between the TPP and the RCEP, TPP negotiators should focus on optimizing levels of IP protection, rather than on simply maximizing them.

CONCLUSIONS

Differences not only in levels of ambition, but also in the nature of those ambitions, loom as potentially the largest obstacles to convergence between the TPP and the RCEP. In a number of areas, convergence is likely to require the RCEP participants to raise their level of ambition to be comparable with that of the TPP. An important question is whether this will be posed as a prerequisite for considering convergence, or whether agreement may be reached on a convergence process that involves phasing of alignment in levels of ambition over agreed periods of time, accompanied by appropriate provisions for capacity-building assistance. But the TPP participants may need to show flexibility in other ways as well. First, they should be prepared to consider RCEP approaches that turn out to be demonstrably superior as instruments for promoting regional economic integration, which may be the case with rules of origin and scheduling of commitments. Second, they should avoid locking in provisions that are unlikely to win acceptance in the overall regulatory architecture for Asia-Pacific regional economic integration, whether because the approaches are conceptually flawed as instruments for maximizing economic welfare in the region, or because they raise insuperable political obstacles for some of the region's economies.

SOURCES

Association of Southeast Asian Nations. 2011. "ASEAN Framework for Regional Comprehensive Economic Partnership."

Association of Southeast Asian Nations. 2012. "Guiding Principles and Objectives for Negotiating the Regional Comprehensive Economic Partnership," August.

Fukunaga, Yoshifumi, and Arata Kuno. 2012. "Toward a Consolidated Preferential Tariff Structure in East Asia: Going Beyond ASEAN+1 FTAs." Economic Research Institute for ASEAN and East Asia, ERIA Policy Brief No. 2012–03, May.

Ishido, Hikari, and Yoshifumi Fukunaga. 2012. "Liberalization of Trade in Services: Toward a Harmonized ASEAN++ FTA." Economic Research Institute for ASEAN and East Asia, ERIA Policy Brief No. 2012–02, March.

Lee, Chang Jae, and Misa Okabe, eds. 2011. *Comprehensive Mapping of FTAs in ASEAN and East Asia*. Economic Research Institute for ASEAN and East Asia, ERIA Research Project Report 2010–26, March, Jakarta.

Medalla, Erlinda. 2011. "Taking Stock of the ROOs in the ASEAN + 1 FTAs." In *Comprehensive Mapping of FTAs in ASEAN and East Asia*, edited by C.J. Lee and M. Okabe. ERIA Research Project Report 2010–26, March, Jakarta.

Ministry of Trade of Indonesia. 2014. "A Perspective on Regional Comprehensive Economic Partnership." Presentation at the APEC Dialogue on Information Sharing on Regional Trade Agreements and Free Trade Agreements in the Asia-Pacific Region, Qingdao, China, May 8.

Office of the US Trade Representative. 2011. "Outlines of the Trans-Pacific Partnership Agreement."

Petri, Peter A., Michael G. Plummer, and Fan Zhai. 2012. *The Trans-Pacific Partnership and Asia-Pacific Integration: A Quantitative Assessment*. Policy Analysis in International Economics No. 98. Washington, DC: Peterson Institute for International Economics and East-West Center.

20

Asia-Pacific Economic Integration

Projecting the Path Forward[1]

Jeffrey J. Schott, Senior Fellow, Peterson Institute for International Economics

INTRODUCTION

Almost two decades ago, the leaders attending the Asia-Pacific Economic Cooperation (APEC) Summit in Bogor, Indonesia, agreed to achieve free trade and investment in the region by 2010 for developed economies and 2020 for developing economies. The deadlines for those ambitious ventures might have seemed distant to the APEC leaders in November 1994, but the first marker has already long past and the second is fast approaching.

APEC gets a grade of "A" for its vision of regional economic integration and an "incomplete" for its execution. Nonetheless, progress toward an Asia-Pacific free trade region over this period has been notable, even though much of it has taken place outside the scope of APEC deliberations. The network of bilateral and regional free trade agreements (FTAs) in the Asia-Pacific region has expanded dramatically over the past decade, interconnecting almost every major trading nation in the region, with one notable exception: neither the United States nor China has pursued an FTA initiative involving the other. Most APEC economies now participate in a variety of integration arrangements, and all are committed to the long-run APEC goal of creating a Free Trade Area of the Asia-Pacific, or FTAAP.

That said, the pathway toward economic integration in the Asia-Pacific region is still uncertain. Several options for crafting the FTAAP are under review. As a practical matter, the two mega-regional integration arrangements in the APEC region—the Trans-Pacific Partnership (TPP) and the Regional Comprehensive Economic Partnership (RCEP)—will substantially inform the APEC debate. [2] This short chapter assesses the prospects for achieving an FTAAP via the mega-regional pathways.

THE MEGA-REGIONAL PATHWAYS: MERGING OR CONVERGING?

The TPP and RCEP initiatives cover a large number of economies that cumulatively account for a substantial share of world output and exports (see Table 1). Both involve more than half of the APEC membership, and a growing number of economies are participating in both the TPP and RCEP negotiations. Both have ambitious agendas to dismantle barriers to trade and investment in goods and services.

To date, APEC discussions about potential pathways toward an FTAAP have looked at each mega-regional. At first blush, similar negotiating agendas and overlapping membership of the TPP and the RCEP seem to suggest that an FTAAP could be crafted from the convergence of the two. However, merging these arrangements into a common FTAAP would be difficult, for two reasons.

First, the mega-regionals have different time horizons for completion of the negotiations. The TPP talks are likely to conclude in 2014, while the RCEP talks still are in the early stages of a multi-year negotiation. Accommodating the least-developed economies in the Association of Southeast Asian Nations (ASEAN), and avoiding delays provoked by current foot-draggers, like India, to trade liberalization will be stiff tests for the RCEP negotiations, and will likely result in the talks extending

TABLE I   *TPP and RCEP: Overlapping Membership*

	TPP	RCEP	In both TPP-12 + RCEP	In both TPP-16 + RCEP	In both TPP-17 + RCEP
Number of economies	12	16	7	11	12
Aggregate share of world GDP (%)	38	29	12	15	27
Aggregate share of world exports (%)	24	30	10	16	28

TPP = Trans-Pacific Partnership; RCEP = Regional Comprehensive Economic Partnership
Notes: A TPP-16 scenario would include Korea, Indonesia, the Philippines, and Thailand.
A TPP-17 scenario would include China.
Sources: IMF WEO database and IMF Direction of Trade Statistics, 2013.

well beyond the targeted completion date of late 2015.

Second, and more problematic, is that the TPP deal is likely to be much more substantial in terms of the depth of prospective trade liberalization and the scope of rule-making obligations than the RCEP. The TPP aims to develop a twenty-first century rulebook for trade that goes beyond current WTO obligations in important areas, such as labor and environment, intellectual property, investment and competition policy, and disciplines on state-owned enterprises, with enforcement of most obligations covered by binding dispute settlement procedures similar to those in the Korea-US (KORUS) FTA.[3] Though the RCEP also aims to expand the liberalization commitments contained in existing FTAs between ASEAN and its six bilateral partners, it has less lofty ambitions regarding the depth and scope of reforms, far more exemptions for sensitive products and for broad development considerations, and more consultative rather than binding dispute resolution procedures.

Harmonization of the two mega-regionals would inevitably require a dilution of the reform commitments mandated by the TPP. Most TPP economies would regard the return on such an investment to be inadequate.

To be sure, the overlapping membership of the TPP and the RCEP will promote the convergence of the two agreements. To date, seven of the sixteen RCEP economies also are negotiating the TPP. In addition, four RCEP economies—namely Indonesia, the Philippines, South Korea, and Thailand—are already performing "due diligence" on the TPP to assess the potential benefits and domestic policy adjustments that would be required if they join in the coming years. It is thus quite possible that eleven of the sixteen RCEP economies could be engaged in the TPP before the end of this decade.

Since the TPP is expected to conclude well before the RCEP, the TPP outcome could well affect RCEP negotiations. For those economies involved in the two talks, it will be easier to implement RCEP standards if they already have committed to more comprehensive TPP obligations. From this perspective, there already seems to be a convergence of the two mega-regionals. But it is not the merging or harmonization of the TPP and the RCEP that poses the biggest challenge; rather, it is a convergence toward the TPP template!

However, not all APEC economies participate in the two mega-regionals, and some non-APEC members are involved. Russia, Chinese Taipei, and Hong Kong don't participate in either initiative, and the RCEP involves four economies that are not in APEC.[4] Restrictions on participation in each mega-regional pose problems for the broader application of the pact to the entire APEC membership. The TPP is limited to APEC economies, while the RCEP is limited to ASEAN FTA partners. In practice, membership restrictions etched into these pacts will need to be overcome if the FTAAP, as broadly envisioned, is to build on these initiatives.[5]

In sum, APEC economies seem to be "voting with their feet" for the TPP pathway. Yet, as in any infrastructure project, the site preparation may need some modification to deal with specific challenges. The following sections suggest two scenarios for going forward with the construction of the FTAAP.

TPP: THE PATHWAY TO ASIA-PACIFIC ECONOMIC INTEGRATION?

From the outset, the TPP has been a dynamic initiative, evolving from an agreement of the P4 economies (Brunei, Chile, Singapore, New

Zealand) to an agreement of 12 economies, with new members added throughout the course of the talks and prospects for additional members after the deal enters into force. TPP architects envision building an eventual FTAAP on the comprehensive foundations of the TPP accord, with other APEC economies joining the pact in coming years through an accession process similar to that provided in the World Trade Organization (WTO) for new members—even though there are few precedents for such docking. TPP economies have said that the pact will be open to the accession of other APEC members; however, the procedures have still to be clarified.

As noted earlier, there already are prospective candidates for TPP expansion in a "second tranche" of negotiations once the TPP enters into force. Indonesia, the Philippines, South Korea, and Thailand are primary contenders for boosting the TPP-12 to a TPP-16. These economies have been motivated to consider joining the TPP primarily for two reasons: the perceived larger payoff from TPP reforms, and the cost of nonparticipation in terms of trade and investment diversion.

Another major trading nation carefully weighing the advantages (and disadvantages) of the TPP is, of course, China. If China asks to join the TPP, it would boost the TPP's prospective additional members to 5, potentially creating a TPP-17—one step closer to a TPP covering all 21 APEC economies.[6] While China is currently considering how the TPP could complement and reinforce domestic reforms approved by the Third Plenum in November 2013, the broad consensus is that China is not ready to accept TPP obligations, particularly those on transparency and disciplines on government intervention in the market. Participation in the TPP would require significant narrowing of the gaps in China's current record of liberalization commitments. However, China is making incremental strides toward this end as it deepens pacts with its Northeast Asian trading partners, including its current FTA negotiations with South Korea. China's willingness to make meaningful commitments within key plurilateral WTO initiatives—the Trade in Services Agreement (TISA) and Information Technology Agreement (ITA), among others—would also provide important signals of progress.[7]

If China is willing and able to join the TPP in the coming years, then it seems clear that the TPP will be the standard not only for the FTAAP, but also for the global trading system. A TPP-17 would be an irresistible attraction to other trading partners; in that context, it would be relatively easy to accept special TPP arrangements to encourage the participation of nonmember least-developed economies (Cambodia, Laos, and Myanmar). Participation by Chinese Taipei and Hong Kong, both with existing bilateral pacts with China, could follow a similar path to their accession to APEC. However, if the high standards and reforms required by the TPP prove to be significant barriers to crafting an APEC-wide regime, consideration should be given to an umbrella agreement that overlays the hard and soft integration approaches of the TPP and the RCEP without requiring revision of either arrangement.

A HYBRID APPROACH

If China does not participate in the TPP later this decade, then another option for a pathway to an FTAAP would be a hybrid approach that links the "hard" elements of the TPP and the "soft" elements of the intra-Asian approaches to trade integration. Under such a scenario, the hybrid pact—the FTAAP—would be an umbrella providing reciprocal obligations applying to TPP and RCEP economies, while the more comprehensive and legally binding TPP provisions would remain in force among the TPP signatories. Importantly, under this scenario, the United States and China could continue to deepen their commercial relationship without the strain of trying to directly incorporate China into the TPP, or the cost of diluting the vitality of the TPP on trade and investment among its signatories to accommodate China. Indeed, China and the United States, each for its own political reasons and economic objectives, might find it attractive to pursue such a hybrid approach to an FTAAP.

What should a hybrid Asia-Pacific integration pact cover? As a first approximation, it is worth looking at China's most recent trade and investment initiatives in the region. A prospective middle ground between the TPP and RCEP approaches seems to be evolving within those concurrent Northeast Asia initiatives. South Korea and China launched FTA talks in May 2012, and in 2013, a parallel negotiation between

China, South Korea, and Japan was launched. Although a bilateral or trilateral trade pact among these economies would comprise obligations less comprehensive than those negotiated in the Korea-US FTA—which served in many respects as the foundation for the TPP—these initiatives could produce a deal in the large middle zone between the two sharply distinctive integration paths of the Asia-Pacific region. Precedents for the deal could also be drawn from economic cooperation provisions under construction in the RCEP and from the environment chapter of the TPP, among others.

CONCLUSIONS

The TPP and RCEP countries are pursuing parallel tracks toward the APEC vision of economic integration that could be mutually reinforcing and prepare Asia-Pacific economies for accession to a broader FTA-AP. That said, the TPP seems to have a first-mover advantage in terms of setting important precedents for economic integration in the region that could critically shape the pathway toward the FTAAP. Increasingly, more and more economies are looking into the benefits and adjustment demands of gradually adopting TPP norms. The rationale is straightforward: adopting the TPP's "high standards" would complement prospective domestic economic reforms and help boost productivity growth across the economy. In so doing, it would create new opportunities for trade and investment, while improving the quality of economic institutions and governance.

To be sure, participation in the TPP entails adherence to high standards and binding obligations that would constrain the use of politically popular policies, a fact that has already slowed the integration of China and other economies. If that presents intractable economic or political problems, APEC members should consider a hybrid approach to constructing an FTAAP in the form of an umbrella agreement that serves as an overlay to the RCEP and the TPP.

First-mover effects could prove to be important and encourage convergence toward the TPP as the primary platform for regional economic integration. This will largely depend on TPP's success in attracting and incorporating new members after the talks conclude. If China decides to participate in the TPP in the coming years, it will cement the TPP as the template for both an FTAAP and an upgrading of the world trade rules. Of course, in this regard, the political and economic climate within the United States and China will play key constraining (or enabling) factors.

NOTES

1. Peterson Institute for International Economics, 2014. Used with permission.

2. For an economic analysis of the prospective gains, see Peter A. Petri, Michael G. Plummer, and Fan Zhai, *The Trans-Pacific Partnership and Asia-Pacific Integration: A Quantitative Assessment*, Policy Analyses in International Economics 98 (November 2012), Peterson Institute for International Economics, Washington, DC.

3. In so doing, the TPP will achieve a substantial upgrading of existing trade pacts among participating economies.

4. All 12 TPP economies are APEC members; 4 of the 16 RCEP economies (India, Cambodia, Laos, and Myanmar) are not in APEC.

5. For details, see Jeffrey Schott, "Revisiting APEC's Membership Freeze," *Boao Review*, November 21, 2013.

6. At present, Russia's participation is problematic. Hopefully, current frictions will abate, allowing trade relations to normalize in the coming years and FTAAP participation by all APEC members.

7. See "Froman Says China ITA Stance Does Not Bode Well for TISA, Cites Other Factors," *Inside US Trade*, October 29, 2013, www.insidetrade.com (accessed on March 21, 2014).

21

Regional Economic Integration Strategy of South Korea

Sangkyom Kim, Senior Research Fellow (on leave),
Korea Institute for International Economic Policy

INTRODUCTION: SOUTH KOREA'S TRADE LIBERALIZATION POLICY[1]

The South Korean economy has been highly dependent on trade. As shown in Figure 1, South Korea's dependency on international trade reached 73 percent in 2012.

As one of the beneficiaries of global trade liberalization, South Korea has emphasized trade liberalization at all levels—bilateral, regional, and multilateral. Despite the volatile economic environment, South Korea has kept its trade policy adherent to the principles of an open and rule-based multilateral trading system, and participated in international efforts for a conclusion of the Doha Development Agenda (DDA) negotiations.

South Korea considers free trade agreements (FTAs) and regional economic integration (REI) to be complementary tools for accelerating the Doha negotiations. Therefore, South Korea has pursued FTAs

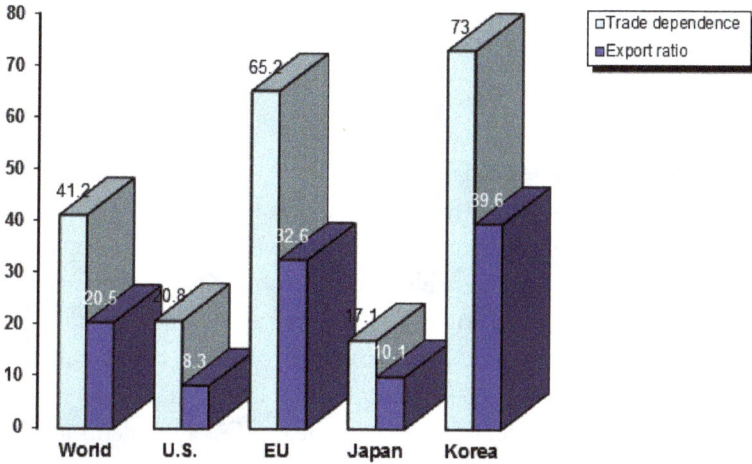

1) *Trade dependence degree = (total exports + total imports) / total value-added*
2) *Export ratio = total exports / total value-added*
Source: *Oh-Seok Hyun, "New Korea-US Economic Relations: Recommendation for a Mature Partnership," presentation file, 2013.*

FIGURE I   *Trade Dependency and Export Ratio*

actively, not only to improve access to foreign markets, but also to secure market access amidst multiplying FTAs with other economies. In particular, South Korea has assumed a leading role in regional economic cooperation, such as ASEAN-Plus-Three, the RCEP, and the TPP, in the belief that they are pathways to multilateral trade liberalization.

This paper proceeds as follows. As a device to accomplish trade liberalization, the second section introduces South Korea's FTA strategies and the progress of free trade agreements. The third section discusses the importance of regional economic integration and presents strategies for accomplishing this. The fourth briefly discusses several negotiations on regional economic integration. A final section concludes with providing policy directions from a South Korean perspective.

FTA STRATEGY

South Korea's FTA Strategy

South Korea has actively engaged in FTA negotiations since 2003, and it has developed its own FTA strategies. First, South Korea uses a multi-track approach, conducting simultaneous negotiations with other players in the global arena and mitigating political opposition by putting several deals simultaneously on the table. Second, South Korea pursues comprehensive and high-level FTAs in terms of contents, which are consistent with the WTO rules and comprehensive in coverage: commodities, services, investments, government procurement, intellectual property rights, technology standards, etc. Third, South Korea's FTAs are widely supported, as public endorsement based on national consensus has been obtained.

FTA Roadmap

An FTA roadmap was formulated in September 2003, and revised in May 2004. This roadmap forms the basis of the FTA agenda. Based to this roadmap, South Korea classifies target economies for negotiating FTAs. Short-term FTA partners include Japan, Singapore, ASEAN, the European Free Trade Association (EFTA), Mexico, Canada, and India. Large economies such as the United States, the EU, China, the South American Common Market (MERCOSUR), and Northeast Asia are mid- and long-term FTA partners. Further FTA partners being considered are the Gulf Cooperation Council (GCC), Russia, Australia, New Zealand, Peru, Israel, Morocco, Algeria, and the Southern African Customs Union (SACU).

Progress of the FTAs

Since the establishment of the FTA roadmap in 2003, Korea has actively pursued FTAs with its major trading partners. So far, FTAs with Chile, Singapore, the EFTA, ASEAN, India, Peru, the EU, and the United States have gone into force. The South Korea–US FTA was signed in June 2007 and entered into effect on March 15, 2012. On April 8, 2014, South Korea officially signed a prolonged FTA with Australia (KAFTA), less than a month after the announcement of the conclusion of negotiations with Canada.

South Korea is under negotiation with Indonesia, Gulf Cooperation Council, New Zealand, and China. South Korea and China announced the launch of FTA negotiations on May 2, 2010. Of particular note, the start of the China-Japan-Korea FTA (CJK FTA) and the Regional Comprehensive Economic Partnership (RCEP) negotiations were announced officially on November 20, 2012.

Prior to official negotiations, South Korea has conducted, and is in the process of conducting, preparation talks or joint feasibility studies with MERCOSUR, Israel, Vietnam, Central America, Malaysia, and Indonesia. Efforts to reopen pending negotiations with the GCC, Japan, and

TABLE 1   *South Korea's FTAs*

	Partner	Dates in effect
FTAs in effect (9 FTAs, 46 economies)	Chile	April 2004
	Singapore	March 2006
	EFTA	September 2006
	ASEAN	June 2006 (goods) May 2009 (service) September 2009 (investment)
	India	January 2010
	EU	July 2011
	Peru	August 2011
	US	March 2012
	Turkey	May 2013
FTA signed	Colombia	June 2012
	Canada	March 2014
	Australia	April 2014
FTAs under negotiation	China, Indonesia, New Zealand, Vietnam, CJK, RCEP	
FTAs under joint research	Central America, Israel, Malaysia, MERCOSUR	
Pending FTAs	GCC, Japan, Mexico	

Source: *http://www.fta.go.kr.*
Note: *Constructed by author.*

Mexico are also expected to make progress if unfavorable eco-political environments and conditions are improved.

REGIONAL ECONOMIC INTEGRATION STRATEGY

South Korea's REI Strategy

As noted above, South Korea considers regional economic cooperation to be a pathway to multilateral trade liberalization. Although bilateral FTAs seem to be better in terms of considering trading partner–specific sensitive sectors, the level of liberalization in the scope in services trade and investment is still low in bilateral FTAs. On the other hand, regional economic integration (REI) can bring more benefits by providing common rules and increasing competitiveness. First of all, externality and network effects are expected to be achieved under REI since the benefits to economies joining a network depend on the number of members in the network. Besides, common and cumulative rules of origin (ROO) prevent the "spaghetti bowl effect" from harming supply chains. South Korea, which has supply chains spreading out widely across regions, can exploit its comparative advantages by dividing production processes.

For those reasons, South Korea values REI as another track for trade and investment liberalization and facilitation across regions, which will eventually strengthen the multilateral trading system.

TABLE 2   *FTA vs. REI*

	Bilateral FTAs	REI
Exclusive preference (e.g., market access)	Differentiated concession	Single concession
Non-exclusive issues (e.g., rules, standards, regulations)	Mutual recognition	Network effects
Rules of origin	Bilateral (spaghetti bowl effect)	Common/cumulative in region

Source: *Young Gui Kim, "Korean Perspectives on the Trans-Pacific Partnership," presentation file, 2013.*

REI in the Asia-Pacific Region

The Asia-Pacific region has been emerging as the nucleus of the global economy, given the region's many fast-growing markets. Figure 2 shows that the economic growth rate of East Asia is expected to increase up to 7.2 percent in the period from 2010 to 2015. This market, therefore, provides huge trade opportunities. Presented with these opportunities, South Korea is eager to sustain its growth momentum by building cooperative networks with emerging economies.

In addition, strong production networks, which are achieved through high intraregional trade and investment between Asia-Pacific economies, allow members to enjoy the benefits of their comparative advantages. As shown in Figure 3, the share of intraregional trade between Asia-Pacific economies—such as that reached in the RCEP and ASEAN—has increased to 43.7 percent and 24.2 percent, respectively.

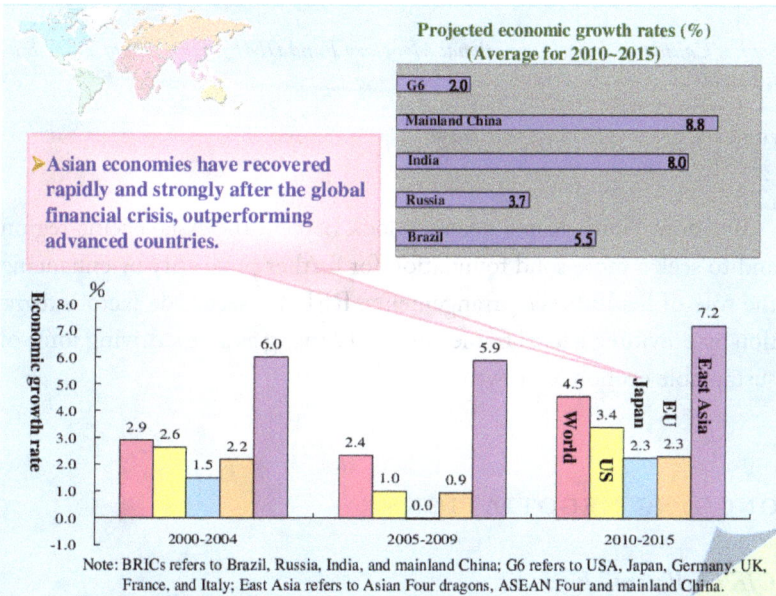

Note: BRICs refers to Brazil, Russia, India, and mainland China; G6 refers to USA, Japan, Germany, UK, France, and Italy; East Asia refers to Asian Four dragons, ASEAN Four and mainland China.

Source: Young Gui Kim, "Korean Perspectives on the Trans-Pacific Partnership," presentation file, 2013.

FIGURE 2 Economic Growth Rates

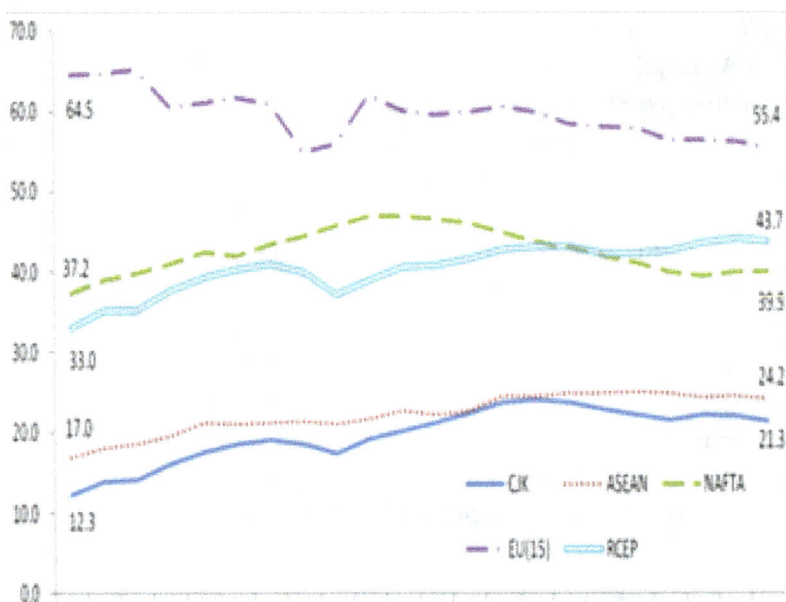

Source: Calculated from International Monetary Fund (IMF), Direction of Trade Statistics, 2012.

FIGURE 3 *Share of Intraregional Trade*

But now, South Korea needs to look beyond the Asia-Pacific region and to seek a more solid foundation for further prosperity by enhancing the role of institutional arrangements. REI can secure de facto integration by providing a legal framework and serving as a new driving force of sustainable economic growth.

ONGOING NEGOTIATIONS

CJK (Trilateral) FTA

Following the APEC Leaders' Meeting at the summit of 1999, three entities—the Development Research Center (DRC) of the State Council of China, the National Institute for Research Advancement (NIRA) of Japan/Institute of Developing Economies of the Japan External Trade Organization

(IDE-JETRO),[2] and the Korea Institute for International Economic Policy (KIEP)—began trilateral joint research on establishing an FTA among China, Japan, and South Korea.[3] From 2003 to 2009, they conducted the joint research on the CJK FTA (China-Japan-Korea FTA), and announced the launch of CJK FTA negotiations in November 2012.[4] Most recently, the fourth round of negotiations was held in March 2014 in Seoul.

The CJK FTA aims at establishing a milestone for economic integration in Northeast Asia.[5] To attain a comprehensive and high-level FTA, the CJK FTA wants to bring consistency to the WTO rules, to balance competing interests, and to allow for consideration of sensitive sectors.[6]

South Korea's strategy for the CJK FTA is linking it to existing FTAs and the RCEP. thereby promoting coherence and avoiding the "spaghetti bowl effect." Coordination is needed in terms of modalities, rules of origin, and customs procedures.

The RCEP

In the context of ASEAN centrality, an ASEAN framework on the RCEP was adopted at the 19th ASEAN Summit in Bali, November 2011. The negotiations were also launched by ASEAN and its six FTA partners (Australia, China, India, Japan, South Korea, and New Zealand) at the East Asia Summit in November 2012. The RCEP aims to be a comprehensive, high-quality, and mutually beneficial economic partnership agreement among the ASEAN member states and ASEAN FTA partners. Srinivasa Madhur (2013) of the Asian Development Bank stated, "RCEP aims primarily at harmonizing existing rules and their application within the various ASEAN FTAs."[7] The RCEP would lead to greater economic integration, support equitable economic development, and strengthen economic cooperation among the economies involved.[8]

The official home page of ASEAN states the following: "Consistent with the RCEP Leaders' Joint Declaration on the launch of negotiations for the RCEP of November 20, 2012, and the guiding principles and objectives for negotiating the RCEP endorsed by RCEP ministers on August 30, 2012, the RCEP negotiations will aim to:

- achieve a modern, comprehensive, high-quality, and mutually beneficial economic partnership agreement establishing an open trade and investment environment in the region to facilitate the expansion of regional trade and investment and contribute to global economic growth and development; and

- boost economic growth and equitable economic development, advance economic cooperation, and broaden and deepen integration in the region through the RCEP, which will build upon our existing economic linkages."[9]

Yoshifumi Fukunaga and Ikumo Isono (2013) suggested that the RCEP should introduce many convergent rules, such as a common concession approach, a clear definition and approach about nontariff barriers, a general rule for establishing specific ROO (rules of origin), a region-wide approach to trade facilitation and economic cooperation, and a prioritization of service sectors to strengthen East Asia's links with global production networks.[10]

South Korea will play an active role in the RCEP negotiations, especially in light of its high intraregional dependency, its accumulated experience in forming FTAs with major economies, and its role as a middle-rank power in the context of regional economic cooperation. Whereas South Korea should pursue bilateral FTAs with the RCEP participants and coordinate with the CJK FTA, it is necessary to take a strategic approach to deepen and make use of the production networks in East Asia through the RCEP, rather than focusing on concessions. To penetrate China's domestic markets, with ASEAN members as a production base, South Korea should build not only a competitive relationship, but also a win-win relationship with China.

The TPP

The Trans-Pacific Partnership (TPP) was originally conceived in 2003 by Singapore, New Zealand, and Chile as a path to trade liberalization in the Asia-Pacific region. Then known as the Trans-Pacific Strategic Economic Partnership Agreement, it grew when Brunei joined negotiations in 2005, and the agreement was concluded in 2006. In March 2008, the United States joined the negotiations to conclude the still-outstanding investment and financial services provisions.

The trans-Pacific option for region-wide trade liberalization was developed further, resulting in the emergence of the TPP initiative. On November 12, 2011, the leaders of nine Trans-Pacific Partnership economies—Australia, Brunei, Chile, Malaysia, New Zealand, Peru, Singapore, Vietnam, and the United States—announced the achievement of the broad outlines of an ambitious, twenty-first century TPP agreement that would enhance trade and investment among the partner economies; promote innovation, economic growth, and development; and support the creation and retention of jobs.[11] With Canada, Mexico, and Japan now joined, the 12 members are involved in shaping trade and investment rules.

A Congressional Research Service report (Fergusson 2013) described the TPP as a "comprehensive and high-standard" FTA that aims to liberalize trade in nearly all goods and services, and to include commitments beyond those currently established in the World Trade Organization (WTO).[12] It also stated that the "TPP could help promote and ensure the longevity of domestic economic policy reforms...TPP is viewed as an important element in the US rebalancing toward Asia... TPP could serve as a building block for a more viable multilateral trade system that responds to trade challenges of the twenty-first century."[13]

In November 2013, South Korea expressed its interest in joining the TPP. With regard to South Korea's accession to the TPP negotiations, Sangkyom Kim (2011) stated, "as one of the main objectives of the TPP is setting a new standard for global trade by incorporating a wide range of crosscutting issues, the opportunity cost South Korea should pay will be substantial when the TPP is successfully formed."

CONCLUSIONS: POLICY DIRECTIONS FROM A SOUTH KOREAN PERSPECTIVE

South Korea maintains the stance that an open regime is vital for every trade arrangement with its trading partners. The thought is that one of the final goals of trade liberalization is the achievement of an FTAAP (Free Trade Area of the Asia-Pacific). As a pathway to an FTAAP, ongoing negotiations such as the CJK FTA, the RCEP, and the TPP become

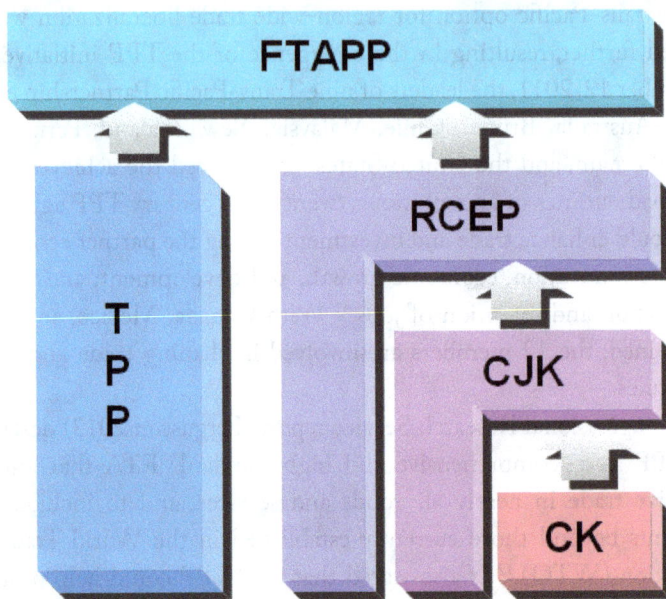

Source: Younggui Kim (2013), "Korean perspective on the Trans-pacific partnership." Presentation material.

FIGURE 4 *New Trade Roadmap*

important. In view of the current political and economic situation of South Korea, conditions seem ripe for achieving national consensus on joining the TPP. The TPP might emerge as one of the premier rule-setting processes shaping new global trade norms, and, in my opinion, South Korea needs to participate. It should strive to become a regular contributor to the process of harmonizing regional trade arrangements. In fact, just as South Korea was able to smoothly move forward with its consultations with TPP members, so too will South Korea's official engagement into the TPP facilitate and trigger the realization that it is a meaningful endeavor, and that significant regional trade agreements will eventually lead to a broader Asia-Pacific community.

In the development of REI negotiations, South Korea will play the role of incubator to harmonize regional trade arrangements, and as linchpin in the regional integration in the Asia-Pacific region.

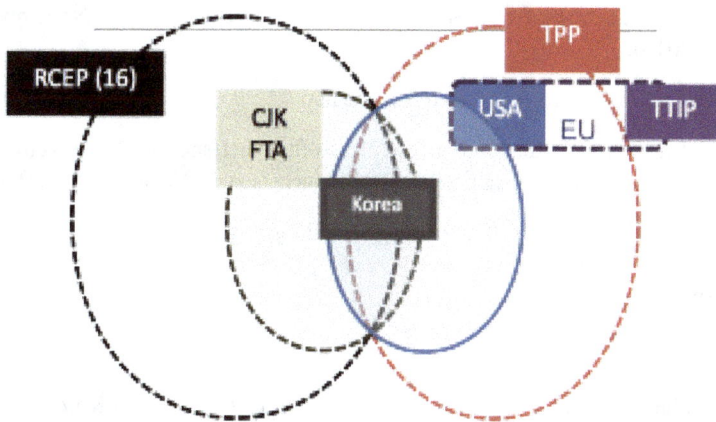

Source: Younggui Kim (2013), "Korea-US FTA and Prospects of Korea-China FTA."
Presentation material.

FIGURE 5 *South Korea's Role in Regional Economic Integration*

NOTES

1. I thank Hyeri Park and Kyungsoo Lim. I also thank Young Gui Kim for helpful discussions. This paper was prepared for a CNPECC (China National Committee for Pacific Economic Cooperation) conference presentation.

2. NIRA was replaced by JETRO in 2009.

3. See Jae Lee Chang in reference list.

4. See http://www.fta.go.kr/new2/ftakorea/ftakorea2010_c.asp (accessed on November 11, 2013).

5. Ibid.

6. See http://www.fta.go.kr/kcj/policy/meaning.asp (accessed on November 11, 2013).

7. See Srinivasa Madhur in reference list.

8. See http://www.fta.gov.sg/press_release%5CFACTSHEET%20ON%20 RCEP_final.pdf (accessed on November 11, 2013).

9. See http://www.asean.org/news/asean-statement-communiques/item /regional-comprehensive-economic-partnership-rcep-joint-statement-

the-first-meeting-of-trade-negotiating-committee (accessed on November 11, 2013).

10. See Fukunaga and Isono in reference list.

11. See http://www.ustr.gov/about-us/press-office/fact-sheets/2011/november /united-states-trans-pacific-partnership (accessed on November 11, 2013).

12. See Ian F. Fergusson, et al. in reference list.

13. Ibid.

SOURCES

Chang, Jae Lee. 2013. "CJK Economic Trilateralism: A South Korean Perspective." *Joint US-Korea Academic Studies* 24, 2013, Korea Economic Institute of America.

Deardorff, Alan V. 2013. "Trade Implications of the Trans-Pacific Partnership for ASEAN and Other Asian Countries." Paper presented at the 2nd Asian Development Review Conference, August1-2, Manila.

Fergusson, Ian F., William H. Cooper, Remy Jurenas, and Brock R. Williams. 2013. *The Trans-Pacific Partnership Negotiations and Issues for Congress.* CRS Report No. 7-5700, April 15. Washington, DC: Congressional Research Service.

Fukunaga, Yoshifumi, and Ikumo Isono. 2013. "Taking ASEAN+1 FTAs towards the RCEP: A Mapping Study." Economic Research Institute for ASEAN and East Asia, ERIA Discussion Paper, No. 2013-02. January.

Hyun, Oh-Seok. 2006. "New Korea-US Economic Relations: Recommendation for a Mature Partnership." PowerPoint presentation made to the American Enterprise Institute.

Kim, Sangkyom. 2011. "Korea and TPP: Options and Strategy." Unpublished paper.

Kim, Young Gui. 2013 "Korean Perspectives on the Trans-Pacific Partnership." Presentation file.

Madhur, Srinivasa. 2013. "China-Japan-Korea FTA: A Dual Track Approach to a Trilateral Agreement." *Journal of Economic Integration* 28 (3): 382.

22

How to Push the WTO Doha Round in the Current RTA Talks?

Winichai Chaemchaeng, Director of the International Institute for Asia-Pacific Studies, Bangkok University

Since the World Trade Organization (WTO) launched the Doha Development Agenda (DDA) in 2001, the global economy has grown larger and the trading system has become far more complex. In turn, solutions through multilateral negotiations have proved elusive. While progress has been recently made at the Bali Ministerial Conference, many critical issues remain open. Meanwhile, a large number of smaller bilateral and regional trade agreements (RTAs) have been concluded addressing similar agendas. These developments raise urgent questions about the future of the world trading system and about potential complementarities between global agreements and RTAs.

The DDA Work Programme of 2001 covered a wide range of issues divided into several negotiating clusters: agriculture, services, market access for non-agricultural products, trade-related intellectual property rights (TRIPS), trade facilitation, WTO rules, dispute settlement understanding (DSU), trade and environments; and non-negotiating issues, i.e., investment, competition policy, transparency in government procurement, implementation issues and concerns, electronic commerce, small economies, trade debt and finance, trade and transfer of technology, technical cooperation and capacity building, less developed countries, and special and differential treatment.

Meanwhile, WTO membership has increased from 143 members with China's accession at the Fourth Ministerial Conference to 159 members at present. The WTO Doha Development Round that was to be concluded by 2005, or within four years, has been negotiated and extended for 12 years, but the conclusion is still far away.

THE CHALLENGES OF THE DOHA NEGOTIATIONS

It was hopeful in the Seventh Ministerial Conference in December 2009 that the Doha round could be wrapped up by the end of 2010. However, while the negotiations brought promising agreements concerning nonagricultural market access (NAMA) and agriculture, two major members were unable to bridge their disagreement on the threshold or import triggers for the operationalization of agriculture's special safeguard mechanism for developing economies. At the same time, advancements in other areas, such as services, rules, and trade facilitation, seemed to be forthcoming.

At the conference, there was broad agreement that the growing number of bilateral and regional trade agreements (RTAs) was an issue for the multilateral trading system, and that there was a need to ensure that the two approaches to trade opening continue to complement each other. Some support was expressed for the eventual convergence of the two approaches. However, the idea of extending to all members the benefits offered in a regional context was questioned by some.

There were suggestions that while the WTO RTA transparency mechanism had worked quite well, there was still room for improvement, through making the mechanism permanent, highlighting the common elements in different RTAs, and introducing an annual review.[1]

At the Eighth Ministerial Conference, ministers recognized that the negotiations were at an impasse, and that not all elements of the Doha Development Round could be concluded simultaneously in the near future. Members recognized that they needed to fully explore different negotiating approaches, looking at the possible results that could be achieved in different areas. This was done by taking advantage of the ministerial declaration that allowed members to reach provisional or definitive agreements, based on consensus, before they had fully concluded the single undertaking.

Ministers stressed the centrality of development. Many underlined the need to give priority to issues of interest to least-developed economies (LDEs), including cotton. Many mentioned the importance of all three pillars—market access, domestic support, and export competition—in the agriculture negotiations. They also mentioned trade facilitation, special and differential treatment (S&D), an S&D monitoring mechanism, and nontariff measures. To unlock the current impasse, agreements would have to be reached about the balance in contributions and the responsibilities between emerging and advanced economies.

In addition, the ministers pointed to the growing number of RTAs and stressed the need to ensure that they remain complementary to, and not a substitute for, the multilateral trading system. In that regard, many ministers stressed the need for the WTO to address the systemic implications of RTAs for the multilateral trading system, and to study trends in RTAs and report to the Ninth Ministerial Conference.[2]

THE BALI PACKAGE

The WTO Ninth Ministerial Conference, held December 3–6, 2013, in Bali, Indonesia, produced an outcome called the "Bali Package," which is comprised of three main issues: trade facilitation, some agriculture, and some development issues.[3] The possibility that an accord might be reached that covered only a part of the full agenda was anticipated early on in the Doha negotiations. Ministers agreed in launching the round that "agreements reached at an early stage may be implemented on a provisional or a definitive basis."[4]

On Trade Facilitation

The ministers agreed to the draft Trade Facilitation Agreement (TFA), which was designed to facilitate the importation, exportation, and transit of goods, and has been divided into two sections. The first section includes 13 detailed customs rules, such as shortest possible time for the release of perishable goods; fees and charges for customs procedures, which are not in excess of the service cost; a risk management system for customs control on high-risk consignments, and procedures to expedite the release of low-risk consignments. The second section is about flexibilities, or special and differential treatment, given to developing economies and least-developed economies (LDE). The principles are applied through the implementation of three categories of provisions, namely, to implement on the date the agreement takes effect, on a date after a transitional period, and on a date after a transitional period that included capacity building. The WTO members were required to complete internal legal procedures before the ratification period, extending from July 31, 2014, to July 31, 2015, and requiring two-thirds of WTO members to legalize it as a WTO agreement.[5]

On Agriculture

The ministers agreed upon the Tariff Rate Quota Administration Provisions of Agricultural Products, as defined in Article 2 of the Agreement on Agriculture. The agreement required transparency in tariff rate quota (TRQ) administration, and for those with unfilled quota to improve their TRQ administration methods to allow for more imports. WTO members that had imports of less than 65 percent of quota for three successive years needed to adopt a "first come, first serve" method of TRQ administration, or to initiate automatic licensing for a period of at least two years. Such requirements are not applicable to developing economies, which may choose other TRQ administration methods or maintain their current methods. However, the flexibility for developing economies will be reviewed in the Twelfth Ministerial Meeting as reservations have been made by the developed economies on extending the provision.[6]

In addition, the Ministerial Declaration stated that WTO members would proceed with the elimination of all forms of agricultural export subsidies, and would maintain export subsidies at a level significantly lower than the commitments under the Agreement on Agriculture.[7]

The ministers also enacted an interim solution, which was termed "due restraint," allowing developing economies to take exceptions on the public stockholding of food for security purposes. Members were instructed to refrain from challenging these exceptions through the WTO dispute settlement mechanism. Members of developing economies would be considered compliant in meeting their obligations under the Agreement on Agriculture, even though the subsidies were in excess of WTO commitment levels, provided the following requirements were met: notification of relevant information, including stocks, prices, and quantities bought, as well as prices and quantities sold, production, and exports; the program could not distort trade or have an adverse impact on food security in other economies; affected members had to be consulted; and the Committee of Agriculture could monitor the program until a permanent solution was achieved. The requirements for implementing the program were designed so that developing economies could not adversely impact the world market in the period between the Ministerial Decision on December 7, 2013, and a permanent solution being reached at the WTO Eleventh Ministerial Conference.[8]

Moreover, the ministers recognized that general services programs under "green box," or subsidies having no or minimal trade distortion, could be made on the grounds of rural development, food security, and poverty alleviation, particularly in developing economies. The decision was made to include programs related to land reform and rural livelihood security, such as: land rehabilitation, soil conservation, and resource management; drought management and flood control; rural employment programs; issuance of property titles; and farmer settlement programs that promote rural development and poverty alleviation.[9]

With respect to cotton issues, the ministers decided to enhance transparency and monitoring in relation to the trade-related aspects of cotton, and to hold dedicated discussions on a biannual basis. The discussions would take place in the context of the Committee of Agriculture, with special sessions called to examine relevant trade-related developments across the three pillars of market access, domestic support, and export competition in relation to cotton. The development partners were urged to give special focus to such needs within existing aid-for-trade mechanisms/channels, such as the European Investment Fund (EIF) and the technical assistance and capacity-building work of relevant international institutions.[10]

On Development Issues

Including LDEs, the ministers agreed to establish a monitoring mechanism on special and differential treatment (S&D). This would be a focal point within the WTO for analyzing and reviewing the implementation of S&D provisions and to complement, not replace, other relevant review mechanisms and/or processes in other bodies of the WTO. The goal is to facilitate integration of developing and least-developed members into the multilateral trading arena. As appropriate, the mechanism could make recommendations to the relevant WTO body proposing actions to improve the implementation of S&D provisions, or it could initiate negotiations aimed at improving the provisions.[11]

The ministers stipulated that developed-economy members not yet providing duty-free and quota-free market access for at least 97 percent of products originating from LDEs, defined at the tariff line level, should improve access for such products. Developing-economy members that were in a position to do so should also provide duty-free and quota-free market access for products originating from LDEs, or seek to improve their existing duty-free and quota-free coverage for such products.[12]

Continuing, the ministers decided that members should develop or build on their individual rules of origin arrangements as they apply to imports from LDEs. While the provided guidelines should be consulted, members may wish to draw up preferential rules of origin for imports from LDEs under the duty-free, quota-free arrangements.[13]

The Council for Trade in Services (CTS) was instructed to initiate a process for promoting the expeditious and effective operationalization of LDE service waivers, and to periodically review the operationalization of the waivers and make recommendations on steps that could be taken toward enhancing operationalization. At high-level meetings of the Council for Trade in Services, members have been instructed to indicate sectors and modes of supply where they intend to provide preferential treatment to LDE services and service suppliers. They are encouraged at any time to extend preferences to LDE services and service suppliers, consistent with the waiver decision, which deliver commercial value and economic benefits. Also, preferences can be granted to improve market access for LDE services and service providers, including the elimination of economic needs tests and other quantitative limitations.[14]

On Customs Duties Moratorium on Electronic Transmissions

In the area of electronic commerce, the ministers decided to maintain the current practice of not imposing customs duties on electronic transmissions until the next session, which has been scheduled for 2015.

On TRIPS Non-Violation and Situation Complaints, members have been instructed to not initiate complaints under the TRIPS agreement until recommendations have been made to the 2015 session.

The ministers recognized the continuing aid for trade need of developing economies, particularly LDEs. [15]

They also requested that work continue on developing the relationship between trade and the transfer of technology, and that recommendations for increasing flows of technology to developing economies be considered. [16]

The Committee on Trade and Development was instructed to continue its work on small economies and make recommendations in dedicated sessions.

The outcome of the WTO Ninth Ministerial Conference, the so-called "Bali Package," could serve as confidence-building measures, as they mostly covered issues concerning developing economies, particularly least-developed economies (LDEs), on agriculture, development, trade facilitation, and implementation-related issues. The negotiations on major issues concerning market access and agricultural domestic subsidies, as well as rules, have not yet produced outcomes. However, it is expected that the package will build momentum for the advancement and possible conclusion of the Doha Development Agenda.

REGIONAL TRADE AGREEMENTS AND FURTHER PROGRESS

Whether RTAs are complementary or a substitution of the multilateral trading system (MTS), trade liberalization is needed to satisfy demand for larger markets for goods and services, including the elimination of restrictive trade measures and effective rules that are responsive to the changing international trading environment. If the MTS does not respond quickly and effectively to the needs of the business sector, RTAs become second best for that sector, and it no longer matters whether they act as substitutes or complementary forces of the MTS.

However, there are some rules and dispute settlement mechanisms that cannot be dealt with in the RTAs, but only in the MTS. In bilateral FTA negotiations, it was not practical or possible to impose agricultural domestic support levels between the two parties, as the commitments would have put them at a disadvantage with respect to WTO third parties. Instead, such commitments are best undertaken on a multilateral basis. In addition, even though both parties could conclude a dispute settlement agreement on a bilateral basis, adhering to the WTO dispute settlement mechanism, this path would not be as effective as a WTO dispute settlement system where greater peer pressure from all WTO members is exerted, not just from the counterpart in a bilateral trade agreement.

Most RTAs focus on market access of agricultural products, nonagricultural products, and services far beyond the level normally agreed to within the framework of the MTS. Tariff eliminations of at least 90 percent of tariff lines and trade volumes are expected for developing economies, and 95 percent for developed economies, while some RTAs have gone even further to specify the total elimination of tariffs. Service liberalization in RTAs has also been much more ambitious. For example, the ASEAN Framework Agreement on Services targets unconditional liberalization of cross-border trade and consumption abroad, and sets the foreign equity participation for ASEAN member states to at least 70 percent. This participation rate includes negotiations on liberalization parameters, such as the movement of natural persons, as well as mutual recognition agreements (MRAs) regarding professionals, particularly skilled labor.

However, many controversial issues cannot be agreed on in RTA negotiations among WTO members, particularly the Singapore issues—competition policy, government procurement, investment, e-commerce, agricultural export competition, investor-state dispute settlement,

WTO-plus trade-related intellectual property rights, the environment, labor, etc. Even though most provisions on the aforementioned issues might be limited to cooperation and require the parties to become members of the related international conventions, many imposed additional obligations and commitments to the parties, beyond that required of the WTO.

Once WTO members are engaged in RTAs, which usually require deeper and wider commitments than those under the WTO, their ability to commit to further liberalization within the framework of the WTO becomes enhanced. Most-favored nation (MFN) extensions are only required for other WTO members, particularly in regards to trade in services. With respect to ASEAN members, they should be comfortable with negotiated outcomes concerning market access of goods and services, as agreed upon in the Doha Development Agenda. They are expected to be in a strong position for negotiating their most important issues. In Thailand's experiences negotiating the ASEAN-Japan Comprehensive Economic Partnership (AJCEP) or the ASEAN–Australia–New Zealand Free Trade Agreement (AANZFTA)—which concluded bilateral negotiations with Japan, Australia, and New Zealand—there were fewer obstacles and limitations, and greater efforts to reach ambitious goals.

CONCLUSIONS

It was no secret that a conclusion of the Doha Development Agenda would be difficult to achieve in a single undertaking, where consensus of 159 economies on a wide range of issues would be needed. Since the Doha round of negotiations has been at a standstill for too long, members have begun to investigate different approaches, such as those termed "sequential." Agreements on the least controversial issues, such as trade facilitation, development, and some agricultural issues in the "Bali Package," could provide momentum for members to go further on more difficult issues. If WTO members are still not able to find well-balanced outcomes and continue to prolong negotiations, they might have to be content with the administration of existing agreements, dispute settlement procedures, and the trade policy review mechanism. But those developing economies that did not participate in any regional trade agreements might be at a disadvantage and feel marginalized in world markets.

On the contrary, RTA participants, though limited in number, have normally negotiated agreements on a wider range of issues. In the near future, issues taken up by the Doha Development Agenda could be expanded to cover all areas mandated by the WTO Ministerial Declaration, following a confidence-building process accorded to developing economies, particularly LDEs. And some regional trade agreements are in the process of expanding their membership by new agreements, as in the case of the Trans-Pacific Partnership (TPP) and the Regional Comprehensive Economic Partnership (RCEP); of enlarging, as in the case of the EU; of docking, as in the case the Japan-Thailand Economic Partnership Agreement (JTEPA) and the ASEAN-Japan Comprehension Economic Partnership (AJCEP); and merging, as in the case of the ASEAN community. Beyond that, the Free Trade Area of the Asia-Pacific (FTAAP) grows more prominent on the horizon.

The RTAs were exempted from WTO MFN treatment, but were subject to conditions provided in the provisions of the relevant WTO agreements. When it came to rules, most RTAs agreed to apply WTO rules *mutatis mutandis* (with necessary changes having been made). However, RTAs are free to apply higher standards or value-added mechanisms, such as the creation of joint committees to solve problems on issues relating to sanitary and phytosanitary (SPS) measures and technical barriers to trade (TBT), or on more wide-ranging issues such as investment, the environment, and labor.

It would be useful for the WTO Secretariat to keep records of RTA commitments on various issues, by all parties to the agreements, and to carefully analyze how effectively those commitments were working. The WTO Secretariat could conduct the same kind of simulation as was done in NAMA areas to assure positive outcomes once negotiations have been concluded. An ideal solution would be to extend most-favored nation provisions crafted in these RTAs to the design of WTO provisions, docking them in any way possible.

Negotiated RTAs, however, could not serve as a substitute for the multilateral trading system in the case of rules, particularly rules on agriculture, trade policy reviews, and dispute settlement mechanisms provided by the WTO, but they could remain complementary or exist as building blocks. Given the time it took for the WTO to develop new rules addressing modern trade issues, the RTAs might be better equipped to respond in a more timely way to fast-changing trade environments, especially in the fields of e-commerce, paperless trading, global supply chains, consumer protection, investment, competition policy, government procurement, trade and finance, trade and technology, and many other areas.

NOTES

1. Chairman's Summary of the Seventh WTO Ministerial Conference on December 2, 2009, in Geneva, Switzerland.

2. Chairman's Concluding Statement of the Eighth WTO Ministerial Conference on December 17, 2011, in Geneva, Switzerland (WTO Doc. WT/MIN(11)/11).

3. The Bali Ministerial Declaration of the Ninth WTO Ministerial Conference, adopted on December 7, 2013, in Bali, Indonesia (WT/MIN(13)/DEC).

4. The Doha Ministerial Declaration of the Fourth WTO Ministerial Conference, adopted on November 14, 2001, in Doha, Qatar (WT/MIN(01)/DEC/1).

5. WTO 9th Ministerial Conference, Bali, 2013, Agreement on Trade Facilitation Ministerial Decision (WT/MIN(13)/36, WT/L/911).

6. WTO 9th Ministerial Conference, Bali, 2013, Understanding on Tariff Rate Quota Administration Provisions of Agricultural Products Ministerial Decision (WT/MIN(13)/39 - WT/L/914).

7. WTO 9th, Export Competition Declaration (WT/MIN(13)/40WT/L/915).

8. WTO 9th, Public Stockholding for Food Security Purposes (WT/MIN(13)/38, WT/L/913).

9. WTO 9th, General Services (WT/MIN(13)/37, WT/L/912).

10. WTO 9th, Cotton Negotiations (WT/MIN(13)/41, WT/L/916).

11. WTO 9th, Monitoring Mechanism on Special and Differential Treatment (WT/MIN(13)/45,WT/L/920).

12. WTO 9th, Duty-Free and Quota-Free Market Access for Least-Developed Economies (WT/MIN(13)/44, WT/L/919).

13. WTO 9th, Preferential Rules of Origin for Least-Developed Countries (WT/MIN(13)/42, WT/L/917).

14. WTO 9th, Operationalization of the Waiver Concerning Preferential Treatment to Services and Service Suppliers of Least-Developed Countries (WT/MIN(13)/43, WT/L/918).

15. WTO 9th, Aid for Trade (WT/MIN(13)/34, WT/L/909).

16. WTO 9th, Trade and Transfer of Technology (WT/MIN(13)/35, WT/L/910).

23

The Asia-Pacific Cooperation Agenda

Moving from Regional Cooperation Toward Global Leadership

Charles E. Morrison, President, East-West Center

APEC ACHIEVEMENTS AND CHALLENGES

APEC celebrates its twenty-fifth anniversary in a vastly changed region and world. Since 1989, there has been dramatic economic growth in most Asian developing countries, especially China; regional integration through a combination of reduced political and regulatory barriers and the rise of supply and production chains; and a proliferation of regional institutions and freer trade and investment arrangements. In a context where there is also rising demand that institutions of all kinds, including international organizations, demonstrate concrete outcomes, some would question whether APEC can claim any responsibility for the region's achievements.

In fact, it is very difficult to link APEC as an organization in any specific way to these outcomes. Even the reduction in trade barriers has less to do with Bogor Goals than with obligations undertaken as part of WTO commitments, other negotiations, or unilaterally. However, APEC has been part and parcel of the positive changes that have been occurring in the region, and undoubtedly the fact that first ministers, then leaders were meeting on a regular basis provided a positive atmosphere for international interaction and integration. Prior to APEC, there were no such meetings; regional cooperation was nonexistent or confined to subregional or highly specialized organizations with no sense of broad and converging regional interests; and Asia-Pacific engagement in global issues was fragmented and incoherent.[1]

APEC's achievements are much more visible to foreign and trade ministry bureaucracies than they are to the public, or even to more politically and policy-aware stakeholders. APEC has proved to be an efficient venue for the leaders of the region to meet. It has helped build some common sense of international economic norms and values and strengthened adherence to the international trade system. It has provided a vehicle for economies with once-limited awareness of the WTO system to better understand the rules, obligations, and benefits of the system.

While APEC, as a venue for voluntary, nonbinding cooperation, has not itself been a formal vehicle for negotiating free trade areas, much of the inspiration for such agreements has been associated with the APEC process. Freer trade and investment liberalization have been APEC goals for two decades. Today virtually all the economies in the region are engaged in one or another of the major free trade negotiations—the Trans-Pacific Partnership, the Regional Comprehensive Economic Partnership, and the Pacific Alliance. APEC itself may not be a rule-making organization, but it has both deepened adherence to global norms and rules and inspired more liberal trade rule-making at the subregional or plurilateral levels.

APEC no longer remains the only broad-gauged trans-Pacific organization; it has been joined by the East Asia Summit (EAS), which includes the United States as a member. If we consider APEC and EAS as complementary institutions in a broad trans-Pacific cooperation and integration process, this process faces two critical challenges during the coming decades: Will it effectively generate international cooperation among the region's economies in addressing the many continuing and often deepening challenges of the region? And, perhaps even more significantly, can the Asia-Pacific region assume a leadership role in the global system?

A GLOBAL CENTURY WITH AN ASIA-PACIFIC CORE

East, Southeast, and South Asia, with a little more than half the world's population, are rapidly regaining an equivalent share of world gross product for the first time in two centuries. There are many reasons to believe that despite cyclical variability and a longer-term decline in the growth rates of the more advanced nations associated with the end of catch-up development and demographic aging, the comparative rise of Asia within the global system will continue. Human capital enhancements, increased economic integration, technological leapfrogging, and the growth of middle classes are among the reasons. Projections by the US National Intelligence Council suggest that by mid-century, China will have slightly surpassed the United States as the world's most powerful nation, based on a composite index of the many elements of power.[2] But while the power and influence of China and India will continue to rise, and thus Asia's systemic weight increase, no single country will be as influential in the international system of the future as the United States has been in the last part of the preceding century.

The rise of Asia has led to speculation about an "Asian century." With a continuing diffusion of power, the coming century is much more likely to be a global one. However, the international system will have a trans-Pacific core area with much of the economic power and the potential to provide global leadership for the further development of international norms, rules, and cooperation. In this sense, we may be able to refer to an "Asia-Pacific century." Two questions arise: Is North America, with a relatively small share of global population, and a declining share (less than 25 percent by 2050) of global world product, still relevant? Will the nations on the two sides of the Pacific really be able to use their power effectively to assume global leadership? The answer to the first of these is "yes," and to the second, "it depends."

North America's role is not simply based on its population or economic size, but also on the creative dynamism of the American societies, which are constantly being refreshed by new immigration and a highly entrepreneurial culture facilitated by a unique interplay between business, government, and academic sectors, typified by Silicon Valley. Far from retreating from their historical origins as international "melting pots," the United States and Canada remain open to high and increasingly diversified levels of immigration, drawing from human talent pools all over the world. The foreign born in the United States today is estimated at about 45.8 million of its 310 million people, the highest share for this country in over a century.[3] Canada has an even higher proportion of foreign born, with 7.3 million in a population of 30 million. While helping the United States to remain a global center for higher education, advanced research, and cutting-edge technologies, immigrant communities also inhibit retreat toward "isolationism." The United States is likely to continue to provide a leading share of the world's public goods, especially in such areas as international security, disaster relief, and financial systems.

The second question of whether the Asia-Pacific region will step up to global leadership depends on a number of factors and deserves more attention. It may be likely, but there is no guarantee. To be an effective core leadership area, the region needs to meet a number of requirements.

First, the economies need to be stable and secure units, capable of engaging in cooperation and adhering to international commitments. This appears positive. Despite many challenges, the quality of governance continues to improve in most of the region. Second, there need to be harmonious, cooperative international relations among the societies of the region and intergovernmental institutions capable of creating common values, norms, and action agendas. This is currently questionable. The region's global role will be limited if territorial disputes persist, diverting resources and attention from major regional and global issues and challenges. Only by building a sense of community within the Asia Pacific can the region become a truly effective force for global peace- and order-building. Third, there needs to be a continual process of integration and growing connectivity. This has been occurring and is a key objective of the APEC process. The major economies of Asia are now more integrated in terms of trade flows than those of North America, and almost as much as those of the European Union. Continuing this process, as well as improving the interconnectedness of the region in transportation and communication, is an important force for continued Asia-Pacific growth. Fourth, the economies of the region need to be inclusive domestically, drawing upon the whole of the resources of their own societies. APEC's goal of "inclusive" growth is important in this regard, as well as in contributing to the first goal of a "stable and secure unit." Fifth, the APEC economies need to be inclusive internationally, that is, take into account the sensitivities and interests of nations outside the region. Finally, the region will need intellectual, policy, and educational hubs for creative policy ideas and regionally and globally focused leadership training. Just as an integrating Europe required individuals grounded in their own nationalities but with a European sense of challenges and opportunities, the Asia-Pacific region will require such individuals with broad regional and global knowledge.

This last requirement should be a major objective of APEC's working agenda on education. APEC economies can learn lessons from each other's experiences, a main current theme of this work, but they should also strive to build networks of individuals with a similar understanding of regional and global history, challenges, and desirable pathways to address issues. This will be facilitated by the greater mobility of students, joint venture and multinational educational programs, and a truly regional center for Asia-Pacific leadership education.

THE MEGA-AGENDA FOR APEC

What then are the challenges facing APEC in its twenty-fifth year? The presenters in this collection will undoubtedly offer many useful, specific directions. The focus here is on the longer-term regional challenges most relevant to an emerging global agenda.

The first challenge, and an essential requirement for all else, is to strengthen the international cooperative relations of the region. This requires overcoming issues of history and focusing on issues of common concern to the APEC community as a whole. In the past, APEC and other regional bodies have been used to dampen regional tensions and reassure populations that leaders remain engaged. But in recent years, leaders have not made such use of APEC and this may have contributed to regional misunderstandings and tension.

Secondly, there are architectural questions, both within the Asia-Pacific region and between this region and other regional systems and the global system. There is no particular reason that any institution, including APEC, needs to survive in its current form or with its current name. What is important over the longer term is that the process of Asia-Pacific cooperation and economic integration continue. The current architecture of institutionalized regional cooperation with its different components remains a work in progress. The relationship between the East Asia Summit, with its ASEAN base and politico-security dimension, and APEC, with its socioeconomic agenda, will need to be sorted out. Fragmentation into separate processes, however temporarily necessary, undermines political attention and commitment. Moreover, the subregional building blocks of cooperation will need to be filled in. While healthy cooperation takes place in Southeast Asia, Oceania, and the Americas, regional cooperation in Northeast Asia and the North Pacific is quite limited.

Third, APEC should enlarge its stakeholder community within the APEC economies and demonstrate more forcefully its relevance and benefits for the economies as a whole. For the most part, knowledge of and interest in APEC has been confined to bureaucracies. Most of the nongovernmental outreach has been directed toward segments of the business community, as illustrated by the existence of only one advisory committee, the APEC Business Advisory Council. While the business community is an essential sector to be served through APEC, regional integration processes need parallel structures involving parliamentarians and even local political figures, as well as NGOs. Although such involvement does take place, it is usually in settings peripheral to the "core business" of APEC.

Fourth, it is clear that parts of Asia and the Pacific are in the forefront of some of the world's biggest demographic, environmental, and health challenges. If there are models of cooperation in APEC in these areas, they will quite naturally propel the Asia-Pacific region into global leadership roles. Northeast Asia, for example, has some of the world's lowest fertility rates, and Japan and possibly Russia already have shrinking populations. Urbanization is at very high levels or occurring at very high rates in many of the APEC economies. Integrating new citizens into urban communities, providing robust and equitable services, and retaining vitality in rural areas are significant issues not only in themselves, but also to the overall well-being of societies and the quality of their international relationships. With its dense populations and rapidly changing diets and lifestyles, Asia is also at the forefront of many health and environmental challenges. While the medical aspects of these are best dealt with in other forums, general health policies are a legitimate and important topic for APEC cooperation. Sustainable resource use and the environmental agenda for all of the economies have become very acute issues, as attested by the urgent attention the Chinese leadership has vowed to give clean air and water, but the Asia-Pacific regional cooperation agenda in these areas remains underdeveloped. Finally, as mentioned above, APEC should give much greater attention to its education agenda, particularly addressing the task of how to prepare the people of the region for a twenty-first century economy and for global leadership.

POLITICAL CHAMPIONS

Strengthened cooperation in APEC and global leadership from the Asia-Pacific region will, in the end, be driven primarily by the quality, imagination, and attentiveness of political leadership, especially in the larger economies. Without such leadership, modes of cooperation tend to become routinized and bureaucratized, and progress to become incremental. Unfortunately, today's leaders are often highly distracted by the increasingly complex task of domestic governance, combined with responsive rather than proactive approaches to foreign policy issues. But we have a number of new regional leaders who may look upon APEC and the broader regional integration process with fresh eyes. Perhaps this new team of regional leaders can help to formulate a new and workable Asia-Pacific dream.

NOTES

1. Charles E. Morrison, "Four Adjectives Become a Noun: APEC and the Future of Asia-Pacific Cooperation," in *APEC at 20: Recall, Reflect, Remake,*

eds. K. Kesavapany and Hank Lim (Singapore: Institute of Southeast Asian Studies, 2009), 30.

2. US National Intelligence Council, "Global Trends 2030: Alternative Worlds," Washington, DC, December 2012.

3. United Nations, Department of Economic and Social Affairs, "Trends in International Migrant Stock: The 2013 Revision," http://esa.un.org /unmigration/TIMSA2013/migrantstocks2013.htm.

Contributors

Winichai CHAEMCHAENG is director of the International Institute for Asia-Pacific Studies (INSAPS), Bangkok University. During his government service, he was posted as deputy permanent representative of the Permanent Mission of Thailand to the World Trade Organization, later promoted to deputy director-general of the Department of Trade Negotiations and senior commercial advisor to the Ministry of Commerce. He was ASEAN co-chair of the ASEAN-China FTA Negotiating Committee, and Thai leader for the ASEAN-Japan Committee on Comprehensive Economic Partnership, the ASEAN–Australia–New Zealand FTA Negotiating Committee, and the Trade in Goods negotiating team under the Japan-Thailand Economic Partnership Agreement (JTEPA).

Inkyo CHEONG is professor of economics at Inha University, Incheon, South Korea. He was a fellow for eight years at the Korean Institute for International Economic Policy (KIEP), and served as president of South Korea's International Trade Economist Association. Instrumental in establishing the groundwork for South Korea's FTA policy, he has been actively involved as a member of the negotiation team and as an advisor for South Korea's FTAs with Chile, Singapore, ASEAN, the United States, the European Union, Japan, MERCOSUR, and others. Since 2010, he has consulted with the government and private sector to improve South Korea's FTA utilization, and has provided professional consultation for many international institutes and economies regarding FTA issues.

Rodrigo CONTRERAS is an economist with more than 20 years of experience in international economic relations. He currently serves as head of international affairs for the Ministry of Agriculture in Chile, and was chief negotiator of the TPP agreement between 2010 and March 2013. He has been a negotiator for numerous free trade agreements, including those with the United States, the European Union, the EFTA economies, South Korea, Japan, China, India, Australia, Turkey, Peru, and Central America. Among other positions, he recently served in Chile's Directorate of International Economic Relations, Ministry of Foreign Affairs, as both the director of economic bilateral affairs and as chief of the Market Access Department.

Peter DRYSDALE is emeritus professor of economics in the Crawford School of Public Policy at the Australian National University. He is widely acknowledged as the leading intellectual architect of APEC. He was founding head of the Australia-Japan Research Centre, and is recipient of the Asia Pacific Prize; the Weary Dunlop Award; the Japanese Order of the Rising Sun, with gold rays and neck ribbon; and the Australian Centenary Medal. He is also a member of the Order of Australia, and received an honorary doctor of letters from the Australian National University. He is presently head of the East Asia Forum, the East Asian Bureau of Economic Research, and the South Asia Bureau of Economic Research. In 2011–12, he served on the advisory and cabinet committee of the *Australia in the Asian Century* white paper, and was a member of the strategic advisory board for its implementation.

Deborah Kay ELMS is director of the Asian Trade Centre in Singapore. She is also a senior fellow in the Singapore Ministry of Trade and Industry's Trade Academy. Previously, she was head of the Temasek Foundation Centre for Trade & Negotiations (TFCTN) and senior fellow of international political economy at the S. Rajaratnam School of International Studies at Nanyang Technological University, Singapore. Her research interests are negotiations and decision making, and her current research involves the Trans-Pacific Partnership (TPP) negotiations. She has provided consulting on a range of trade issues to the governments of United Arab Emirates, Sri Lanka, Cambodia, Chinese Taipei, and Singapore. Dr. Elms received a PhD in political science from the University of Washington, a MA in international relations from the University of Southern California, and bachelors degrees from Boston University.

Christopher FINDLAY has served as executive dean of the Faculty of the Professions at the University of Adelaide since 2011. He is also vice chair of the Australian Committee for Pacific Economic Cooperation (AUSPECC). Previously, he was professor of economics and head of school at the University of Adelaide. Professor Findlay received doctoral and master's degrees from the Australian National University, and an honors degree in economics from the University of Adelaide. He became a member of the Academy of the Social Sciences in Australia in 2002, and a member of the General Division of the Order of Australia in 2007. His research focus is Australia's economic relations with Asia.

Matthew P. GOODMAN holds the William E. Simon Chair in Political Economy at the Center for Strategic and International Studies (CSIS) in Washington, DC, where he focuses on economic policy issues in the Asia-Pacific region. Previously, he served in numerous US government positions, including at the White House, the State Department, and the Treasury Department. He also has extensive private sector experience.

Masahiro KAWAI is a project professor at the Graduate School of Public Policy, University of Tokyo. Before assuming his current position, he was dean and CEO of the Asian Development Bank Institute (ADBI), and a special advisor to the ADB president in charge of regional economic cooperation and integration. Prior to working with the ADB and ADBI, he was a professor of economics at the University of Tokyo, among other positions. His recent books include *Asian Regionalism in the World Economy: Engine for Dynamism and Stability*, *Asia's Free Trade Agreements: How is Business Responding?*, *Asia and Policymaking for the Global Economy* and *The Global Financial Crisis and Asia*. He holds a PhD in economics from Stanford University, and serves as editor of the *Asian Development Review*.

Sangkyom KIM is a deputy director of the Directorate for Financial and Enterprise Affairs for the OECD, where he works on development of the international investment agenda and promotes OECD standards across a range of subjects, including investment, responsible business conduct, global value chains, anti-corruption, corporate governance, and competition. Prior to joining the OECD, he worked for the Korea Institute for International Economic Policy (KIEP), including twelve years as director of international studies and two years as director of research planning and coordination. He has served as vice-chair of the Korean National Committee for Pacific Economic Co-operation, secretary-general of the APEC Education Foundation, and an expert to the APEC Secretariat for peer reviews of Chile and Mexico, among other roles. He holds a MA in political science from Hankook University of Foreign Studies in Seoul and a PhD in economics from the University of Pennsylvania.

LIU Chenyang received his master's degree and PhD in economics from the Institute of International Economics of Nankai University, China, and serves as director and professor of the APEC Study Center of China at Nankai University. His academic interests lie in APEC issues, regional economic integration and cooperation, and international relations. He is the author of over 30 journal articles, 7 books on APEC and Asia-Pacific economic integration issues, and over 20 consultative reports provided to the Ministry of Foreign Affairs and the Ministry of Commerce of China. He has been invited to serve as an expert consultant on joint feasibility studies of FTAs between China and Australia, New Zealand, Singapore, and Iceland, as well as the China-Japan-Korea FTA and others.

Charles E. MORRISON has been president of the East-West Center since 1998. He has been associated with the Center since 1980 in various capacities, including heading its former Institute of Economics and Politics. A US Senate aide early in his career, he has also been a research associate at the Japan Center for International Exchange. Morrison served as the international chair of the Pacific Economic Cooperation Council from 2005 to 2012, and is a member of other national and international bodies that promote trans-Pacific security and economic cooperation. His PhD is from the Johns Hopkins School of Advanced International Studies, where he also once taught on Southeast Asia. He speaks and publishes widely on US-Asia policy issues and the countries of the region, and gives special emphasis to regional cooperation, particularly the APEC process.

Peter A. PETRI is the Carl J. Shapiro Professor of International Finance at the Brandeis International Business School (IBS), a senior fellow at the East-West Center in Honolulu, and a visiting fellow at the Peterson Institute for International Economics in Washington, DC. He was founding dean of IBS from 1994 to 2006, and has held visiting appointments at the Asian Development Bank, the Brookings Institution, the OECD, the World Bank, and universities in China and Japan. He serves on the editorial boards of several economics journals, is a member of the US Asia Pacific Council and the PAFTAD International Steering Committee, and was a former chair of the US APEC Study Center Consortium. He received AB and PhD degrees in economics from Harvard University.

Michael G. PLUMMER is the Eni Professor of International Economics at the Johns Hopkins University, School of Advanced International Studies (SAIS). He is also editor-in-chief of the *Journal of Asian Economics*, president of the American Committee for Asian Economic Studies (ACAES), and (non-resident) senior fellow at the East-West Center. Until recently, he was head of the Development Division of the OECD (2010–2012). Previous to these positions, he was a tenured associate professor of economics at Brandeis University. He has also been a Fulbright Chair in Economics and Pew Fellow in International Affairs at Harvard University, and a research professor at Kobe University. Professor Plummer has worked on numerous projects for international organizations, development and other government agencies, and regional development banks. His PhD in economics is from Michigan State University.

QUAN Yi is editor-in-chief of the *Asia-Pacific Economic Review*, and research fellow and deputy head of the Institute of Asia-Pacific Studies, Fujian Academy of Social Sciences, China. He is also a member of the China National Committee for Pacific Economic Cooperation.

Jeffrey J. SCHOTT is a senior fellow working on international trade policy and economic sanctions at the Peterson Institute for International Economics. He has been a visiting lecturer at Princeton University and an adjunct professor at Georgetown University. Earlier in his career, he was a senior associate at the Carnegie Endowment for International Peace and an official of the US Treasury Department in international trade and energy policy. During the Tokyo Round of multilateral trade negotiations, he was a member of the US delegation that negotiated the GATT Subsidies Code. He is a member of the US Trade and Environment Policy Advisory Committee, as well as the Advisory Committee on International Economic Policy of the US Department of State. Mr. Schott is the author, co-author, or editor of about 20 books, including recently *Understanding the Trans-Pacific Partnership* and *Local Content Requirements: A Global Problem*.

Robert SCOLLAY received his economics education at the University of Auckland, New Zealand, and the University of Cambridge, England. He is director of the New Zealand APEC Study Centre at the University of Auckland, where he is also a member of the Economics Department. He is a former international coordinator for the PECC Trade Forum, and led a number of its research projects. Some of the projects were undertaken for the APEC Business Advisory Council (ABAC), including an early study of the proposed Free Trade Area of the Asia-Pacific (FTAAP). His recent research and publications have largely focused on regional trade agreements and regional economic integration, including recent developments such as the Trans-Pacific Partnership (TPP) and the Regional Comprehensive Economic Partnership (RCEP).

Djisman SIMANDJUNTAK is senior economist and chairman of the board of directors of the Centre for Strategic and International Studies (CSIS) Foundation. He is professor of business economics at Prasetiya Mulya School of Business and Economics and chairman of the executive board of Prasetiya Mulya Foundation. He is a member of Indonesia's National Economic Committee, as well as chairman of the Indonesian National Committee for Pacific Economic Cooperation Council (IN-

CPEC). He obtained his PhD in economics from the Faculty of Economics and Social Sciences of the University of Cologne, Germany. His articles have appeared in the *Jakarta Post*'s Annual Economic Outlook 2014, *East Asia Forum Quarterly*, and other publications.

Hugh STEPHENS has more than 35 years of government and business experience in the Asia-Pacific region. Based in Victoria, British Columbia, he is vice chair of the Canadian National Committee on Pacific Economic Cooperation (PECC), senior fellow at the Asia Pacific Foundation of Canada, and a fellow at the Canadian Defence and Foreign Affairs Institute. He previously served as senior vice president (public policy) for Asia Pacific for Time Warner, after a career of 30 years in the Canadian Foreign Service. He has written extensively on Asia-Pacific trade issues and on Chinese investment with regard to Canada, testified before the Canadian Senate Committee on Foreign Affairs and International Trade, and commented frequently in the Canadian media.

Sherry M. STEPHENSON is a senior fellow with the International Centre for Trade and Sustainable Development (ICTSD) in Geneva. Previously, she worked with the Organization of American States (OAS) in Washington, DC, where she served as director of the Department of Trade and deputy director of the Trade Unit during the Free Trade Area of the Americas (FTAA) negotiations. She has served as an advisor to the minister of trade in Indonesia and held positions with the OECD, as well as with the GATT and UNCTAD Secretariats. She is a member of the Global Trade Agenda Council of the World Economic Forum and is actively involved in the international trade policy work of the Pacific Economic Cooperation Council (PECC). She received a PhD in international economics from the University of Geneva, and is the author of two edited volumes on services trade and reform and more than 60 articles.

TAN Khee Giap is co-director of the Asia Competitiveness Institute, and associate professor of public policy at the Lee Kuan Yew School of Public Policy, National University of Singapore. He is also the chair of the Singapore National Committee for Pacific Economic Cooperation.

He graduated with a PhD from the University of East Anglia, England. His research interests are the competitiveness and productivity of Asian economies, and the livability of global cities. He has published more than 10 books and many articles in international refereed journals.

TANG Guoqiang is chair of the China National Committee for Pacific Economic Cooperation. Previously, he served in the Ministry of Foreign Affairs of the People's Republic of China for 38 years. He was China's ambassador to Norway from 2009 to 2012; China's permanent representative and ambassador to the United Nations in Vienna; China's permanent representative to the UN Industrial Development Organization and the International Atomic Energy Agency from 2006 to 2009; China's ambassador to the Czech Republic from 2002 to 2006; deputy commissioner of the Commissioner's Office of the Ministry of Foreign Affairs of the People's Republic of China in Hong Kong Special Administrative Region from 1998 to 2002; deputy director-general of the Information Department and spokesman of the Ministry of Foreign Affairs; and counselor of the Chinese Embassy in the UK.

Shujiro URATA is professor of international economics at the Graduate School of Asia-Pacific Studies, Waseda University, Japan; faculty fellow at the Research Institute of Economy, Trade, and Industry (RIETI); research fellow at the Japanese Centre for Economic Research (JCER); and senior research advisor at the Economic Research Institute for ASEAN and East Asia (ERIA). Professor Urata received his PhD in economics from Stanford University. A specialist in international economics, he has published widely on the topic. His recent co-edited books include *Bilateral Trade Agreements: Origins, Evolution, and Implications*; *Multinationals and Economic Growth in East Asia*; *Free Trade Agreements in the Asia-Pacific*; and *Economic Consequences of Globalization: Evidence from East Asia*.

Ganeshan WIGNARAJA is the director of research of the Asian Development Bank Institute in Tokyo. Previously, he worked for the Asian Development Bank, the Commonwealth Secretariat, the OECD, Oxford University, the UN, and a UK consulting firm. He has a DPhil in economics from Oxford University and has published 13 books, including

Asia's Free Trade Agreements: How Is Business Responding? and the forth-coming *A WTO for the 21st Century: The Asian Perspective.*

YAP Xin Yi is currently a manager and research assistant at the Asia Competitiveness Institute, Lee Kuan Yew School of Public Policy, National University of Singapore. She graduated with a banking and finance degree from the University of London.

Fan ZHAI is managing director and head of the asset allocation and strategic research department of the China Investment Corporation (CIC). He is responsible for the overall allocation strategy of CIC's overseas investment. He also oversees macroeconomic research and market analysis to support strategic asset allocation and tactical investment views. Before he joined CIC in November 2009, he was a research fellow at the Asian Development Bank Institute in Tokyo and an economist in the Economics and Research Department of the Asian Development Bank in Manila. He has also worked at the Ministry of Finance and the Development Research Center of the State Council in China. He holds a PhD in systems engineering from Huazhong University of Science and Technology, China.

ZHANG Jianping is director of the Department of International Economic Cooperation at the Institute for International Economic Research at the National Development and Reform Commission (NDRC), China. He is also a member of the expert panel for the Ministry of Commerce (MOFCOM) and the State Forestry Administration; professor of economics of Nankai University; PhD adviser at the University of International Business and Economics; member of the China National Committee of PECC, the Chinese People's Institute of Foreign Affairs, and the Chinese Association for International Understanding; and executive member and deputy secretary of the Asia-Pacific Institute of China. He has chaired more than 30 academic study projects, consulted with leading organizations, and written more than a hundred papers and four books. He received his bachelor's and master's degrees from Peking University, and a PhD in economics from the Chinese Academy of Social Sciences.

ZHANG Yunling is a professor, academy member, and director of international studies at the Chinese Academy of Social Sciences (CASS); a member of the National Committee of Chinese Political Consultants Conference; and president of the China Association of Asia-Pacific Studies. He is also vice chairman of the China Committee of PECC, vice president of the China-ROK Friendship Association, and a board member of ERIA. He was director of the Institute of Asia-Pacific Studies from 1993 to 2007, and has served as a member of the East Asia Vision Group, the Official Expert Group on China-ASEAN Cooperation, the ASEM Task Force, and many other groups. His recent publications include *China and Asia Regionalism* and *Seeking a Benign Relationship between China and the World.*

www.ingramcontent.com/pod-product-compliance
Lightning Source LLC
Chambersburg PA
CBHW061237220326
41599CB00028B/5453